WRITING AND PUBLISHING

ALA GUIDES FOR THE BUSY LIBRARIAN

Hiring, Training, and Supervising Library Shelvers, by Patricia Tunstall

WRITING AND PUBLISHING

THE LIBRARIAN'S HANDBOOK

EDITED BY **CAROL SMALLWOOD**

AMERICAN LIBRARY ASSOCIATION
CHICAGO   2010

Carol Smallwood received her MLS from Western Michigan University and her MA in history from Eastern Michigan University. She is the author or editor of eighteen books for Scarecrow, McFarland, Libraries Unlimited, Pudding House Publications, Peter Lang, and others. Some other credits include *The Writer's Chronicle, Journal of Formal Poetry, Detroit News, Instructor, English Journal,* and *Michigan Feminist Studies.* The novel *Lily's Odyssey,* the coedited anthology *Contemporary Women: Our Defining Passages,* and a short story in *Best New Prose Writing 2009* are forthcoming. A 2009 National Federation of State Poetry Societies Award Winner and a finalist for the 2009 Eric Hoffer Award for prose, Smallwood has experience in school, public, and special libraries and has served as a library consultant. She appears in *Contemporary Authors* and *Who's Who in America.*

The paper used in this publication meets the minimum requirements of American National Standard for Information Sciences—Permanence of Paper for Printed Library Materials, ANSI Z39.48-1992. ∞

Library of Congress Cataloging-in-Publication Data

    Writing and publishing : the librarian's handbook / edited by Carol Smallwood.
       p. cm. — (ALA guides for the busy librarian)
    Includes bibliographical references and index.
    ISBN 978-0-8389-0996-6 (alk. paper)
    1. Library science—Authorship. 2. Library science literature—Publishing. 3. Authorship. I. Smallwood, Carol, 1939–
  Z669.7.W75 2010
  808'.06602—dc22

                                   2009025047

ISBN-13: 978-0-8389-0996-6

Printed in the United States of America
14 13 12 11 10   5 4 3 2 1

PART I WHY WRITE?

PART II EDUCATION OF A WRITER

GETTING STARTED

WRITING WITH OTHERS

REVISE, REVISE, REVISE

LESSONS FROM PUBLISHING

PART III FINDING YOUR NICHE IN PRINT

PART IV FINDING YOUR NICHE ONLINE

PART V MAXIMIZING OPPORTUNITIES

M̲ost libraries love to share with one another. Whether they offer reciprocal bor-
rowing or interlibrary loans, it all comes down to sharing resources. This sharing, in effect, greatly enlarges a single library's collection. What the library does
not own, others do, and a patron can obtain a book from as close as the library one
town over or as far away as a library in another country.

Likewise, librarians generally love to share ideas with their colleagues—an action
that greatly enhances the profession's knowledge base. At the local and regional levels, news travels quickly about a program that was particularly well received or well
done, often through the grapevine and e-mail or at meetings of regional groups, such
as an adult reading roundtable. More broadly, librarians present ideas that turned
into terrific projects, procedures, or practices. They share these ideas in a number
of ways, such as table talks, displays, and formal presentations at state and national
conventions.

But it is the written word that likely is the most widely used way that librarians
share their ideas. Some librarian-authors may have cut their teeth writing for their
libraries' newsletters. Others have written for the professional journals of various
state groups, such as the Illinois Library Association's *Reporter,* or of national associations, such as the American Library Association's *American Libraries.* Librarians
also contribute articles, columns, book reviews, and letters to *Library Journal.* And
librarians write books or chapters in books about the profession's myriad topics,
including management, technology, intellectual freedom, and innovative services.

Being the creative and innovative people they are, librarian-writers may not necessarily limit themselves to writing about their profession. Many also write short
stories, novels, and poetry, not only expanding their imaginations but also entertaining or edifying the reading public. This is another facet of librarians' sharing
their thoughts and ideas.

The book you have before you is a unique collection of articles by and about
librarians whose work has been published in one form or another. Here, the writers

talk about their writing processes, the thinking behind their works, and their feelings about sharing with others their experiences in the library and literary worlds.

I hope you enjoy the compilation and, in the nature of librarianship, that you share it with a colleague.

—**Bob Blanchard**, adult services librarian, Des Plaines Public Library,
and contributor to *Illinois Library Association Reporter* and
Thinking outside the Book: Essays for Innovative Librarians (2008)

Librarians tend to be creative people, and what profession other than library and information sciences could be more encouraging for writers? We are surrounded by books, technology, and people, which provides the opportunity to write not only for the profession but also poetry, novels, short stories, and creative nonfiction for children and adults.

Writing and Publishing: The Librarian's Handbook was prompted by a desire to acknowledge the many contributions by librarians who write and to encourage beginning librarian-writers. A great benefit from writing, as observed by the well-known writer Natalie Goldberg, whom one of my creative writing classes studies, is that "when we write we begin to taste the texture of our own mind."

In compiling this book, we asked published librarians to submit two 1,900- to 2,100-word unpublished pieces to show their writing range, and we encouraged them to follow Gustave Flaubert's advice in order to help readers: "Whenever you can shorten a sentence, do. And one always can. The best sentence? The shortest."

Calls for submissions went to school, public, academic, and special librarians, as well as library and information sciences faculty from the United States and Canada who have been published in librarianship as well as outside the field. The ninety-two chapters are grouped by topic in the table of contents and indexed by subject and author. It has been a pleasure working with these forty-seven creative librarians who are willing to share their hard-won success.

PART I
WHY WRITE?

KNOW YOUR AUDIENCE

How Writing Helped Me Be a Better Librarian

ELIZABETH A. STEPHAN

Librarianship is a second career for many librarians—it was for me. Before attending library school, I was a price guide editor. I edited price guides that covered antiques, collectibles, and toys—toys were what I spent most of my time on and what I knew best. The organizational and project management skills I learned as an editor have been invaluable to me as a librarian, but the most helpful has been learning how to write for a specific audience. Writing and editing for a specific audience mean that you have to identify that audience and understand their needs. And identifying that audience and knowing what they want and need tie directly into librarianship. As outreach and marketing become more important to libraries, knowing who our users are and how they use the library is becoming core to our mission.

As an editor, I had to know who read our books. Our reading audience included two main groups: serious collectors and dealers as well as novice collectors. Serious collectors and dealers generally had large collections or had an interest in building large collections. Many of them made their living—or part of their living—by buying and selling toys. They bought multiple price guides to get a well-rounded picture of the market. They would acquire every book available just to have a comprehensive in-home library. Novice collectors were those with only a passing interest in toys. They were more likely to buy only one book for a specific purpose and not buy multiple books. They may not have been the core audience, but they were still readers and potential customers.

Working in publishing taught me how important it was to know my audience. This translated directly into librarianship—to be a better librarian I need to know who my user is. Just as with price guides, there is a primary audience for my library—university students. If I know who they are, what they need, and how they research, I can better serve them. Marketing the library and my services has been one of my goals as a librarian. I have surveyed students about our services. I listen to not only what students are asking at the reference desk but also what they aren't asking. I reach out to faculty to find out what they need but also what they think their students need. One of the things I heard most often from faculty was that students weren't using library sources.

In an effort to reach out to students, I took the library outside of the building. I offered a satellite reference service to the business school, my subject specialty. I wanted to make both students and faculty aware that I existed and that the library existed. At the end of every instruction session, I told students about how the library had the resources they needed to complete their assignments—and one of those resources was me and every other librarian on campus. Everything I did as a librarian represented the library and was a way to reach out to my core user.

Why did I put so much effort into marketing myself and the library? From getting to know my core audience through questions, observation, and research, I knew that I needed to market the library. I needed to reach out directly to my user—and that has helped me be a more effective librarian.

NARRATIVE AND LIBRARIANSHIP

JOHN GLOVER

Writing stories can improve your effectiveness in many areas of library work, and you do not have to be Austen, Chabon, Shakespeare, or Woolf for this to happen. The process of writing, along with what the writer learns along the way, boosts skills ranging from instruction to presentation and interviewing. As someone who wrote long before ever thinking of library school, I use tricks and techniques learned from writing every day in my work as a humanities reference librarian. Although I write fiction, any kind of narrative stories, whether autobiographical anecdotes or narrative nonfiction of the kind written by Krakauer or Wolfe, should be effective for the purposes I describe here.

WRITING AS AN AID TO PRODUCTIVITY

One of the best aids to the creation of good stories is writing regularly. Some authors write two pages per day and some write fifteen, but most have a daily goal. In addition, most authors develop certain habits to aid their productivity: writing at roughly the same time and in the same place, drinking the same beverage from the same mug, listening to the same music. All of these things combine to put the writer in the proper mental space to write.

If you write in your spare time, you will find that all writing becomes a little easier. Some librarians dislike writing for publication, but there are ways to conquer writing anxiety. When you write regularly in another setting, you will find that your "writing muscles" are warmed up more than they are if you go for long periods writing nothing other than e-mail. While library work often doesn't allow for writing at the same time every day, or even necessarily a room of your own, every little bit that you can do to create a writing habit will be useful when it comes time for you to write on the job.

COPING WITH CRITICISM

Different people take criticism in different ways, but learning how to listen to and profit from criticism is essential for anyone who wishes to work effectively. The process of writing stories typically involves revision to improve one's writing. At some point in the revision process, one often asks for feedback from others, and this can come in a variety of formats.

Most writers develop some ability to take criticism impersonally, which can be very helpful when the time comes, for example, to propose a change in your library. Most such proposals do not pass management uncritiqued and require some measure of refinement. Coping with this can be difficult, especially if one takes criticism to heart. New librarians are often prone to take a lack of unbounded enthusiasm hard, but experience with criticism in one arena may translate well into another.

HELPING PATRONS

Daily journaling can be useful as a tool to help you with regular writing, but there are certain advantages to writing in the form of stories. Whether the stories are made up or based on events from your day-to-day life is not as relevant as setting them down on paper.

Reference transactions. When you are working with a patron, trying to explain how to use resources, or talking about the research process, it can be helpful to talk in terms of stories. People often ask for examples when they are trying to understand something, and even if they do not ask, an example might help the patron understand something in a nonabstract way and put him or her at ease. If you are accustomed to thinking in terms of stories, then good, well-rounded examples will come to you quickly when you are trying to describe aspects of the research process. For instance, an analogy about grocery shopping—finding the right aisle, reading labels, picking your type of shopping bag, not buying the first thing you find but rather carefully shopping—might help a patron trying to understand sorting citation database results.

Illustrations for instruction. Many techniques can enliven library instruction, but I have found stories to be particularly effective at catching patrons' attention. This works for all the reasons mentioned for reference transactions, but there are a couple of things to keep in mind. First, because you prepare for instruction sessions in advance, it can be useful to test the story on colleagues first. This will give you the chance to ensure that the story is interesting and that it makes the point that it's supposed to. Second, make sure that the story is broadly applicable. When working with a patron one-on-one, a story can be more specialized, but in a one-to-many situation, it behooves you to tell a story the whole class will be able to generalize from to research more effectively.

JOB INTERVIEWS

Learning how to tell stories can be an effective tool in helping you learn to interview more effectively, as I have discussed previously (Glover 2007). Framing your experiences as stories can help you to remember all the relevant parts more easily, give interviewers a convenient point of discussion during and after the interview, and provide you with a readily available story to use for behavioral questions. If this seems difficult to you, remember that you are the main character in the story that is your life, and an interview lets you tell that story.

Writing regularly will help your ability to encapsulate your experience in stories. While some people come by storytelling skills naturally, most of us have to practice.

REACHING OUT

We hear stories from our earliest childhood, and we are accustomed to consuming stories as part of communication, whether in the news, at the movie theater, or sitting around a table with friends. Because librarians are always striving to find a way to connect more effectively with patrons, it behooves us to explore all the methods available to us to meet that goal. Sometimes this involves the use of new technologies (e.g., short message service, instant messaging, virtual worlds), but it can also take the form of extended exposure to other methods of interaction.

Employees often attend workshops or retreats designed to improve their ability to collaborate. By the same token, a focused attempt to improve communication skills can lead to an improvement in our ability to work successfully. If librarians can take language courses to reach non-English-speaking populations or practice with new technology to ensure smooth operation in the classroom, it follows that practicing skills like telling stories is an appropriate, useful technique for improving effectiveness in the workplace.

REFERENCE

Glover, John. 2007. "Telling Stories to Get the Job." LIScareer.com, June 6. www.liscareer .com/glover_stories.htm.

WRITING FOR PROFESSIONAL DEVELOPMENT

DAWN LOWE-WINCENTSEN

Professional development can be expensive. It can take time away from your other work duties, but it is often required to some degree. Some ways to reduce this cost include watching webcasts as a group and keeping current on professional literature. Another inexpensive form of professional development is writing. Writing for professional development can mean a number of things, but it always means getting out of the day-to-day and exploring something new. Tips here range from where to get ideas to how to write about the unknown and where to take the material when it is time to publish.

Starting off into the unknown can be daunting. Not sure where to go? Think you should write only what you know? If you work only with what you know, or with what you see around you, you will not have the opportunity to grow. Plan the direction to the best of your ability, and be flexible enough to change when you find something that does not fit into your plan. Change and our dislike of it is the topic of another paper in another anthology. It is important, though, to remember that change can be scary and to combat that with an adaptable plan and an open mind. Try some of these tips for getting started into new areas:

Follow hot topics in the field. When something comes along that is inspiring, follow up. You not only will catch up on professional literature but also will have the opportunity to explore cutting-edge topics and develop new programs, projects, or techniques in your professional environment.

Partner with a colleague in a different field. Create a joint program or research project and see where it goes.

Make a list of the fields of your professional strengths and weaknesses. Pick a weakness and study it. Do some research in that area and get to know it better.

Partner with a colleague who is more experienced than you. Learn from what that colleague is doing, and create a joint project.

There are many ways to branch off from the usual paths. Start by working with a colleague. Once you are on a path to new knowledge, explore how that matches with what you already know. Making connections will help to reinforce your knowledge and make it more useful.

Becoming comfortable with a new material can take time. To use your new knowledge in writing, you will need to become familiar enough with the area to articulate your knowledge of it on a level that a newbie—such as you, before this project—could understand. When you are comfortable enough to articulate your new knowledge, write it out and have someone not related to the field read it to see whether he or she understands it. It is sometimes helpful to have more than one person read your work. Find people whom you trust, whom you know can give you constructive criticism when needed. Be open to making changes based on this new information, and remember how little you knew about the subject when you started. It is always important to get constructive criticism but even more so when you are working in a new area. If you have the opportunity to do so, find an expert to review your paper and someone who does not know the subject. This will help your article to be marketable to both levels of expertise.

After you make changes and have a final product that you are interested in publishing, start looking for places to publish. If you do a project or research with a partner who has more experience than you, either in a new field or in librarianship, look to your partner for ideas to publish. There is no need for you to reinvent the wheel when the person you are working with already has one. Build off his or her knowledge, and the two of you can grow together. If you are working alone, you have another opportunity to develop knowledge in a new area. Use resources such as *Writer's Market* or *Literary Market Place* to find places to publish. If you are delving into a new academic field, look up some of the key publications in that discipline and check their submission guidelines. If you have done extensive literature searches, try instead citation searches for the articles you used. Check out the other people who have cited the articles you reviewed, and count those as other possible publishers to send your article to.

When you find a couple of places to submit your work, follow the submission guidelines carefully. Pay attention to the words used in the guidelines and in any calls for submissions. When appropriate, use those words and phrases in your proposals. If the call for submissions asks for articles on clockwork toys, don't use the phrase "wind-up playthings" instead. If you are not successful getting new material published the first time, try again. Do not be afraid of failure, and be willing to adapt your subject if the publisher is looking for something different. Even if the article is not successful, you will have learned something new and can expand on that for further articles.

Writing for professional development does not stop with publication. Continue to research your new discipline or hot topic until you find a new path to go down. You will find that you continue in the front of the pack in terms of professional development, and you will have more opportunity to see your name in print while doing so.

WHY WRITE ON NONLIBRARIAN TOPICS?

VALERIE J. NYE

All writing projects require commitment. Whether a book is based on personal interest or professional success, writing a book on any subject requires an enormous allocation of time for research, time for thinking, and time for writing. The thought of spending an immense amount of time on creative writing topics without professional merit might seem like time ill spent to career-driven librarians. While writing for the library profession is a means to increase your professional or academic credentials, writing a book on a nonprofessional topic can be an extremely rewarding commitment that may, in the end, have a significant impact on your library career.

As librarians, we know what questions people are asking, and as librarians, we are often the first people to notice when there is a lack of information in a subject area. With persistent questions (and creative inspiration), librarians have been known to write creatively on any number of subjects. Librarians have published romance novels, children's books, cookbooks, restaurant guides, religious studies, and mysteries. Many of these books have enriched peoples' lives and have granted librarian-writers the opportunity to reach out from behind the reference desk and into the lives and minds of readers around the world.

REASONS TO WRITE

Your life will be enriched. Writing in an area outside of your professional comfort zone is a stimulating challenge and will give you the opportunity to enhance interests in your life that you may have yet to fully examine.

Your professional life will be enhanced. Many people spend a great deal of time consumed with work stress, employee conflict, and short deadlines. A new project outside of your daily work will enable you to focus on something new, and maybe avoid work-related burnout. The creative energy you develop on a project outside of your job description will eventually allow you to lend more creativity and energy to your job.

Your network with people who appreciate books will grow. Writing a creative work will open doors to new experiences and relationships. In short order, you may find yourself at an author association meeting talking with an award-winning author about the joyous day he saw his newly published first book on display at the library.

Your professional identity will change. You will become an expert on something new. Becoming an expert in a new field has the potential to bring you great satisfaction and personal accomplishment. Taking a step away from your job may give you the freedom to appreciate librarianship more or be the inspiration you need to try something new.

AT THE INTERSECTION OF LIBRARIAN AND AUTHOR

The connection between being a published author and working as a professional librarian does not begin and end with the quest to fulfill unanswered questions. As librarians, we are aware of the details that can make a book popular to a wide audience. For instance, librarians know that people do judge a book by its cover, we recognize the names of reliable publishers, and we know the companies and publishers that review books. In short, we know how to get books into readers' hands.

In an effort to find readers for your newly published book, you may find your life as a writer boldly intersecting with your life as a librarian. As a guest speaker at bookstores and libraries, you might be surprised by the ways librarianship and your life as a writer connect.

You'll meet future librarians. Touting yourself as a writer and a librarian will attract fellow librarians and people who have thought about attending library school to your book signings. This new platform as an author-librarian will give you the opportunity to share valuable information about the library profession with people who are interested in entering the profession. Be prepared to answer the questions "Where is the nearest library school?" and "Do you think earning a library degree online is a good idea?"

You'll find new books. As a new author, you will inevitably join writers groups or have speaking engagements with other authors. The new writers you meet will give you insight into and information about the books they are writing, books that may be appropriate for your library's collection and of great interest to library patrons.

You'll reach nonlibrary users. As publicity about your writing is released, you may find yourself invited for interviews with newspaper reporters or talk-radio hosts. If the interviewer knows you are a librarian, he or she will certainly ask about reading, literacy, or librarianship. Interviews are a perfect opportunity to speak about the work of librarians.

You'll have new professional writing opportunities. While you may write a work that is of personal interest, once you are a published author, new doors will open. Library publishing companies or library journals might approach you to write literature that will contribute to the profession.

Writing a book in a nonacademic subject area will allow you to explore interests that you may have submerged as you fashioned your library career. As a librarian and a writer, publishing any book will renew your professional energy by enriching yourself and by serving readers' needs. The freedom to examine and rethink creative areas will help you recharge and bring you full circle—back through the doors of your local library.

WRITING FOR TENURE

ROBERT P. HOLLEY

Imagine that you have successfully completed an innovative project in your academic library that implements some key features of Web 2.0 and has received positive feedback from your user community. You wish to write a report on the project. Which of the following two strategies should you choose? The first option is to prepare an easy-to-read and relatively informal report for *American Libraries* or *Library Journal*. You can be sure that thousands of librarians will at least glance at your article. Some will borrow portions of your project to make changes in their own libraries. Your peers will learn who you are and respect your Web 2.0 skills. The second option is to write a scholarly article with all the formal conventions of the genre— literature review, endnotes, statistics, charts, tables, and formal prose with as little of your personality as possible. The journal will have some pretentious, scholarly name and about three hundred subscribers. You expect that the publication delay will be at least six months to a year as your article wends its way through the peer-review process. If accepted, your article will enter into the scholarly canon but is unlikely to have much practical effect before the findings become dated.

If you hope to meet the tenure requirements at many colleges and universities, you obviously choose the second option because nonrefereed publications, however widely read, do not count much, if at all, for tenure. I would hasten to add that your first step is to pay no attention to this article until you find out what the rules are at your institution. My advice is based on nearly thirty years of active publication, but publication requirements for academic librarians vary much more than they do for the teaching faculty. Double-check with your director, the academic administrator in charge of the review process, a current or former member of the review committee, or someone who has gone through tenure review to discover both the official and hidden rules of the local tenure process. I also advise you not to gamble on the future of your career by believing that, for some reason, you are special and thereby exempt from these rules.

AUTHORSHIP AND PUBLICATION TYPE

The first author gets the most credit for any publication. Your tenure portfolio should include a majority of publications for which you are the sole author or the first author. Some review committees might like to see a mix of solo and joint articles to show that you have the ability to work with others, but librarianship is not a field like some of the sciences in which the publishing tradition includes research teams and dozens of authors even for short publications.

Editing a book or special issue of a journal is also probably not worth your effort for tenure. My institution considers such editorial activities more service than research. Editing the work of others is a specialized and needed skill, but few consider it scholarly research. You will also spend much time tracking down authors and encouraging them to meet deadlines.

I also caution against writing a book before you get tenure. In the same amount of time, you can write multiple articles so that you do not put all your eggs in one basket. Although some books are reviewed,

many aren't; and common wisdom states that books are less likely to be cited than articles.

Nonrefereed articles count somewhat, especially if an editor reviews them before publication; but internal documents, blogs, training materials, and textbooks normally have little worth for tenure.

CHOICE OF JOURNAL

The key decision in writing for tenure is thus to make sure that you choose a refereed journal. You can find such information easily in Ulrich's Periodical Directory (available at www.ulrichsweb.com/UlrichsWeb/). Some journals have both a refereed and a nonrefereed section, so you must look carefully at any correspondence from the editor about the placement of your article. If the designation *refereed* is accurate, the editor will send your article out for review by one or more experts. The tenure review committee gives greater weight to such articles precisely because of this external review.

Other factors come into play but have less importance. A good tenure portfolio emphasizes the positive factors and minimizes the others. Journals, like universities, have more prestige if they reject a higher percentage of articles. If your article will date quickly and lose its potential for publication, consider sending it to a lower-prestige journal, because getting your article published is the most important consideration for tenure. Other quality factors include the reputation of the publisher and the journal's impact factor as judged by experts in the field. The journal's circulation and appearance in indexing and abstracting services are important because they are a factor in being cited, as I discuss a bit later.

CHOICE OF SUBJECT

Getting your article published is only the first step in improving your chances for tenure. Review committees will most likely judge your scholarly impact, so it is important for others to cite your work. Librarians who publish moderately good papers on hot topics are more likely to be cited than are those who publish excellent papers on cold topics. I doubt that the best paper in the world on the history of filing rules in the card catalog would be cited much. Once your article has been cited a few times, other authors will find those citations and confirm your scholarly reputation. You will then have an excellent citation record to include in your tenure dossier. In fact, I will contradict here what I said earlier because a paper in *American Libraries* may acquire an excellent citation record, and so have more value in the citation part of your dossier that it did as a publication. While citations in standard sources such as Web of Science count the most, most review committees will give some credit for citations in other publications, including in blogs and web documents.

CONCLUSION

I could write much more on this subject, but I'll conclude by repeating that the most important point in writing for tenure is to know what counts and what doesn't at your institution. Find out what the rules are and follow them. Most of all, don't waste your time on publications that won't help you reach your goal. You can write the great American library study after you get tenure.

COAUTHORING FOR TENURE

VALERIE J. NYE

Early in my professional career as a tenure-track librarian, I received sage advice: to consider coauthoring with another faculty member as a way to meet some of the tenure requirements. About a year into my tenure-track job, I found myself in a meeting with a colleague who wanted help with an appendix for a book he was on the verge of publishing. The details of writing the appendix grew into a full-length research project that we eventually coauthored and published together.

Working on a writing project early in my career allowed me to develop a friendship and a mentoring relationship with an experienced colleague. Coauthoring helped build my confidence as a researcher, writer, and professional librarian. Six years later, I found myself thinking about another collaborative writing project, and I have enjoyed the benefits for the second time of working with a fellow librarian to publish a book.

THE PROS OF PARTNERING

For most writers, writing with a partner offers some overwhelmingly positive benefits.

Continuous energy to keep the project moving forward. When one person hits a low moment in the writing, research, or publication process, there is another dedicated person to pick up the pieces and keep the project moving in the desired direction.

Developing a solid mentoring relationship. The relationship building and continual communication required to publish a book can form a long-lasting professional relationship.

Building on ideas. A colleague who is familiar with the depths of your research can be a welcome sounding board for inspiration.

Expanding your network. For new writers or people who are new to the library profession, writing a book with a more experienced professional may open the door to an array of professional experiences.

Strengthening your research. Talking about the numerous details involved in writing and research can help both authors focus unclear ideas. Coauthoring also opens up possibilities of working on an interdisciplinary project with an expert in a field outside of librarianship. A professor in psychology or in business may have significant expertise to add to your professional writing.

Creating new writing opportunities. Publishing book-length research has a way of opening doors to new writing projects or spin-off projects based on your original research.

Sharing the pain. When rejection comes, you have someone with whom you can empathize. No matter what kind of book you are writing, there will be times when you feel disappointed or rejected. When times are hard, it helps to share the disappointment with someone who really understands.

THE CONS OF COOPERATION

A good coauthoring relationship will reap all of the foregoing benefits and more. With those collaborative advantages firmly in mind, it is worthwhile to consider some of the potentially negative aspects of the coauthor relationship.

Sharing the author line. In some academic circles, coauthoring may not carry the same prestige as being the single author on a publication. In other academic situations, however, coauthoring is measured as a strength if you are working interdepartmentally or with students.

Breaking up. The coauthor relationship can fall apart in the midst of a project for any number of reasons. Publishing a book necessitates a relationship that lasts for years. If the relationship between the authors falls apart at any point before, during, or after the publication of a book, the project may suffer and end up much more complicated than a solo publication.

Downed communication lines. Communication is a key aspect of a good relationship, but it is also time consuming. If one or both authors are not willing to devote substantial time to communication, insurmountable problems may arise.

THE SEARCH FOR AN IDEAL COAUTHOR

Coauthor relationships generally begin when two people have a shared interest or curiosity in the same subject matter. Once the idea for the writing project is forged, communication is critical throughout the planning, research, writing, and publishing process. Here are some things to consider before launching into a full-scale coauthored writing project.

Commit to the project. Both authors need to have a commitment to seeing the project through to the end. As events unfold during the production of a book, the commitment may fade and be revived again for both writers. However, an initial commitment to the final product is crucial.

Share information. As the research process progresses, both writers need to share all of their information. Providing each other access to all research materials allows both writers the freedom to think about things together and individually. Ultimately, sharing information will permit both authors to work together to create the best work possible.

Divide up the work. There should be an agreement about the division of labor. With both of my book projects, my coauthors and I agreed that our goal was to have fun. This goal helped ease the way through painful issues with publishers, contracts, and money.

Acknowledge strengths and weaknesses. As committed partners, it is essential to realize that you can balance each other along the journey. Every contribution should be acknowledged as having an equal part in the success of a book.

Identify goals. What do you and your coauthor each want individually from the project? While each author's desired outcomes may be different, it is important to be aware of each one.

Discuss expenses. There are almost always monetary costs associated with the research, writing, and production of a book. A basic agreement about expenses will save hours of heartache.

Although all of these items are worth consideration and discussion, writing a book with a coauthor can be a very rewarding accomplishment. Dividing the labor of writing and research will lighten individual responsibility, and passionate conversations between coauthors will add to the depth and complexity of the final work. In a successful coauthoring relationship, both authors benefit by expanding their personal intellect, building new relationships, and successfully publishing a high-quality resource.

POETRY AND LIBRARIANSHIP

JOHN GLOVER

The twentieth century brought many changes for librarians, including the revolutionary advent of computers in the library, and the twenty-first promises everything from digital libraries to the gradual disappearance of printed books. Even as we strive to maintain the values of our profession, many librarians have job descriptions that are increasingly interchangeable with those of web developers, student services administrators, community liaisons, and intellectual property lawyers. In the face of this sea change, the ancient practice of writing poetry can help librarians work more effectively at the same time that they celebrate their humanity.

A USEFUL SENSITIVITY

Writing personal poetry tends to connect you to the world. To write well, you must use effective, fresh detail that has not been used the same way in the past. You have to understand something about the human heart—its joys and its sufferings. At the risk of trafficking in stereotypes, it is important to be sensitive as a poet, and the writing of poetry itself often leads to sensitivity. This can be useful when working with patrons, especially after you have answered the same questions a thousand times.

From "Where's the stapler?" to "When's the next Stephen King coming out?" librarians get many repeat questions. We also get repeat problems, from children curious about and afraid of puberty to parents afraid of the effects of violent images on the community, to people suffering from incurable diseases who want current research. As in all helping professions, librarians sometimes become deadened to the concerns of the people they serve.

Reading and writing poetry exposes you to a kind of emotional experience that even the best of novels or movies do not provide, thereby renewing your capacity for sympathy to patrons. Reading poetry can attune you to the language patrons use and help alert you to those moments when they most need care. And while writing a poem about a Grecian urn or a road not taken might be helpful, more useful is writing the kind of personal poems in which you try to articulate the great joys and pains of your life.

Personal experiences often inspired confessional poets like Sylvia Plath or Robert Lowell, or more recent ones like Sharon Olds. By putting personal secrets on the page, and by trying to give them more structure than the raw form of a journal entry or blog post, you are forced to remove yourself somewhat from the experience. This ability to handle deep emotion can help you in working with those patrons who come to the library with concerns that are unique and serious for them but concerns that you may have seen a dozen times, or a hundred.

CONCISE LANGUAGE

Information overload is a major problem in most professions today, and this is especially true in librarianship. A busy librarian may receive hundreds of e-mails in a day, sort through piles of catalogs and vendor offers, contact dozens of people about something or another, and manage patrons' information needs. Clarity and conciseness are useful traits generally, but they are especially useful in written communication with colleagues.

Learning to write concisely can happen in many different ways. Some people learn by observation, reading countless e-mails or articles and learning what works best. Some people take courses on effective communication. But another way you can learn to write effectively is through the process of revising poetry. Revision is important for books, essays, articles, and short stories, but it is essential for poetry, where a poem's success can rest on a single word.

Poets learning their craft can spend weeks, months, and sometimes years revising a single poem. They substitute words, exchange lines, and rewrite entire stanzas. Gradually, they learn not to overwrite, avoiding duplication and florid prose. For example:

> *Rays of sun flashed and flickered vividly, flooding her dying husband's sallow gray cheekbones.*

becomes

> *Those sundrops rippled*
> *across her husband's ashen cheek.*

Librarians do not need to be poets to communicate concisely and effectively, but the pains that you are forced to take when learning how to revise poetry can translate into other areas. When examining an e-mail before sending it, you will notice clusters of awkward words that you can profitably diminish— "the planned departmental reorganization that will be coming soon" becomes "cataloging's impending reorganization."

CLEAR VISION

Anyone who has ever taken the time to read a number of mission or vision statements knows how badly many of them are written, often in language that seems only marginally literate. At some point, we all wind up involved in planning institutional missions and goals. While framing them in sonnet form is not necessarily more helpful than using business English, familiarity with poetry can be useful.

Individually we turn to poetry at times of change and crisis: births, deaths, commitments, and anni-versaries. This is not because we think that wispy-haired aesthetes daydreaming on an idyllic plain are inherently transitional, but because poets observe life and recount the parts of it that matter using condensed, strong language. While knowledge of the principles of good writing is helpful when composing mission statements or other guiding language, an awareness of poetry may prove useful when trying to condense a large set of goals and values.

Vague or unclear language is inherently weak. The linguistic sensitivity that comes from writing poetry may help to combat the tendency to obfuscate or to use library jargon when it is of the utmost importance to be clear.

Finding time for poetry between all the tasks that face us every day can be difficult. While writing daily can make you a better poet, if your goal is simply to improve your skills as a librarian in the ways described here, you may only need a couple of hours every week or so. Over time, those hours will build up, increasing your verbal ability and keeping you attuned to the importance of language in our daily work.

DON'T FIND TIME TO WRITE—MAKE TIME

GABRIEL MORLEY

If you're always trying to find time to write, you're probably on a wild goose chase. Chances are that you'll never find time to sit down, collect your thoughts, and actually write something. The key to being a successful writer is to make writing part of your everyday schedule. It's not always easy to do, but the discipline will make you a better writer and much more prolific.

Most of us are too busy with our "real" jobs during the day to even think about writing. And, if you're like me, when you get home you just want to decompress and relax. You don't want to think about work or anything as mentally challenging as writing.

The key is to incorporate writing into your daily routine. Mornings work best for me. I dedicate the first two hours of my day as writing time. I don't do anything else during those two hours. No phone. No e-mail. No Internet surfing. No staff problems. No interruptions. I just sit, think, and write for two hours.

I've even devised a unique timer that lets me keep track of my writing schedule. I downloaded two hours of music on my iPod. The sound is turned down low enough to block out the noise in the office, but it is not loud enough to distract me. When I hear certain songs, it's a clue that my two-hour limit is approaching.

Occasionally, I'll catch myself falling into the Internet trap. I have a bad habit of checking the Internet for the correct spelling of a word and then thirty minutes later realizing that I've been "doing research" on the Net and avoiding writing. This is particularly common when I'm blogging or writing online content for a website.

I won't argue that it's difficult to change your routine and incorporate writing into your daily activities. You might think it's impossible to squeeze any more time out of your day. I understand that excuse. I used it for years and didn't get much writing accomplished either. Just admit to yourself that it won't be easy and then block off fifteen minutes—or more—per day at the same time every day. I wrote the first draft of a genre novel during my twice-daily fifteen-minute breaks while I was working as a circulation clerk. Once you get in a groove and make writing part of your standard routine, you'll be amazed at your output. Recently, when I got back to work from vacation, I was out of my routine and worked hard to reestablish the habit of writing first thing in the morning. It took a few days to get back on track, but now I'm in the groove again.

Some writers prefer to set a goal of writing a certain number of words per day instead of writing for a specific length of time. Some prefer to write late at night. Whatever works best for you is fine. The point is to dedicate the time to writing and to avoid being bogged down with other things—whether it's work or family related.

Often, when trying to write, it's difficult to concentrate because there is other "real" work to be done. On those days, I could sit in front of the computer for eight hours and not write one useful thing. So I don't fight it. I make a deal with myself to do some of my other work and then spend thirty minutes writing. Take those thirty minutes several times throughout the day and you'll meet your writing goal.

Over the years, a number of individuals have complained to me that they have trouble getting started writing. When I had been a daily newspaper reporter, I didn't have the luxury of procrastination. I learned quickly that the only way to write something is to sit down and pound it out. You can always go back later and add things or edit what you've written. That philosophy has remained with me after transitioning into library management.

Don't waste your writing time trying to figure out what to write about each morning. Jump-start your day by preparing in advance. I have a little notebook I carry with me, and I jot down words and sentences and, sometimes, whole paragraphs whenever I think of them. If I'm at the grocery store, I make notes. Even when I'm in a meeting, if I think of something, I'll take out my little notebook and start writing. No one else knows I'm not taking notes about the meet-

ing. Similarly, I drive an hour to work each way. I do some of my best thinking during that drive. Rather than trying to take notes while I'm driving, a digital recorder preserves my notes until I can transcribe them later. I've even thought about calling myself at work and leaving a long voice mail message.

Here are some tips to get you writing and to keep you on track:

- Set aside a certain time to write every day. Figure out when you're most alert and ready to write—early in the morning, late at night, or during your lunch hour.
- Don't overload yourself by trying to do too much—set reasonable, attainable goals.
- Parcel your time. Even fifteen-minute increments will suffice.
- Turn off your phone, the Internet, and any other distractions.
- Try writing the old-fashioned way—by hand. It slows you down and makes you concentrate and really focus on what you're writing.

A PEP TALK ON WRITING THE AWFUL FIRST DRAFT

PAUL BLOBAUM

So you want to write and get your work published. Or maybe you don't really want to write—you have to write because you need to publish given the conditions of your employment. We librarians have important perspectives to contribute to the world, and publishing is one of the best ways to give our ideas a voice. Whether you have been writing for years or are wet behind the ears, you must do what all writers do. All writers write the Awful First Draft; there are no shortcuts.

You already have done the background work, the research, the brainstorming. You already have decided what you want to write about, and you know what you want to say or explore. The challenge of the Awful First Draft is to finally give your ideas a voice, and to do that, you must get that pen moving, channeling your "inner Hemingway." Or

maybe it's not a pen but a keyboard. Whether you write on a legal pad or sit at a computer screen, your job is to get material written in a fixed medium, whatever is expedient. More experienced writers expect that there will be many revisions after the first draft, but the Awful First Draft has to come before that hallmark moment when the editor's letter arrives, congratulating you on your forthcoming publication.

Don't let your fears paralyze you. Writing for publication is a different animal from a term paper assignment. You aren't writing to please anyone or impress an instructor. You are writing to communicate with an audience, and it is scary to put your reputation at risk. Perhaps no one will read it. Perhaps they will read it and laugh themselves silly, and you will have to change your name.

You have to fearlessly battle your irrational feelings of inadequacy, fear, and loathing and just plan on writing something that's going to be awful at first. You must overcome your paralysis and face that blank page, transforming it with the strange symbols that make up what we call the English language (hopefully before rigor mortis sets in). Doing so requires courage but also discarding almost all you believe about writing in the English language. In the first draft, don't worry about spelling, grammar, or whether the text makes actual sense. These should be the least of your worries. Perfectionism is the enemy.

The Awful First Draft is not going to be pretty. Unless you are using a computer (in which case the Awful First Draft is always disguised as a neat final manuscript), the Awful First Draft is going to look really messy, as if a poorly trained, angry monkey wrote it. But who really cares what the draft looks like? After all, you aren't going to let anyone else look at it! The Awful First Draft is for your eyes only! Vladimir Nabokov, the author of *Lolita,* said that showing your first draft "is like passing around samples of one's sputum."

A thesis statement here, some background information there, and conclusions and recommendations are framed and articulated for the first time. The first draft is the laboratory for working things out, for experimenting with characters, plot, subtext, and point of view. The first draft is a work in progress.

Avoid the temptation to use a dictionary, thesaurus, or Google to check spellings or facts. You aren't wasting creative energy with technical details, and you aren't flipping through the American Psychological Association's style manual for your citations: you are just working. As you get into your Awful First Draft, you possibly will have enough of an idea of where you want to go with your writing that you can detect an emerging framework or revise the one you had started out with. Focus on one area at a time instead of becoming overwhelmed with writing the whole work all at once. Don't worry if you find yourself revising in the next writing stage because the lines are blurry.

Writers argue about whether there is truly such a thing as writer's block. Paul Silvia argues in *How to Write a Lot* (2007) that there is no such thing: there is only writing or the avoidance of writing. Whatever your experience of writer's block, you will struggle with your writing and will experience emptiness. Creation is the work of forming something out of nothing. As long as you are writing, you are accomplishing something useful that you can work with later (or not). Keep moving and writing, paying no attention to how bad it is. The poet William Stafford once said, "There's no such thing as writer's block for writers whose standards are low enough."

Unmotivated or uninspired? Some writers set goals of word counts or the number of lines that they are going to write each day. Some reward themselves for meeting their writing goals. Ice cream works for me. But even the reward of ice cream does nothing to speed up the process of writing or make it easier.

Writing the Awful First Draft will take a lot out of you. Expect emotional turmoil and obsession with your work. Expect your progress to be laborious and slow. When I wrote my first draft of this chapter, I spent five hours on it and ended up with only half a page.

The house will be a mess and dishes will sit in the sink. Remember to eat something. Hang in there: you aren't losing your mind; you are giving it a workout. If you have written at least something and have been working at it for a while, switching gears to other activities can be a way to enter into the writing process at a deeper, subconscious level. It may be useful to do something physical. Cook a meal, ride your bike, or go for a walk. Work on some problem that is solvable: pore over a jigsaw puzzle or walk a labyrinth. My seminary's preaching professor advised keeping scrap paper and a pen handy for odd moments of clarity and insight when you were going about your business.

The Awful First Draft is one of the several stages of the writing process that moves the imagined idea into final published form. The publishing process has no guarantees of success at any stage, but no one publishes without writing an Awful First Draft.

REFERENCE
Silvia, Paul J. 2007. *How to Write a Lot: A Practical Guide to Productive Academic Writing.* Washington, DC: APA LifeTools.

WRITING 101
Reading with a Writer's Eye

JAN SIEBOLD

The facilitator of my community-education writing workshop assured my group that the more we wrote, the more we would begin to read with a writer's eye. Knowing how engrossed I could become in reading, I doubted that I could compartmentalize my reading into the two categories of unconscious enjoyment and conscious observation of writing strategies and techniques.

I also had misgivings about the possibility of analyzing a book to death. E. B. White once wrote, "Humor can be dissected as a frog can, but the thing dies in the process." I felt the same way about books.

Shortly after my writing workshop ended, while reading E. Annie Proulx's *The Shipping News,* I read the sentence "Quoyle smiled, his hand went to his chin" (1993, 60). I remember thinking about how the use of the character's simple gesture spoke volumes. I realized that I was doing it. I was starting to read with a writer's eye.

Since then, I have noticed more and more that while I read I am noticing techniques that the writer uses to promote my enjoyment and understanding of the book. This awareness of the writer's writing decisions does not detract from my enjoyment of the book, as I had feared. Instead, it adds to my awe and respect for the power of the written word.

As an avid reader and a school library media specialist, I have had a lifelong relationship with words. My training as a writer has come primarily from the unconscious internalization of language and grammar that comes from my own reading for pleasure and from years of reading aloud to children.

I believe that there is an important distinction between those two types of reading. When we read silently for pleasure our brain allows us to skip over many words while preserving the uniqueness of the particular story and style of that work. However, when we read aloud, we are given the luxury of speaking every single word that the author has written.

That practice has been especially helpful in my writing for children, as it has trained my writing voice in the use of transitional words, sentence fluency, language choice, rhythm, dialogue, pacing, and style. Most librarians who read aloud have come across texts that stay with them. Vivid words, sentences, and phrases from books like William Steig's *Sylvester and the Magic Pebble* (1969) or Mordicai Gerstein's *The Man Who Walked between the Towers* (2003) will resonate in my mind forever.

I have begun to notice how writers organize their story lines. Are they written in a linear manner or through a series of flashbacks? What scenes move the story forward?

As a beginning writer, two areas that challenged me were point of view and pacing. As I was starting to write *My Nights at the Improv* (2005), I couldn't decide whether to use a first- or a third-person point of view.

I reread some of my favorite middle-grade novels and discovered that those that were written in the first person gave me a more intimate knowledge of the character's thoughts and feelings. Those that were written in the third person gave me the feeling of being an observer rather than a confidante. I decided that I wanted a first-person relationship between my readers and the character of Lizzie.

I still struggle with pacing, and I admire authors who know just the right amount of dialogue, gestures, and actions to include before moving their characters to a new place or time. Their transitions seem effortless. I take note of them whenever possible.

A simple way to consciously begin to read with a writer's eye is to take notice of a book's beginning. Does the story pull you in immediately? In the case of E. B. White's *Charlotte's Web* (1952, 1), the opening sentence immediately creates tension and foreboding: "'Where's Papa going with that ax?' Fern asked as her mother was setting the table for breakfast."

In Beverly Cleary's *The Mouse and the Motorcycle* (1965, 11), the reader must keep reading to find out who is doing the watching: "Keith, the boy in the rumpled shorts and shirt, did not know he was being watched as he entered room 215 of the Mountain View Inn."

Other books begin with a character or setting description, or with a piece of dialogue. Because the opening sentence largely determines how the reader will first connect to a story, it can serve as an effective teaching tool.

I once attended a writing seminar at which the presenter urged us to read with the eyes of both an eagle and a mouse. Her point was that an eagle sees the big picture from above, and the mouse sees the details up close—an interesting and useful metaphor for writing and for life.

I have found that reading has provided me with a lifetime of preparation and training for being an author. Most of that training happened without my knowing it. Now that I am more conscious of reading with a writer's eye, the phrase "hitting the books" has taken on a whole new meaning.

REFERENCES

Cleary, Beverly. 1965. *The Mouse and the Motorcycle.* New York: William Morrow.

Gerstein, Mordicai. 2003. *The Man Who Walked between the Towers.* New York: Scholastic.

Proulx, E. Annie. 1993. *The Shipping News.* New York: Charles Scribner's Sons.

Siebold, Jan. 2005. *My Nights at the Improv.* Morton Grove, IL: Albert Whitman.

Steig, William. 1969. *Sylvester and the Magic Pebble.* New York: Simon and Schuster.

White, E. B. 1952. *Charlotte's Web.* New York: Harper and Row.

BECOMING AN EXPERT—FINDING YOUR NICHE

BRUCE R. SCHUENEMAN

A niche begins with an interest—or even a love. Like the student writing a thesis or a dissertation, a niche must be an area that will maintain your interest for a long time, possibly even an entire lifetime. A niche usually implies a narrow interest. Shakespeare may be an interest, but a niche is performing editions of *Hamlet* or eighteenth-century performing editions of *Hamlet*.

My own niche is related to my love of classical music, which I discovered as a teenager. At the age of twenty-five, I took up the violin and was fortunate to be able to study under Dr. Thomas Pierson at my place of work—Texas A&I University (now Texas A&M University–Kingsville).

As a commentator on classical music in general, I had no real qualification except my love of music. As a player, I began to discover music and composers who were not well known and were in fact entirely obscure. Soon I discovered an entire subspecies of composer called the violinist-composer. Some of these composers are moderately well known, but many of them are completely unknown.

THE FRENCH VIOLIN SCHOOL

Some of the best-known violinist-composers (relatively speaking) were a group of French violinist-composers active during the period 1780–1830. The Italian Giovanni Battista Viotti, who settled in Paris in the 1780s and was one of the first concert violinists to use the modern Tourte bow, founded the so-called French school. Chief among the group of composers following Viotti's example was Pierre Rode, a native of Bordeaux who traveled to Paris as a boy and quickly became Viotti's star pupil.

In the late 1980s, I discovered that the French musicologist Arthur Pougin, perhaps best known for his work on opera, had written a short biography of Pierre Rode titled *Notice sur Rode* (1874). No English translation had ever been published, and the French original was hard to find. Eventually, I found a copy and began work on a translation—first as a lark, but as I progressed that became the serious intention of "doing something with it." I had found a niche—the French violin school that flowered from

Viotti's example, and more particularly Pierre Rode as its finest representative—and now I had acquired enough expertise to use my niche as a platform for publication.

A NICHE LEADS TO EXPERTISE

Before I had finished the English translation of Pougin, I had begun seeking outlets for articles concerning my new passion. In 1990, I published an article in *ViolExchange.* The subject of the article, Rode's Sixth Concerto, gained traction precisely because I was now an expert on Rode, and as such, I owned numerous versions of his best-known concerti. The article was essentially a comparison of published versions, and it particularly demonstrated that one version (still in print at the time) had been brutally edited and was quite at variance with all other published versions. It was the sort of insight that is at once elementary yet entirely obscure, because few violinists owned any Rode concerti, let alone numerous versions of the same work. My niche made me an expert.

By then, I had finished my painstaking translation of Pougin's *Notice sur Rode,* which I self-published in 1994. As translator and publisher, I wrote my own expert introduction and created an index that hadn't existed in the original. The book eventually appeared in *RILM Abstracts of Music Literature.*

OPPORTUNITIES

In the same year that I published my work, I contacted *Music Reference Services Quarterly* about a possible article on Rode. Eventually seven articles, all styled "The Search for the Minor Composer," appeared between 1994 and 1996. Already my niche was expanding. Besides articles on Rode and Viotti, the series included articles on other obscure composers, including Charles de Bériot, Samuel Coleridge-Taylor, Félicien-César David, and Riccardo Drigo.

All the *Music Reference Services Quarterly* articles had been written for the editor William Studwell. Studwell had material on several musical topics, most of which actual scores could immeasurably enhance. Beginning in 1997, I was able to collaborate on six books for Haworth Press (these usually also appeared as double issues of *Music Reference Services Quarterly*). My task, except in the case of the first book (*Minor Ballet Composers,* which I authored), was to produce camera-ready musical scores for publication (via music notation software), though I occasionally wrote small portions of text. This material was pretty far afield from the French violin school: state songs, college fight songs, circus songs, and other popular music. But it was a new way to publish, and while tangential to my main interest, it was also a refreshing break from the French school.

This led to other opportunities. Knowing from my work on Rode that score editions are even more suspect than book editions, I wrote an article on the subject of various printed editions of the same work; this article grew directly out of the experience of my first publication on the French school.

Having discovered that several French school composers, among them Rode, had started their own publishing and retail music firm, a colleague and I successfully submitted a conference proposal: "Legacies: 500 Years of Printed Music Conference." An article in *Fontes Artis Musicae* was the eventual result.

When *Notes: Quarterly Journal of the Music Library Association* asked for suggestions for their Sound Recording Reviews section, I naturally suggested a review article on the French violin school. This represented another variation on my usual French violin school theme, as the article mainly concerned current recordings of the French violin school.

UNSOLICITED INQUIRIES

Most surprising of all, as my niche has developed over the years, are the unsolicited inquiries that resulted in publication. A music professor in Italy contacted me about a chapter for his book on Viotti (*Giovanni Battista Viotti: A Composer between the Two Revolutions*). Again I was able to highlight Rode in yet another way, this time in relation to his mentor Viotti. In 2007, Naxos Records contacted me and asked me to contribute liner notes for a new series of CDs featuring nineteenth-century violin music, including several French school composers.

My niche has developed slowly (partly because of my job responsibilities), but over the years, it has afforded me numerous opportunities for publication in a narrow area of intellectual interest. The necessary condition for a niche is the ability to persevere, and that chiefly requires a love of the subject. If you are true to your love, your love will be true to you, and your niche may even make you an expert.

FIND OUT WHAT'S CURRENTLY BEING PUBLISHED IN CHILDREN'S BOOKS

MARY NORTHRUP

If you are interested in writing for children, you need to know what children are reading *now*. Read the children's classics to help you in your writing, but know that they will not help you identify what will sell. For that, you need to check other sources to find out what is being published currently. When you get your hands on these current books, first read them for content. Read in your area of writing and outside; for example, if you are interested in writing historical fiction for eight- to twelve-year-olds, read everything you can find in historical fiction for eight- to twelve-year-olds, plus other historical fiction books and other books in that age group. Second, read for marketing. Discover what is being published and which companies are publishing.

To find new children's titles, you have a wide variety of resources, print and electronic, to consult.

PERIODICALS

Book Links. www.ala.org/booklinks/. This monthly magazine features articles for librarians, teachers, and parents on how to use books with children. Most articles contain lists of books pertaining to that article's theme. The website includes articles, the magazine's archives, blogs, and an e-newsletter.

Booklist. www.ala.org/booklist/. If you are familiar only with the adult book reviews in this semimonthly magazine, check out its "Books for Youth" section, which reviews titles in three broad age groups. Browse the current issue and indexes of reviews. You can subscribe to Booklist Online for the reviews.

The Bulletin of the Center for Children's Books. http://bccb.lis.uiuc.edu. Published eleven times a year, this publication reviews many children's books. Check out the Monthly Dozen (twelve books on a particular topic), as well as the Blue Ribbon Archive (staff-chosen "best of") and the annual Children's Book Award winners.

The Horn Book Guide. www.hbook.com/guide/. A semiannual guide to almost every children's and young adult book published in the United States, this source rates the books on a six-point scale. View indexes, a gallery of covers, the rating system, and more.

The Horn Book Magazine. www.hbook.com/magazine/. This bimonthly publication, begun in 1924, offers articles and reviews of new children's literature. You can find reviews by themes and authors, and the website includes a blog and podcast.

January Magazine. www.januarymagazine.com. This e-zine, begun in 1997, reviews all types of books. Click on Children's Books for current juvenile titles.

Kirkus Reviews. www.kirkusreviews.com. This biweekly features special issues on children's books (November 15) and young adult books (December 1) each year. Click on Children's to view the list of reviews (you need to subscribe for full reviews).

LMC: Library Media Connection. www.linworth.com/lmc/. Published seven times a year, *LMC* reviews children's books and software in a large section following the feature articles and columns. You can read some of the reviews online.

The New York Times Book Review. www.nytimes.com/pages/books/. This section of the *Times* features a pullout of children's books in May and November and other children's book reviews throughout the year. Includes Children's Books Best Sellers list and a section on children's books under Browsing Books.

Publishers Weekly. www.publishersweekly.com. This is *the* source on publishing news, featuring special issues on children's books in mid-February and mid-July. Click on Children's Books to find book reviews.

School Library Journal. www.schoollibrary journal.com. The standard review source for school media specialists is issued monthly. The journal features lots of reviews, as well as other information for school librarians and media specialists.

NEWSPAPERS

Your local newspaper may occasionally feature an article on new children's books, perhaps geared toward a holiday, season, or a special event (such as Black History Month).

PROFESSIONAL JOURNALS

Publications for educators may include a column on current children's books, such as "Childhood Education," "Instructor," and "Teaching K–8."

WEBSITES

Cooperative Children's Book Center. www.edu cation.wisc.edu/ccbc/. Click on Books for Children and Young Adults to view many lists: by theme, by age, CCBC Choices (best of year), and more. A must-read is the Current Publishing Trends essay.

KidsReads and TeenReads. www.kidsreads.com, www.teenreads.com. Check out the Cool and New section for new books each month.

MARKETS SOURCE

Children's Writer's and Illustrator's Market. This book is published annually by Writer's Digest Books. Take a look at this standard source for marketing your work, as the companies in the Book Publishers' section list their recently published titles.

OTHER SOURCES

Bookstores. Bookstores are probably the best place to find what is currently in the market and selling. Talk to the booksellers, preferably those who are familiar with the children's section.

Libraries. Check the new book display or section in your local public library and ask the children's librarian what he or she thinks are the popular new titles. If you know a school librarian or media specialist, do the same.

Conferences. Any conference that attracts public or school librarians will have exhibits by children's book publishers. The American Association of School Librarians conference is a good one.

Publishers' catalogs. When you read a new book, note the publisher. Then study the company's catalog, either in print or on the Web.

BEST OF THE BEST

Children's books, authors, and illustrators collect many awards each year. Major media sources announce the big ones, the Caldecott and Newbery. Others can be found on websites such as the following:

American Library Association. www.ala.org. Click on Awards for access to literary awards and children's notable lists.

Database of Award-Winning Children's Literature. www.dawcl.com. Read about seventy-nine awards in the "Explanation of Awards" section, then connect to each award's website.

Write what you love, but realize that publishers will accept only what they can sell. Determine what is selling by keeping up with current books, then see how your book idea fits in. It can be a delicate balance: you don't want to be a trend follower, but you also have to be aware of publishing trends. It can also be great fun to keep up with current children's literature, especially if the area is not part of your daily job. So investigate all the sources for new books—and imagine the possibilities for your own!

BUILDING A WRITER'S PORTFOLIO

KRIS SWANK

Whether searching for a job, pursuing tenure, or seeking personal growth, there are simple, effective techniques you can use to build a portfolio of professional publications. Novice writers, as well as experienced authors, should cast a wide net and employ multiple strategies.

KICK-START YOUR PORTFOLIO WITH LOCAL AND NONTRADITIONAL PUBLICATIONS

Writing for local, regional, and nontraditional publications is a great way to get your portfolio growing. The articles in these sources are typically shorter and less formal than those in scholarly journals. This allows less-experienced authors to experiment and develop their own unique voices.

State and regional library associations, public library systems, and academic institutions often produce their own newsletters, newspapers, or magazines featuring articles of interest to their communities. These publications are always searching for contributions, and the editors won't shun new authors as long as they have good story ideas and solid writing skills. Write concise, upbeat articles on personal experiences or the latest events at your library, such as special programs, grants received, or new technologies. My first professional publication was an informative piece for my state association newsletter about a study tour I'd taken to Japan. I also created a library newsletter at my college and contributed articles to our alumni magazine. By using multiple strategies, I was quickly able to start a professional portfolio.

Today, technology provides even more avenues for publication. You could edit a web page, start a library blog or podcast, or create innovative electronic resources. For example, Bob Baker, the library director for distance education at Pima Community College, recently developed a series of YouTube videos on information literacy.

GOING NATIONAL MAY BE EASIER THAN YOU THINK

There are more than 1,500 library and information science periodicals currently published in the United States, according to *Ulrich's Periodicals Directory.* Only about a hundred of them are refereed, and most need a steady supply of interesting, well-written pieces. Develop articles from conference presentations, poster sessions, or even library-school research projects. When Connie Forst, a public librarian from Vegreville, Alberta, was selected to attend the 2006 Thinking Outside the Borders library leadership institute in Champaign, Illinois, she took pen and camera along to record her experiences. The Canadian Library Association's national magazine, *Feliciter,* published her article about the institute. Be sure to check a periodical's submissions policies on its website or inside a recent issue.

A massive collection of library documents resides in ERIC, the U.S. Department of Education's digital library. ERIC actively seeks submissions of high-quality education-related materials, including research reports, conference papers, dissertations, and theses.

Writing book reviews is another good vehicle for building a portfolio. Publications like *Booklist, Choice, Library Journal, Midwest Book Review,* and *School Library Journal* routinely seek reviewers. But according to Donna Seaman, associate editor of adult books at *Booklist,* some areas of expertise are needed more than others. "Many reviewers want to review fiction, for example, but few are qualified to review arts and science books," she says. In past years, *Library Journal* has called for reviewers on such diverse topics as child rearing, pop psychology, business, do-it-yourself, and religion. Writing book reviews is fun, but it's a serious commitment. Editors may expect you to review a book per month, and periodicals have strict deadlines. Visit magazine websites for specific guidelines and application information.

USE THE BUDDY SYSTEM

Novice writers may not feel ready or qualified to pen an entire paper on their own. Collaborating with more experienced authors is an effective solution. Look for coauthors both inside the library and in complementary fields such as educational technology, information technology, and student services. Or propose a partnership with those who use your library services, such as professors or community organizers.

Contributing to an edited volume is another way to collaborate. When Gwen Meyer Gregory, then a librarian at Colorado College, considered publishing a book, she knew that writing long works was not one of her strengths. But coordinating projects and motivating others were things she did well. So Gregory opted to edit a volume of papers that other librarians contributed. She wrote the outline and introduction, solicited authors with specific expertise, edited the submissions, and coordinated with the publisher. The result was *The Successful Academic Librarian,* a critical success and a 2005 Colorado Book Award finalist.

Calls for papers (CFPs) can come from a variety of sources: word of mouth, publishers' websites, or even online. Yahoo! Groups and CataList can help you identify and subscribe to electronic discussion groups on library topics, where CFPs may be posted. The website *A Library Writer's Blog* also regularly posts CFPs.

ADDITIONAL ADVICE

Recycling. You may be tempted to grow your writing portfolio by submitting the same project to multiple outlets. It's an ethical no-no and can damage your reputation unless you change the material substantially for each publication or acknowledge in writing that the work was previously published elsewhere. Some periodicals accept only previously unpublished material.

Tenure. If you're building a portfolio for tenure review, keep in mind that universities often weigh various publications differently. For instance, research articles in peer-reviewed journals may earn more points than newsletter stories. Carefully read your organization's tenure policy.

New technologies. Keep an eye open for emerging channels of professional communication. Five years ago, who would have heard of podcasts or blogging? Who knows—soon you may be publishing articles straight to cell phones or using Ajax web applications to customize your data for each reader.

Until that future, employ the strategies discussed here and your professional writing portfolio will soon be growing.

FOR MORE PRINT AND ONLINE INFORMATION

Bob Baker's "Info Literacy" video series on YouTube

Booklist

CataList, catalog of electronic discussion lists

Choice

ERIC, U.S. Department of Education

Connie Forst, "Thinking outside the Borders," *Feliciter,* no. 3 (2007): 151–152

Gwen Meyer Gregory, *The Successful Academic Librarian: Winning Strategies from Library Leaders,* Medford, NJ: Information Today, 2005

Library Journal

A Library Writer's Blog

Midwest Book Review

School Library Journal

Ulrich's Periodicals Directory Online

Yahoo! Groups, online discussion groups

MLS, MFA

The Working Librarian Pursuing a Degree in Creative Writing

COLLEEN S. HARRIS

Finding the time to pursue a master of fine arts (MFA) in writing is challenging for anyone. In particular, as a working librarian, you don't have the luxury of schooling full-time without the responsibilities of your job looming over you. If you take the low-residency route for an MFA program, which is increasingly the route that already-employed would-be-writers take, you dedicate approximately ten days in the spring and ten in the fall (though this varies from program to program) to actually being on campus and immersed in a retreat and classroom setting. You spend the rest of your time writing from home and corresponding with faculty and other students while living your real life. The great thing about this system is that you are forced to dedicate yourself to writing even while bombarded by the daily stresses of work and family. While attending full-time sounds great, it insulates you from the rigors of real life. The low-residency program allows you to develop your craft while acclimating to squeezing in dedicated writing time, which can easily fall to the bottom of the list when life gets hectic. When deadlines loom and you are paying tuition, excuses of "I don't have time to write" lose their power, and you learn to incorporate writing into your daily routine.

In addition to work, committee meetings, various projects, and keeping up with professional development and technology changes, many librarians write professional articles; participate in organizations at the local, state, and national levels; attend and present at various conferences throughout the year; and are busy keeping up with new developments and literature in the field. Committing twenty-five to thirty hours a week (as most programs recommend) on such a personal pursuit as creative writing is no small feat, particularly because the residency part of the program likely comes out of hard-earned vacation time.

Given those considerations, however, pursuing an MFA in creative writing can be a rewarding and ful-filling experience. Your MLS is a terminal degree in a professional field that qualifies you to be a librarian. The MFA, while it is also considered a terminal degree and qualifies you to do particular things (like teach creative writing), may be a much more personal achievement because you are working on your own personal craft that nurtures your unique talent and style, and what you leave the program with has been uniquely tailored to your individual needs.

There are three essential factors that contribute to the librarian's successful pursuit of an MFA in creative writing that will contribute to your success in completing the degree: mind space, time, and commitment.

MIND SPACE

Writing professionally occurs in a completely different mind-set from sitting down to work on your creative writing, and you'll get frustrated if you try to swap from one to the other without recognizing that your brain needs some form of transition. While professional writing and projects can be somewhat formulaic in their construction, creative writing is often less so. It helps to have a dedicated space away from librarian work where you don't have to worry about any of your library projects bogging you down. Allowing space in your schedule between work and writing may help, as may collecting a file of writing prompts that allow you to switch from analytical and critical thinking to a more creative mind-set. Regular meetings or correspondence with fellow writers either locally or via the Internet may also help you create this sphere of creative mental activity.

TIME

You have to be willing to take the time your writing requires and deserves. Your supervisors and coworkers are not going to tell you that you work too much (and if they do, it's likely because you've gone so far around the bend that they felt obligated to mention it). It is your responsibility to schedule some sacred time for yourself outside of work and other life obligations. This may mean getting up a few hours early and stealing time to write or specifically blocking out time on your personal calendar for uninterrupted writing time in the afternoon or evening. Whatever method works best for you, remember that, much as the time you spend on your professional life is important to your future and the attainment of your goals, the time you spend on your creative writing may be equally important for you to feel fulfilled. The time you spend writing is just as important as the time you spend on "real" work, and it deserves to be honored. Writing is a habit that needs to be nurtured.

COMMITMENT

As a professional, you likely make the commitment to get to work on time, to complete projects on or before a due date, and to be responsible for your actions and inaction. Your personal life as a writer deserves no less. Committing to the pursuit of the MFA doesn't just require you to carve out separate physical and mind space and a good deal of time; it also requires acceptance that this is an important personal commitment that will take energy. Yes, looming deadlines can be frustrating, particularly if the words aren't coming and research won't fill the gap. It can also be difficult to split yourself between conference attendance for professional development as a librarian and conferences that may hold great value for you as a writer. Understand that some form of compromise on each side will be necessary.

The MFA in creative writing is a natural addition for the librarian who is naturally curious, organized, and enjoys the thrills and challenges of creation. With the right mind-set and preparation, pursuit of the MFA can be a fulfilling addition to an already-rich career.

BRINGING CREATIVE WRITING LESSONS TO THE LIBRARY LITERATURE WORKTABLE

GEORGIE DONOVAN

Every year, dozens of books are published, targeted at creative writers who want to try their hand at everything from poetry to creative nonfiction to romance novels. In addition, hundreds of students graduate with degrees in creative writing annually. What lessons do these books and graduate programs teach about writing that apply to scholarly writing for library journals?

In 2000, I finished an MFA in creative writing with a book of poetry as my thesis project. After teaching college English, I returned to school for an MLS and have been working in libraries ever since. When I started my current tenure-track position at midyear, my dean offered the option to add a year to my tenure clock because of my late start date. At the time, I declined because I thought about how I generally like writing. She may have been surprised, but having coursework in creative writing helped to alleviate some of the anxiety that many early-career librarians feel when facing their first publication. With this in mind, several strategies that creative writing and composition students learn are applicable to writing for a scholarly audience in library and information studies.

LEARN TO FREEWRITE

Writing for publication requires using different mental muscles and therefore requires getting into shape. The writing we do on a daily basis consists of e-mail and short reports with bullet points. However, the rhetorical structure of an academic journal article looks quite different. To exercise those writing muscles, professors of writing recommend freewriting every day. In the creative world, carving out a specific time to write without editing is crucial to developing fluency and the ability to concentrate for long stretches. In our library, a group of colleagues started a "writing buddies" group in which researchers schedule a short time to come together in a quiet room and work on their current writing project. Setting aside time regularly to write helps train the mind to approach the blank page with less anxiety and effort.

PUT ASIDE THE CRITICAL VOICE WHEN DRAFTING

It's impossible to get anything on the page when a voice in the back of your mind insists that the project is worthless, that your writing is terrible, and that television has permanently stunted your vocabulary. A time and place exist for that inner critic, but during the drafting stage, that voice should be ignored. All writers, even the most brilliant ones who write award-winning books, write terrible first drafts with awkward phrasing, inelegant diction, and paragraphs of meandering thoughts. The first goal is to get something down on paper, and later, the inner critic can edit, revise, and rearrange everything.

WRITE CONFIDENTLY

Frequent advice to creative writers is "write what you know." This comes to bear on all writers as they approach their topic with confidence. In coediting a book of stories from new librarians, I frequently counseled authors who felt that they could talk about their own experience but weren't sure how that might relate to other librarians. As I reminded them, when we read journals, librarians are always eager to adopt best practices, to take programs and anecdotes of other libraries and turn them into success stories in our home institutions. As authors, we should have the confidence to talk about what we know in a way that encourages others to learn from our success, to understand our findings, and to extrapolate our research into systems and ideas that apply elsewhere.

EDITING YOUR WORK CRITICALLY

If you've only ever written a few pages of text, then each sentence you wrote may be very dear to you. Once you have written more, though, it is easier to edit and scratch through entire paragraphs of mediocre writing. Poets may salvage one good phrase from pages of freewriting and use that to create an entirely new work. Stories abound of writers who shave hundreds of pages from a manuscript to create a tighter, more cohesive novel. In the same way, librarians who write must be able to turn a critical eye to their own work, ensuring that each paragraph adds to their argument and helps the reader understand and follow logically to the conclusion. Time spent away from a piece is one recognized strategy, but having a colleague read your work critically can be helpful as well, especially if you toughen up enough to take his or her edits cheerfully.

BE DIRECT

The best writers express this idea differently, but all talk about the need to be concrete, direct, and vivid. In some texts, this idea is expressed as "show, don't tell," meaning that an image is a more direct communication than a vague circumlocution describing the emotion or insight. Other writers focus on the power of strong nouns and active-voice verbs, and most who are writing textbooks implore the writer to avoid adverbs. In library literature, make every word count, and edit with an eye toward clarity and conciseness. Elegant prose may be rare in library journals, but readers appreciate it when it appears and share those articles widely.

The only way to learn to write is to write often. Moreover, the only characteristic of a writer is someone who writes. For librarians, publishing can be a chore or it can become part of each person's identity as a professional: someone who writes and shares that work in the wider field of librarianship. Employing specific strategies to develop creativity in that facet of a librarian's professional life can be the catalyst that turns writing from an unpleasant task to something that gives great pride and an outlet for professional curiosity and passion.

NURTURING THE WRITER WITHIN USING MENTORS AND GUIDES

PAUL BLOBAUM

Librarians are from a community of organizers and researchers. Our professional theories do not address authorship: Ranganathan's laws of librarianship do not mention writing. I know a lot of librarians who are readers, devouring several books a week (which I find intimidating), but relatively few who are writers. We are experts at implementing technological solutions and providing top-notch service to our users, but writing is low on our priority list. Librarians who write and publish stand out from the crowd. It is going to be lonely, you and that blank page. Finding companions and guides on this journey will be important.

The Buddhist proverb "When the student is ready, the teacher will appear" seems to be a useful metaphor for us. The more you become interested in writing, the more the universe will spin writing-related things your way. You will start noticing things like writers' groups in the community. You will discover books as well as websites and blogs for writers. When you go to a bookstore, through a cosmic coincidence, you will find yourself by the shelves with writing and publishing books on them.

Librarians are world-class networkers. Tell your friends and colleagues that you are interested in writing, and the word will get around. Friends and colleagues will recommend books on writing to you, and you will make connections.

Although you cannot learn to write by reading books about writing any more than you can learn to play the piano by reading a book about playing the piano, books on writing can provide significant companionship and guidance. The writing process can be isolating and disruptive, and people in your life aren't going to understand what you are going through, so you will want to connect with people who do.

My dad is a fine writing role model for me. Before he retired after forty years of ministry, he often could be found tapping away at his typewriter and scribbling on legal pads at his desk. He wrote a sermon every week, wrote copy for church newsletters and bulletins, and carried on correspondence.

My dad introduced me to one of my favorite books on the writing process. It describes the technical components of writing and the emotional and psychological aspects. Despite his years of extensive writing (and mentoring), my dad took a workshop on writing memoirs at his local community college when he retired. The workshop leader recommended Anne Lamott's *Bird by Bird* (1995) as a good book about the writing process. Lamott writes about her brother's childhood difficulty of completing a school report about birds. He was overwhelmed with the writing assignment. His mother advised him to write it "bird by bird," thus the title. Dad asked me if I would locate a copy for him, and I read it first, naturally.

I immediately became a Lamott devotee and read several of her books. Later, while flipping channels one day, I found Anne Lamott on the Book Channel talking about writing one of her books. Even though Lamott never reviewed one of my manuscripts, I benefited greatly from her insight and experiences as a writer and teacher.

Another author whom I consider a mentor is Paul Silvia, author of *How to Write a Lot* (2007). Silvia describes the scholarly writing process for freshly minted psychology professors and offers practical advice. He is an advocate for setting aside regular times for writing and for designating space for writing. Even though I likely will never meet Silvia, he joined my personal pantheon of teachers and guides. Your job is to arrange your own.

Peer reviewers are also crucial for successful writers. In addition to connecting to books about writing, making connections with real people with whom you can collaborate and have read your drafts is a great gift. These opportunities often come disguised as hard work.

While I was in library school at the University of Illinois, I was fortunate that my graduate assistantship supervisor, a faculty librarian, invited me to do some research and coauthor an article. Years later, in the early years of my tenure-track library faculty career, I serendipitously found a grant-proposal-writing mentor while having coffee one day. Later, my dean, who has a master's in English, noticed that I was sweating details over a book chapter I was writing and offered to be a peer reviewer. Each mentor appeared right at the time I needed her.

I also have been fortunate to find a writing "pal," a junior faculty colleague who teaches language arts and the writing process to preservice teachers. We mentor each other. She reviews my writing and gives constructive feedback, and I help her with technology skills. This works out nicely. A lot of our work of mutual support can be done while at home and at odd hours, thanks to the miracle of computer technology and broadband Internet.

Nurturing the writer within you is a lifelong process, and connecting with others, especially mentors, will help you become better with this calling. I wish you much satisfaction and success as you move ahead with your writing.

REFERENCES

Lamott, Anne. 1995. *Bird by Bird: Some Instructions on Writing and Life.* New York: Anchor Books.

Silvia, Paul J. 2007. *How to Write a Lot: A Practical Guide to Productive Academic Writing.* Washington, DC: APA LifeTools.

WRITING WITH COLLEAGUES
Strategies for Getting the Work Done

GEORGIE DONOVAN

Starting a writing project with a friend may seem like a clever idea until you're in the midst of things, when any number of problems arise: You've e-mailed your coauthor, but suddenly she is missing in action. You're not sure whether she's lost interest, is procrastinating, or has dropped off the planet. Your coauthor is mailing you, but you haven't finished the work, and instead of confessing to your delay, you've been letting his e-mail fester at the bottom of your in-box. Both of you were excited about the project initially, but now your passion for the piece has fizzled. Although you and your cowriter agreed about the initial idea, now that you're in the midst of the writing project, you realize that your two perspectives are misaligned.

This short list of possible scenarios alludes to the countless challenges involved in writing with a colleague. Nevertheless, partnering with someone to accomplish the research can create a stronger published piece, help your ideas evolve, and ease the overall writing process. By incorporating the following strategies into the work flow, a collaborative research and writing project will run more efficiently and lead to a better finished product.

BUILD A STRONG COMMUNICATION NETWORK WITH YOUR COAUTHOR

As with any collaborative project, regular and open communication is crucial to cowriting for publication. As the coeditor of a book and coauthor of several articles, I have learned to work with librarians who work both down the hall and across the country. Our projects began with a few long conversations about an idea that sparked our curiosity and passion. In the course of these conversations, we moved rather quickly to the practical stage, testing the waters for whether a joint project would work and how. In early discussions, ask your colleague about her strengths, how he likes to work, whether she enjoys deadlines or more flexibility, and other characteristics about his working style. For example, I know that I have a difficult time staring at a blank screen, so I frequently ask a coauthor to start an outline, and I will revise the outline and start writing sections under each heading.

COMING CLEAN ABOUT PROCRASTINATION

Delays can be either the result of sincere scheduling conflicts that arise when juggling work with professional writing or the result of procrastination. In either case, the best policy is to communicate honestly with your coauthor about your needs. For example, when you get an e-mail about the project that you know you cannot respond to immediately, at least write back immediately with a short e-mail, letting your coauthor know that you received his message and will reply next week. If you're the one sending e-mail that seem to die in cyberspace, don't hesitate to resend something or call your colleague before you become frustrated. Like many others, I rely on e-mail as an indispensable communication tool, but a quick telephone call at work can often solve a writing puzzle or get you back in the spirit to write another section of the piece. If you feel procrastination becoming a problem, call and talk to your coauthor. Talking about the research and about your work honestly is often a simple way to solicit advice or end dawdling.

DRAFT AN ACTION PLAN AND KEEP REVISING IT

An action plan, like a time line, has specific tasks or responsibilities accompanied by deadlines for their completion. In addition, the plan should list who is responsible for each task and a notes field for changes or questions that arise. While coauthoring a book, I created three separate action plans that we used at different points throughout the process. Our first action plan was a rough sketch of the chapters and which one of us would be responsible for receiving and editing those chapters. We included a rough time line listing when we would review proposals, the deadline for finished manuscripts, a date to return chapters for revision, and final submission deadlines. Many of these deadlines were revised along the way, but early planning gave us flexibility when the need arose. We used action plans later in the process to handle the dozens of edits from the publisher and manage the proofreading process efficiently.

To create a basic action plan, start a table with four columns. The column headings should include the responsibility, who is responsible, deadline for the task, and comments. The more detail used in listing tasks, the easier it will be to bite off small chunks of work incrementally. On the action plan for my book, my coauthor and I included tasks such as "work on introduction with elements: why authors were selected; audience for the book; preview of each chapter." Whenever I had free time to work on the book, I had a few manageable tasks to do rather than having to dive into the book fresh each time.

USE AN OUTLINE

Starting in third-grade English, we created outlines for our research papers as part of the writing process. For a while, I left this step behind, trying to save time by diving straight into the draft stage. As a coauthor, however, it is much easier to begin by compromising on an outline of the article, chapter, or paper. At this point, many thorny problems can be avoided, such as spending a great deal of time on a project only to realize that your coauthor has a radically different take on the issues than you do. Outlines also slice the work into segments that are easier to tackle than a blank page. My outlines frequently have a section heading followed by the number of paragraphs needed on that topic. For an introduction, we might list "two paragraphs" in the outline. Knowing you only have to write two paragraphs, each comprising four or five sentences, makes the work much less daunting.

With strong communication, a plan for accomplishing the work, and an outline that points toward the finished product, writing with a colleague can be easier and more interesting than working alone. Your coauthor can reinvigorate your interest in the project when your energy wanes, and you can polish his or her brilliant ideas by cleaning up less-than-brilliant prose. Although perhaps it is more than half the work of publishing an article solo, the benefits of cowriting are ample, and it is worth taking the time to make the writing process run as effortlessly as possible.

LIBRARIAN WRITING GROUPS

STEPHANIE MATHSON

Do you find scholarly writing a rather solitary pursuit? Do you ever wonder if other librarians will find your research useful or at least interesting? Are your colleagues asking themselves these same questions? If they are, consider establishing a writing group to encourage one another's work and to meet regularly to edit and revise one another's papers.

In April 2007, three colleagues and I attended a workshop conducted by Tara Gray, who, among her many works, wrote the book *Publish and Flourish: Become a Prolific Scholar.* In the book, Gray advises faculty members to write for fifteen to thirty minutes per day, every day, to get into the habit of putting fingers to the keyboard (or pen to paper). Gray, who is the director of the Teaching Academy and an associate professor of criminal justice at New Mexico State University, is a strong advocate for writing groups. She argues that members of such groups who record the amount of time they write daily and hold one another accountable for that task are far more productive than the solitary scholars locked away in their offices who write for good chunks of time but do so only occasionally. She provides statistics to support her assertions, which makes her short book a must-read.

The workshop was a live rendering of the book, complete with a discussion on the how-tos of creating a writing group. Papers, Gray claimed, are stronger when shared early and readily. Laypeople can read drafts, too, so do not worry if someone with no technical know-how reads your paper about the mechanics of adding streaming video content to your library's catalog. It is later in the writing process that you should look for experts with whom you can share your paper for review.

Spurred on by Gray, my colleagues and I decided to establish a writing group after the workshop. We extended invitations to two other coworkers who had not attended the workshop but were interested in joining our group. We all had to commit to writing every single day and charting our progress. Because several of us were working on various research projects at the time, making such a commitment posed no problems—at least not initially.

The next step was to establish a firm meeting date. We attempted to find one period during which all six of us were free every week, but that turned out to be impossible. We settled for the date and time that the majority was available; those who were not free then could meet with the rest of us as their schedules permitted.

Meeting on a weekly basis kept us intently focused on our own writing and much more engaged with one another than we would have been otherwise. It was midspring when we began meeting. With the end of classes around the corner and individual deadlines looming, we were productive.

During our writing group meetings, we limited the amount of work we shared with one another to three or four pages per person each week. That was enough by which we could chart our progress for one another. In addition, that amount of work was the result of the fifteen to thirty minutes of writing we aimed to do each day. At the beginning of each meeting, we discussed when and how we had accomplished our writing output for the week, and we mentioned any hindrances we had encountered. Then we distributed copies of our work to one another, read the text (editing as we went), and discussed each person's work in turn. We spent approximately one hour at each writing session, and there were times we could not finish discussing everyone's work. In those cases, we would return our marked drafts to the author and exchange further comments via e-mail as necessary.

Throughout the rest of last year, our group was quite productive. I completed and shared with my colleagues the better parts of two different articles that I have now published. Another member accomplished the same. A third member finally finished a paper that she had long let languish on her desk, and a fourth member outlined and wrote the introductory matter for the book she conducted research for while on sabbatical.

Our group was far less formal than it might appear. We met only when at least three of the six people involved were available, which meant that as the months wore on and projects came to an end, or vacations (and, in one case, a sabbatical) were taken, we met less and less regularly. As a result, we relied on e-mail more and more.

Despite the fact that communicating via e-mail is not typically as effective as face-to-face interaction, as it allows us to put off doing tasks that meeting in person forces us to complete more quickly, our group has cooperated very well through that means. Case in point: Earlier this year, one of the group members spent four weeks as a fellow at the University of Michigan's Inter-University Consortium for Political and Social Research (ICPSR), conducting research on the role that librarians have played as ICPSR organizational representatives at their respective institutions. My colleague wrote a paper on her research that other members of the group and I reviewed and critiqued via e-mail. This experience provided us with evidence that we do not always have to meet in person to work productively and collegially with one another. With more projects ahead for us, no doubt we will continue to draw on one another's assistance in revising papers and preparing for presentations.

WRITING GROUPS

NANCY KALIKOW MAXWELL

This chapter would have been better if I had taken it to my writing group for critiquing. But how could I? Then Maria would know I think she's a blowhard who knows nothing about writing. Peggy would discover that when she tears into my writing, she tears directly into my heart. Jean, in contrast, would learn that her comments are useless because she loves everything I write. "Great!!! Great!!! Great!!!" she scrawls in the corner of the first page of each manuscript. If my writing was consistently "Great!!!" I wouldn't need to belong to a writing group.

Of course these are not their real names, but each of them would see through my veiled attempt at camouflage. I just hope none of them ever stumbles on a copy of this book. Snide comments aside, I need my Maria, Peggy, Jean, and all the members of my writing group. Despite the suffering they inflict on me, they do improve my writing. At writing workshops I lead, one piece of advice I offer aspiring writers is to join a writing group. "They can be pains to participate in, but writing groups are worth it."

MOTIVATION

Before you even step foot into the room at your first meeting, you will enjoy benefits from the group. As with being given a homework assignment, writing groups impose a subconscious deadline on you. The type of writing that members of critique groups do is usually self-generated and therefore lacking a true timetable. Unless you have a publisher, no one demands that you finish that poem about the sunset over the Adirondack lake or tackle the part in your novel where Harry whacks his former lover. Whether your group meets weekly, twice a month, or monthly—all common writing group frequencies— the structured schedule will generate a deadline for producing pages.

AUDIENCE

Although mechanics differ, one central feature of most writing groups is that authors read works aloud, providing the author a live audience to test the piece. An amazing amount of information can be detected nonverbally from such a gathering. My daughter, a theater major, tells me that stage performers learn how to "read" audiences by paying attention to their reactions. Whether those assembled are engaged, scared, intrigued, or thinking about dinner can be gauged by their responses. The author will know immediately when the piece is working and—more important—when it is not.

CRITIQUING AND EDITING

Because writers are so close to the work, possible improvements may not occur to them. Writing groups provide a method to obtain an outside, objective perspective on how the piece could be better. A good critique not only will point out whether the work is good or bad (or great!!!) but also will contribute constructive comments. Suggestions about relocating paragraphs, changing openings, or defining characters can help change a lackluster manuscript into an engaging piece of writing.

Effective critiques also let the writer know when the picture that appears in his or her head has not been successfully transferred to the reader. From the aforementioned lover-whacking novel, my writing group was presented with a scene describing a steamy sexual encounter between the narrator and a prostitute. Later the action switched to him luridly making love with his girlfriend. Although all of us—especially the men—applauded the character's sexual prowess, we questioned how he could deftly switch sexual partners so quickly. Only then did the author realize that the reader did not know that the prostitute and girlfriend were the same character (who subsequently also became the "whack-ee").

Groups can also be a source of free editing assistance. Margaret, a former high school English teacher, was invaluable to one group for her ability to catch grammatical errors. Before any of us submitted a work for publication, we made sure Margaret read it. We knew that any piece that could pass the Margaret test was punctuation perfect.

FINDING OR STARTING A WRITING GROUP

It may take many attempts to find a group that works for you. The list at the end of this chapter provides places to begin your search. It can be especially difficult to locate a mix of individuals at the appropriate critiquing level. Much like the Three Bears, some groups will be too soft and some too hard. To ensure a uniform level of expertise, groups may limit participation to published writers or admit members by invitation only. People who are just starting out may need to try several groups to find a good fit.

A FEW GOOD MEMBERS

As you embark on your quest, keep in mind that no group will consist of 100 percent useful participants. For several years, I belonged to a group of about fifteen people, but only two of them consistently offered critiques that I found helpful. However, those two people were so astute and improved my writing to such an extent that I continued to participate. I tried to listen to them and ignore the comments of the rest of the group. *Tried* is the operative word here, because ignoring negative comments—even from those you consciously disregard—can be difficult.

If you cannot locate an appropriate group or an existing group is not working, you may want to consider starting your own. Once you have a cadre of participants, schedule a date, sit yourself down, and do some writing. Just be ready to have your work denigrated by a blowhard or two. Or perhaps you will learn that everything you write is "Great!!!" Everything, that is, except your piece about writing groups.

PLACES TO FIND OR START A WRITING GROUP

- local public library
- state or local affiliate of the Library of Congress Center for the Book (www.loc .gov/loc/cfbook/stacen.html)
- major bookstores
- community colleges
- continuing education classes at public schools
- noncredit division of colleges and universities
- parks and recreation departments

NETWORKING AND SERENDIPITY IN PUBLISHING

ALINE SOULES

We network every day through more forms of communication than ever before: face-to-face, telephone, e-mail, online chat, instant messaging, electronic discussion lists, social networking, talk radio, local television, newspapers, conferences, teleconferencing, webinars.

The traditional method of publication has been to write an article, submit it, and wait for results. While this method is still valid, it's time consuming, and if your submission is rejected, you end up with nothing. I write in both the library and the creative writing fields. In creative writing, "no simultaneous submissions" used to be a rule—at that rate, you might never be published. Now that's changed.

GETTING STARTED

Publishing opportunities are increasing all the time. They often come through electronic discussion lists. I belong to about two dozen such lists. While others choose RSS feeds, I prefer to receive e-mail directly. I skim them for information, calls for proposals, and the names and e-mail addresses of major contributors whom I might want to contact some day.

The sooner you see a call for proposals, the sooner you spot opportunity and can act. Sooner is better than later. Your submission may be saved until the deadline, but sometimes proposals are read on arrival. If you are ahead of deadline, your proposal will likely get more consideration.

Be active on campus or in your community and you'll meet interesting people. Any librarian can join the local library and its friends group. You meet people who are interested in libraries and who may also be connected to local government, giving you more potential connections.

Attending conferences is another way to meet people, learn about the organization, and gain opportunities. Talk to the person sitting next to you in a meeting. If you enjoyed the presentation, introduce yourself to the speakers or panel moderator. Can you join the committee? Participate in program planning? Get to know people and let them know

you. As you broaden your scope, you'll reach the tipping point where opportunity starts to find you.

SERENDIPITY

Never underestimate serendipity. People have told me that I'm lucky—and it's true. I don't control luck, but I do control whether I position myself for luck. For years, I've followed the advice I described here and, every once in a while, I'm in the right place at the right time to be lucky.

When I was only a couple of years out of library school, I was at a party and heard that there was a job as coordinator of extramural library services at the University of Windsor in Windsor, Ontario. I applied and got it. It was a low-tech, pretechnology version of distance learning. The director of the library where we placed one of our programs was a real go-getter, and I made sure to meet her every time I traveled there. She asked me to be on a team to write a report for the Ontario government about this new collaboration. I benefited from her mentorship, got my first publication, and was called by my local member of Parliament with another opportunity and connections to more people than I could have imagined. Was I lucky? Yes. Did I help to make that luck? Yes. I was the first library liaison who had sought out that director every time I visited. It paid off.

I've been published in the *Kenyon Review,* a prestigious creative writing journal. If I had just submitted my work, I would probably have been rejected, but I was invited. As part of completing my MFA in creative writing, I read my work to a group. I have a theater degree, I enjoy presenting, and it was fun. I read some prose poems. What I didn't know was that the audience included an editor for the *Kenyon Review.* She came up afterward and asked me to send her my best pieces. Lucky? Definitely. Did I make my own luck? Yes. I read well and my work was good enough to pique her interest. Later, when that editor completed a novel, she contacted me and I returned the favor to some extent by sharing a galley copy with my local independent bookstore owner (yes, I know him, too).

COLLABORATION

You can work alone or find partners. If you work alone, you really need to want to write because it calls for self-motivation that's not always as easy as it sounds. I once read that 80 percent of writers need a deadline and only 20 percent don't. If you are writing on spec, without a deadline, you'd better want it.

One option to counteract this is to join a writing group. If you can find a good one, it is a manifold blessing. You read others' work, you give and get feedback, and you form community. I have never been able to decide whether I gain more from giving feedback or getting it. If you can't find a group, try starting one. Your group could be on campus, in your community, from the organizations you join, even over e-mail. Sometimes it's great; sometimes it peters out. I currently belong to a writing circle at work and a writing group through the California Writers Club. I meet with a local individual once a month and I exchange work monthly via e-mail with another person. Writing doesn't have to be alone.

Another option is collaboration. I generally initiate collaborations after I get the opportunity. I'll call people I hardly know if I think they're the right people. I usually find them grateful. They don't have to hustle up an opportunity—I offer it. We complement each other. Sometimes, I've gone through two or three partners before finding one to see a project through. Occasionally, a project fizzles out, but it's a risk I've never regretted. The end result has always been better, it's easier to stay on track, and I meet new colleagues.

GO FOR IT

I've given you some ideas. Now it's up to you—have fun!

245 FIELD MEETS CHICAGO MANUAL OF STYLE

Formatting Your Manuscript

KATHRYN YELINEK

No matter where in a library you work, an eye for detail gets you through the day. Catalogers: you knew AACR2 inside and out, and by the time this book is published, you'll probably know RDA and FRBR, too. Reference librarians: you routinely walk students through the pitfalls of perfecting a bibliography. Whether you work in technical or public services, not a comma or a period goes unquestioned.

Such attention to detail matters when you're submitting for publication. Following publishing conventions tells an editor that you're a professional who cares enough to make a good impression—and that's one less reason to toss your piece in the reject pile. This article will walk you through the rules of submitting on paper or by e-mail.

For all submissions, you should first read the submission guidelines for your target publication. Most magazines and publishing houses will have a website that includes tips for submitting to them. Take the time to read these guidelines carefully and follow them exactly. If the guidelines say to include your name only in a cover letter and not on the manuscript, then include your name only on the cover letter. There really is no excuse not to follow any given guidelines. You follow the rules for cataloging and citing works—do the same when you submit.

FORMATTING A PAPER SUBMISSION

First, unless the publication guidelines say otherwise, follow standard manuscript format. Standard manuscript format calls for the following:

- Double-space.
- Use white paper with black ink.
- Include at least one-inch margins.
- Print on good-quality computer paper.
- Print on one side of the paper only (do not duplex).
- Indent each paragraph (do not include a blank line between paragraphs).
- Use a twelve-point standard font such as Courier or Times New Roman.

Second, format your first page, which will look different from all of your other pages. On your first page, type your contact information in a single-spaced text block in the upper-left-hand corner. Here, include

- Your real name.
- Your contact information, including address, phone number, fax number, and e-mail.

- The total number of words in the work. Round to the nearest hundred for shorter pieces (4,312 words becomes 4,300 words) and thousand for longer pieces (54,897 words becomes 55,000).

Once you've finished this contact information block, switch to double-spacing. About a third to half of the way down the page, type the title of your piece, centered. One double-spaced line below that, type the word *by*. One double-spaced line below that, type your name. If you're using a pseudonym, type your pseudonym. Two double-spaced lines below that, align your text left, indent, and begin the first line of your piece.

Third, add a header to all pages after your first page. Do not include a header on your first page. The header contains three components: your last name, the title of your piece, and the page number. Formatting this header varies, but in general, include your last name and title (or keywords if the title is long) on the left. For example: "Yelinek/Formatting Your Manuscript." On the right, insert the page number.

Congratulations! You've successfully formatted your print submission.

FORMATTING AN ELECTRONIC SUBMISSION

First, if the publication accepts attachments, format the manuscript as you would for a print submission, following the foregoing guidelines. Be sure to include a meaningful subject line for your e-mail, such as "Submission: [Title of Your Piece]." Pay attention to the file format that the editor wants. If the editor wants rich-text format (.rtf) instead of Microsoft Word (.doc or .docx), then save a copy of your piece in that format before attaching it.

Second, if the publication does not accept attachments, you will need to include the text of your submission in the body of the e-mail. You can't just cut and paste from MS Word, though, because many e-mail programs have trouble reading the Word format. You don't want an editor to open your e-mail and see what looks like hieroglyphics! To avoid this, convert your piece to a plain-text document (.txt).

You will lose formatting such as italics, bold, and paragraph indentations, but you'll ensure that your editor can read your piece, no matter what e-mail program he or she uses.

To convert a Word document to plain text, follow these directions:

- Make sure your text is at least a twelve-point font.

- Select all of the original text.

- Increase the left and right margins to 1.5 inches.

- Choose the option Save As. Under Save As Type, select Plain Text. This will give you a document with a .txt extension.

- If you receive a warning prompt about compatible features, select Yes. Also, check the box that asks whether you want to insert line breaks.

- Open the new document in WordPad or Notepad and read it carefully. If you weren't able to check the box to insert line breaks, insert them manually. Be sure there is a blank line between paragraphs. Make changes, if necessary, as you have lost italic and bold formatting.

Third, cut and paste the new plain text document into your e-mail. Be sure that your contact information, including your address, phone number, fax number, and e-mail address, is added to your signature block. Also, include a meaningful subject line for the e-mail.

Fourth, send the e-mail to yourself as a test. Make sure everything looks as it should.

Last, once the e-mail reads as you want it to, send it to your target publication. Congratulations! You have successfully formatted your electronic submission.

As a librarian, you know how a missing volume number or incorrect subfield can create difficulties. Now is the time to transfer your talent for details to the writing world. Show a prospective editor or agent that you're a professional by submitting a manuscript that plays by the rules.

EDITING YOUR WRITING

BETH NIEMAN

Getting a first draft on paper is quite an accomplishment, but a writer's job doesn't end there; you must edit your work to make it presentable for a publisher and suitable for readers to enjoy.

Make time for editing. Allow yourself plenty of time to write your article, and then let your rough draft sit unread for a day or so before you pick it up to edit it. You'll see it as though you were reading it for the first time. Awkward sentences, spelling errors, and grammar problems will be more obvious to you.

Read your writing aloud with pen in hand. It is helpful to print your work out double-spaced, perhaps with larger-than-normal print, so that you have plenty of room on the page to mark corrections. Circle phrases or paragraphs that sound awkward as you read your work out loud. Head back to the word processor, make the changes you marked, and read the corrected passages aloud again to make sure they flow well and convey your ideas. You can repeat this step several times.

Look for common writing mistakes. The following five areas are troublesome to many writers:

1. Clichéd phrases. Clichés are overused phrases that add absolutely nothing to your writing. Instead of writing "It rained cats and dogs," come up with a fresh way to describe a sudden, intense downpour. Sometimes a cliché is what comes to mind as you're writing your early draft; that's OK, as long as you go back later and remove it during the editing process.

2. Passive sentence structure. A passive sentence here and there isn't going to ruin your writing, but a book or article full of passive sentences often makes for dull reading and adds unnecessary words. "The ball was thrown by Sally" is an example of a passive sentence. To rewrite that sentence, try "Sally threw the ball." This easy rewrite cut out two unnecessary words that added no meaning to the sentence. It also made Sally the subject of the sentence instead of the ball.

3. Weak verbs. Colorful verbs give energy and impact to your writing, while weak verbs make for anemic writing that interests no one. Compare "George drove quickly around the track" to "George sped around the track" and "George raced around the track." "George drove" conveys the basic meaning, but *drove* is a boring verb that needed the adverb *quickly* to help it along. A verb such as *sped, raced,* or even *zoomed* adds zest to the sentence and needs no modifier.

4. Grammar, spelling, and usage errors. When sending your proposals or articles to editors, remember that your writing is the first impression of you that an editor will receive. It's important to proofread your writing carefully. Computer spell-checkers and grammar-checkers can help, but they're not infallible. Writers who want to see their work in print must have an excellent command of standard English and turn in their very best work to editors. If you need help improving your writing, consider taking a community college class to sharpen your skills. Also, there are many reference works available for you to study. Get one. Use it.

5. Fuzzy thinking. If you find it difficult to rewrite an awkward sentence or paragraph, it's possible you just don't know what you're talking about. Are you writing around your idea instead of getting right to the point? Ask yourself, "What is it I'm trying to say in this sentence?" If you can't answer that question, try cutting it altogether; your writing will probably be better for it.

Don't be afraid to rearrange the furniture as you're editing. You may have a lot of great ideas for an article or book chapter, but they don't necessarily emerge from your keyboard in the most effective order. You might find that you wrote the perfect opening sentence somewhere in the middle of your first draft. With the aid of your word processor, it's just a matter of seconds to rearrange your sentences or even entire paragraphs without retyping.

Make sure you have your facts straight before submitting your writing for publication. Check for accuracy on facts and dates, citations, and the spelling of proper nouns and personal names. Don't count on your editor to do this important step for you.

The best thing you can do to improve your writing is to cut unnecessary words for improved clarity.

This step tightens your writing, making it crisp, clean, and readable. The American humorist Mark Twain once wrote to a friend, "I didn't have time to write a short letter, so I wrote a long one instead." It does take more effort to write a well-polished, short article because you must make each word, phrase, and sentence work hard—there simply isn't room for flab. This phase of editing can actually be fun. You'll be amazed at how fresh and clear your lean final draft is.

After you have cleaned up your draft, have a colleague review your work if possible. Choose someone whose judgment you respect and who will be honest with you rather than someone who will just say nice things to make you feel good. Remember, you don't have to use every suggestion your colleague makes—just use what is useful to you. Be prepared to graciously accept whatever criticism is offered and don't take it personally. If you've chosen your reader well, he or she will tell you where your ideas are unclear, where there may be typographical errors, and perhaps even ask a couple of probing questions to draw you out and help you get more information into your article.

Finally, give special attention to the first and last paragraphs of your article. The first paragraph should introduce your topic with an interesting hook to make the reader want to find out more, while the final paragraph should sum up your points in a neat, memorable way.

Creating a solid rough draft is an important step to producing a great article, but good editing is equally important for a professional result. Make time for editing, and editors will make time for you.

THE LIBRARIAN'S GUIDE TO DEALING WITH REVISION REQUESTS

MICHAEL LORENZEN

The manuscript is finished. You have proofread it endlessly and feel good about your work. You then safely put it in the mail or e-mail it to the editor. At this point, you are happy and can already envision seeing your work in print. The manuscript is forgotten and perhaps you have started on your next writing project.

And then it happens. The manuscript is returned to you. Instead of an acceptance notification, you are asked to do more work! In fact, the editor may demand substantial revisions, which may require days of effort. At this point, many authors despair and some never make the revisions, dooming their writing to go unpublished.

After all the work of writing and submitting a manuscript, there is the possibility that you will be rejected or asked to make significant revisions to your work. No matter how good an author is at writing, some manuscripts for some reason will not be accepted at the first place they are submitted. Many more will eventually be accepted but require extra effort to satisfy the demands of the editor. The more an author writes, the more often this will happen.

TIPS BEFORE SUBMITTING

I have been the editor of *MLA Forum* for two years. This journal is the peer-reviewed and indexed journal of the Michigan Library Association. In my role as editor, I have had to reject manuscripts. I have also had to send out requests for revision to authors.

There are a couple of tips that you can keep in mind before you submit in the first place that will cut down on the number of revisions an editor will request. Always check your spelling and grammar repeatedly. A brilliant paper that is poorly written still creates work for everyone involved in the process. Also, be sure to understand the guidelines for authors. Most journals post these online, and editors for books will happily make you aware of what they expect. Ask if you are unsure. Finally, have someone else you trust (like a coworker or friend) read the manuscript, as he or she may catch mistakes you have made.

REJOICE AND REVISE!

As disappointing as a revision request is, it also is a harbinger of good news. If an editor makes requests for changes to a manuscript, the editor is planning on publishing the work. If you get a manuscript back from the editor with the request to rewrite it, do so. If you follow the advice that the editor and referees provide, then the manuscript will likely be accepted. It is highly unlikely that a manuscript rewritten to the specifics of these comments will get rejected.

READ CAREFULLY

If a manuscript is rejected, read the rejection letter carefully. What were the reasons listed for the rejection? In most cases, these will be valid and reviewing them will actually help make the rewritten manuscript better. If you have questions, ask the editor for clarification.

Make sure that the revision makes a good attempt to meet both the spirit and the letter of what is being requested. As a journal editor, I have been frustrated by writers who are sent revision requests and then make weak attempts to address the concerns I have raised. Rather than consider what I as an editor want the author to do, the author has basically sent me the same manuscript the second time. Doing so usually is followed by a rejection letter from me. Take the time to read the comments, revise your manuscript, and then send it back to the editor for what should be an approval as long as you make a real attempt to revise according to the desires of the editor.

DISAGREEING WITH THE REQUESTED REVISIONS

In some cases, you may disagree with the revisions requested. It is possible that the editor misunderstood your research methodology, for example. If you feel that the editor made a mistake, contact the editor to discuss it. It may not get the manuscript accepted as is, but it may be worth it, as it may result in the revision request being rescinded or made less laborious. Or it may give you a better understanding of what is wrong with the manuscript, thus helping you to fix it.

Sometimes an editor will just not accept a manuscript as is. If you feel that you cannot make the revisions requested, thank the editor and move on. Do not send a nasty note back to the editor. This not only is impolite but also could sabotage your attempts to get published in the future! The simple truth is that the library field is not a difficult one in which to publish. Try a state or regional journal or newsletter, as they are usually easier to be accepted at. If you and an editor disagree, move on.

BE PROMPT

There are few things more frustrating to an editor than an author who cannot meet deadlines. Editors have deadlines, too, and tardy authors impede the whole process. When revision requests are made, the editor hopes that the manuscript will be brought up to acceptable standards so that it can be published. The editor may hope to publish it in the near future. For this reason, the deadlines for revisions are often shorter than they are for the original manuscript due date.

Finding the mental energy to make revisions can be hard. For this reason, many authors delay too long when revising a manuscript. Be sure to work promptly on any revision requested by an editor. If you are unsure of the deadline, ask!

WORKING WITH BOOK AND JOURNAL EDITORS TO REVISE YOUR MANUSCRIPT

PATRICK RAGAINS

Revising an article or book manuscript involves as many cycles of reading and rewriting as necessary to satisfy yourself and your editor in the time available. Following the steps outlined in this chapter will simplify the process of writing and revising. I first discuss how to plan an expository article or book and then touch on the main elements of editing, leading up to your manuscript's final submission.

PREPARING YOUR MANUSCRIPT FOR INITIAL SUBMISSION

ARTICLES

Scholarly and professional journals typically publish instructions to authors on their websites and in print issues. Instructions to authors identify editorial policies, including the following:

- whether the editor accepts unsolicited manuscripts

- style manual and edition used (e.g., *Chicago Manual of Style, MLA Handbook*)

- text treatment (e.g., organization, file format)

- illustrations, including color and black-and-white, file format, and resolution

- citation format

Also, examine recent issues of journals that interest you to see how they apply their style requirements.

BOOKS

When you have an idea for a book, contact prospective publishers to discuss it with an editor. Publishers of library-related books almost never accept complete manuscripts unsolicited, but they do offer guidance to prospective authors and assistance in developing book proposals. Here are typical components of a book proposal:

- the book's proposed title

- a succinct explanation of its content

- identification of your target audience

- indication of length

- table of contents

- features (e.g., illustrations, sidebars, accompanying CD or DVD, website)

- a sample chapter or introduction

- a market analysis identifying books on similar topics and how your book will differ

The editor who assists you will likely discuss the idea with a larger editorial team, after which she or he will offer you further guidance. The editor may suggest or require changes to your proposal to strengthen it. Make certain that the final proposal and contract accurately reflect your earlier discussions with the editor and other publisher representatives concerning the expected content, organization, time line, and financial arrangements.

WRITING YOUR NARRATIVE

Tell your readers at the outset what your book or article is about and why the issue is important. Writing from an outline is useful, as it helps you stay focused and move crisply from one set of ideas to the next. The outline also supplies your section headings, which will help readers follow the narrative. Use the active voice as your default (e.g., "We taught eighty freshman English classes in the fall semester using our new instructional model"). Passive constructions often conceal who performs an action and can confuse readers (e.g., "Five of the new librarians were not employed past their probationary periods").

REVISING FOR SUBMISSION

You won't really know what you have written until you've read your first draft from beginning to end and start to revise it. Check for the following:

Words. Conform to your publisher's or editor's required spelling, capitalization, and usage. Define professional words and phrases the first time you use them. Alternatively, replace jargon with everyday words. Remove adjectives and adverbs wherever possible; when overused, they dull your readers' understanding.

Sentences. Each sentence should convey a new idea and move the narrative forward; make your point and move on to the next one. Split run-on sentences. Check for subject-verb concurrence (e.g., "Each librarian and instructor *is* compiling a teaching portfolio").

Paragraphs. Place topic sentences at the beginning of a paragraph (i.e., the first or second sentence). If you find the topic restated at the end of a paragraph, remove it and make certain that its essential points appear at the head of the paragraph.

Float a trial balloon. After your initial revision, ask one or more colleagues to read and comment on your work. This will help you improve the manuscript and prepare for your editor's response.

REVISING FOR FINAL SUBMISSION

After your editor reads the manuscript, he or she may request changes depending on his or her sense of what readers want. As you edit, be sure that any internal references from one part of the narrative to another are correct.

You can often revise effectively with just a few well-crafted sentences or a paragraph. For example, a book editor I worked with asked me to add a discussion of federated searching to a teaching unit on library and information literacy skills I had written. I easily added this to the narrative in three sentences.

Closely follow your editor's style recommendations.

Finally, contact your editor if you don't understand something he or she has requested or appears to misunderstand something in your manuscript. Put yourself in a problem-solving frame of mind when you call or e-mail. Your editor will appreciate a businesslike approach to editing.

REVIEWING PROOFS AND ANSWERING YOUR COPY EDITOR'S QUESTIONS

This is the final step in revising your work for publication, although now you must limit most editing to correcting errors (your own, the copy editor's, or the typesetter's). Most book publishers and some journals send printed page proof of your work for you to proofread, correct by hand, and return. Usually, you must complete this task in a short time frame (forty-eight hours to seven days is common).

Here are some tips for reading page proof:

- Ensure that each page is included. Request any missing pages from the publisher immediately.

- Photocopy the proof. Mark all of your changes on the photocopied pages.

- Proofread the copies from beginning to end. Have a printed copy of your final submission within reach for comparison.

- Once you've corrected your working copy of the proof, copy your marks to the original set of pages you received from the publisher. Review each of your editing marks for correctness.

- For a book, you may be asked to create an index and submit it with the corrected proof. Consider using Microsoft Excel to create and sort your index. Finish the index in Microsoft Word, where you can indent subheadings and insert other formatting.

- Mail the corrected proof, index, and required paperwork to the publisher, using the specified mail carrier and delivery option.

- Keep your working copies of the proof and index as backup copies until the article or book is published.

CONCLUSION

Revising a manuscript for publication requires rigorous proofreading, careful thought, rewriting, and effective time management. Remember, your editors want you to produce a polished, successful book or article, so follow their guidance. Enjoy your accomplishment!

PREPARING FOR PUBLICATION
Strategies for Identifying Potential Library Journals

DEBORAH H. CHARBONNEAU

Research and publishing in library and information science (LIS) contribute to the profession. As such, publishing in LIS journals offers one avenue for library practitioners to share results and experiences that both enhance and contribute to our collective wisdom. In addition, getting published facilitates the sharing of new discoveries, leads to personal growth, and is an excellent way to establish a professional identity.

However, identifying potential LIS journals for publication can be one challenge that librarians encounter. Therefore, the aim of this article is to provide practical suggestions for identifying potential journals for library practitioners to get their work published. Furthermore, the importance of following submission guidelines is also discussed.

SET THE STAGE

Early on, considering the audience for which one will write and how the work fits into a larger context are essential dimensions of preparing a manuscript for publication. Setting the stage involves thinking about the topic and identifying your desired readers before preparing the manuscript itself. The next step is to determine the best way to reach this audience. For example, ascertain whether an editorial, review, how-to, best-practices, or research article is a suitable fit.

Conducting a review of the literature is a crucial step for determining how the proposed work fits into a larger context. By performing a review of the literature, one will be able to determine what work has already been done. Overall, conducting a literature review is instrumental to learning what has already been published and to effectively demonstrating how one's work contributes to the body of literature.

FIND A GOOD MATCH

The key to finding potential LIS journals is to ascertain which journals are the best fit for the proposed article. Key factors involved in the decision to publish a paper include "whether the paper has an original idea worth publishing and whether the journals' readers would want to read it" (LaBorie 1984, 58). Therefore, one useful strategy to help identify potential journals is to examine recent journal issues that have covered related topics. An easy way to accomplish this is to browse journal tables of contents on the World Wide Web.

Another technique for identifying possible journals is to register for tables of contents to be delivered automatically via e-mail or RSS and then to scan them to gain a better sense of the content and scope of a particular journal. Various publishers of LIS journals offer free electronic delivery of tables of contents, including Sage, Elsevier, and Haworth Press. In addition, the previous literature review will help to determine which journals have published articles on similar topical issues. Learning what types of articles a journal publishes, such as review articles or original research, is also important. Often this information can be gleaned in the submission guidelines or directly obtained from the publisher's website.

Another strategy for identifying potential LIS journals for publication is to contact the editor of a particular journal. This time-saving approach is highly recommended, and editors often prefer it. This approach ensures that one's article is appropriate for the journal and allows an editor to offer suggestions for further improvement. Furthermore, several print publications provide acceptance rates for individual journals, such as *Cabell's Directory of Publishing Opportunities in Educational Technology and Library Science* (Cabell and English 2007) or *Guide to Publishing Opportunities for Librarians* (Schroeder and Roberson 1995).

Moreover, academic librarians and LIS faculty are often required to publish in peer-reviewed journals for promotion or tenure. To find out whether an article submission is subject to editorial peer review, check Ulrich's Periodicals Directory. Other alternatives are to consult the journal's front matter, review the submission guidelines, or visit a publisher's website. Moreover, determining the reputation of a journal also requires some investigation. One resource to consult is ISI's Journal Citation Reports for the journal's impact factor, which is commonly considered an indication of a journal's prestige. Asking colleagues for recommendations is another idea.

FOLLOW SUBMISSION GUIDELINES

Attention to detail by carefully following the precise journal submission guidelines is paramount for publication success. Failure to follow the instructions can result in delays in the review of a submission or even rejection. In addition, adherence to standard grammar, writing style, and appropriate citation methods is of chief importance. The Online Writing Lab at Purdue University offers a nice collection of online style guides for formatting manuscripts (http://owl.english.purdue.edu).

Proofreading is an important part of the writing process. The value of getting feedback before submitting an article to a journal cannot be emphasized enough, and you are strongly encouraged to have a peer colleague review a draft for clarity and provide criticism. Finally, keep in mind that it is common practice to submit the article to only one journal at a time.

CONCLUSION

In summary, there are many exciting opportunities for research and publishing in library and information science. According to Brown and colleagues (2002, 18), publishing can be viewed as "a matter of determination, perseverance, and communication." Identifying potential LIS journals for publication entails selecting desired readers and finding a good match for the proposed topic. In addition, contacting the editor is a helpful strategy to ensure that the work is relevant to a particular journal and audience. Furthermore, carefully following the submission guidelines and having a colleague proofread the article for clarity and cohesiveness are also important steps of the writing process. Overall, identifying appropriate LIS journals for publication increases the likelihood of success and can lead to a creative and exhilarating experience.

REFERENCES

Brown, Ladd, Jeff Bullington, Cindy Hepfer, Wayne Jones, and Robb M. Waltner. 2002. "Getting Published: Surviving in a 'Write Stuff or They Will Fire You' Environment." *Serials Librarian* 42 (1/2): 13–18.

Cabell, David W. E., and Deborah L. English. 2007. *Cabell's Directory of Publishing Opportunities in Educational Technology and Library Science*. Beaumont, TX: Cabell Publishing.

LaBorie, Tim. 1984. "Publishing in Library Journals." *Serials Librarian* 8 (3): 55–61.

Schroeder, Carol F., and Gloria G. Roberson. 1995. *Guide to Publishing Opportunities for Librarians*. New York: Haworth Press.

THE PATH TO REPRESENTATION

Finding a Literary Agent

ANIKA FAJARDO

If your goal is publication of a book-length work, chances are you'll need a literary agent. A literary agent helps an author navigate the stormy seas of the publishing industry, and, for many publishers, working with an agent is a required stepping-stone to publication. Fortunately, with a lot of hard work—and some luck—you can enlist the help of an agent to further your writing career.

The first step in securing an agent is to have a good, marketable piece of work, whether this means the next great American novel or a guide to *American Idol*. In my case, I worked with two other writers to create an anthology of stories and recipes called *Let Them Eat Crêpes*. After some basic market research, we were pretty sure we had a solid, unique concept, and we set to work.

I think of literary agents a little like real estate agents; they help bring sellers (the writers) and buyers (the publishing houses) together, and they get to take home a little piece of the pie for their trouble. Of course, the difference is that the book industry is definitely a buyers' market. Imagine if your real estate agent took one look at your house and refused to work with you!

One rule that almost every agent will tell you is not to look for an agent until your work is the very best it can be. Is your novel your best work? Is your book proposal watertight? Have you had multiple readers, dozens of drafts, and a couple of breakdowns? Then you're probably ready to seek out an agent. Agents are looking for work that is ready—now—to be sold to a publisher.

For fiction, you need to have a completed novel that is carefully edited and vetted. Agents and publishers will not generally sell an unfinished novel. For nonfiction, you will either need to have a finished book or a solid book proposal.

Librarians have an advantage when it comes to writing stellar book proposals. With our research skills and ease with information seeking, we can find statistics, comparable books, and data that might be difficult for other writers to find. There are many resources that will help you write a nonfiction book proposal. My two coauthors and I used samples from the Web and Jeff Herman and Deborah Adams's *Write the Perfect Book Proposal* (1993) to write the proposal for our anthology. We set up a website for our project and did a lot of research and work to create the best book proposal we could.

After your piece is in the best shape it can be, it's time to look for an agent. There are many resources both print and online to help you in your search. We relied mainly on *Writer's Market* (2009) and the online Publishers Marketplace (www.publishersmar ketplace.com) listings. *Literary Market Place* (2009) and *Jeff Herman's Guide to Book Publishers, Editors, and Literary Agents* (2009) are other resources to try. You can also find agents by looking at the acknowledgments page in books similar to yours, as authors generally thank their agents and editors.

As you look for agents to whom you might send your work, you will need to learn a little about each one. What kind of track record does he have? How many books has she sold and to whom? Does he represent the kind of material you've written? You can find out a lot about most agents through basic Google searches, and there are many blogs and websites that track agents. Because my coauthors and I had written a food-related book, we looked at agents who specialized in nonfiction, food writing, and anthologies. Querying the wrong kind of agents is a waste of your time and theirs.

Once you've identified a list of agents, a query is your first contact with an agent. This is generally an enticing letter or e-mail that lets them know how great your project is and why you are the one to write it. There are many resources that will help you write a good query. Look through the books listed herein and your own library's collection to find samples of good query letters.

If you're lucky, one or more agents will respond favorably to your query. If their needs, the market, and your project align, an agent may ask to see either more of your work (for fiction) or a proposal (for nonfiction). For *Let Them Eat Crêpes,* we found an agent who was fairly new but had sold a food-related book to Simon and Schuster. When we got the e-mail asking to see our book proposal, we were thrilled.

Because we had our proposal ready to go, we rushed to the copy shop and had a professional color copy printed. We sent it through regular mail in a standard business envelope—we also enclosed that vital SASE (self-addressed, stamped envelope). Agents are often particular about how they want to receive your material. Some of them want manuscripts stapled, some don't; some want a hard copy, others an electronic version. It can't hurt to follow their instructions to a T. If the agent is particularly interested, he or she may ask for an "exclusive," meaning that the agent expects to have your manuscript to him- or herself until a decision is made. During this time, you should refrain from sending your manuscript out to other agents or publishers.

The vast majority of the publishing industry is located in New York City. However, we happened to have garnered the interest of a local agent (we live in Minnesota). This was entirely by chance, but it meant that we were able to meet with her in person. Most of the time, this kind of face-to-face meeting isn't necessary or possible, although it can help both parties make a decision about representation. The two other writers and I met the agent at a coffee shop and were happy to find her to be friendly, knowledgeable, and—most important—interested in our project.

Not every response from agents will be positive, of course. Many will not respond at all; most will send generic notes or e-mail. One agent said no one would be interested in our topic, but our agent clearly thinks differently. The book industry is such a subjective one that it's impossible to know for sure what kinds of topics or projects will interest an agent.

Once you have an agent interested in representing you, you and the agent will need an agent agreement. Most agents have a standard agreement that lays out the details of this business arrangement. Agents typically take 15 percent and 20 percent on foreign sales. The agent agreement is a binding legal contract and is an exciting step in the process.

Signing with an agent, though, doesn't mean that the work is over. After signing with our agent, we then set to work revising our proposal. Even though we had researched book proposals, our agent was able to help us tailor our book proposal for the market reality. We trust her to help us produce the best possible book proposal; after all, we all want to make a sale.

Having an agent is only one step in the long march toward publication. An agent may or may not be able to sell your work, may not have the contacts necessary, or may have misjudged your work and the market, or your project may not meet the needs of the publishers.

In any case, we're hoping that *Let Them Eat Crêpes* will soon be on bookstore shelves. The publishing industry, as librarians know, is unpredictable and changeable, but with luck and a lot of work, you can find success.

REFERENCES

Herman, Jeff. 2009. *Jeff Herman's Guide to Book Publishers, Editors, and Literary Agents: Who They Are! What They Want! and How to Win Them Over!* 19th ed. Stockbridge, MA: Three Dog Press. (Annual publication.)

Herman, Jeff, and Deborah M. Adams. 1993. *Write the Perfect Book Proposal: 10 That Sold and Why.* New York: John Wiley.

Brewer, Robert Lee, ed. 2009. *Writer's Market.* Cincinnati, OH: F&W Publications. (Annual publication.)

Literary Market Place. 2009. New Providence, NJ: R. R. Bowker. (Annual publication.)

TREAT YOURSELF AS A PATRON
Tracking Your Submissions

KATHRYN YELINEK

You've been there: a contact at another organization has promised to follow up with information to answer a patron's reference request, but you wait and wait and wait for the reply. Or you receive a request that your library purchase a specific item. You submit the order, then have to wait for the item to come in.

Following up on requests is par for the course in a library. Whether you're dealing with patrons, vendors, or others in the field, it's crucial that you know how and when to send off a subtle, or not-so-subtle, reminder.

The publishing world is no different, and the rule of the road is often "hurry up and wait." That said, publishing is a business like any other, and it's important to exercise your right to know about the status of your submission. This chapter will show you a simple method of tracking your submissions and will offer tips on when and how to follow up on your work.

TRACKING YOUR SUBMISSIONS

There are a number of ways to track your submissions, but I've found a simple spreadsheet works best. The one I use combines two different spreadsheets described in *Starting Your Career as a Freelance Writer* by Moira Anderson Allen (2003). I create my spreadsheet in Microsoft Excel, but with a little modification, you could create this design in a table in Microsoft Word or even in a ledger book. Experiment to see which method works best for you.

Each submission should have its own row (horizontal line). The columns (vertical lines) record the following information:

Title of piece. An example would be "Tracking Your Submissions."

Title of publication. In this case, *Writing and Publishing*. This column comes second, so if an article is rejected, you can simply insert a second row under its initial entry and record the new publication information. This way you keep all of the submissions for a single article together.

Action. Record here all of the activity that occurs for a submission. Actions would include submitting to a publication, receiving a rejection or acceptance, following up with an editor, or getting a check. This column can be repeated as many times as needed. In my spreadsheet, I have three separate columns all labeled "Action," so I can keep a chronological record of what has happened. If I need more than three columns for a submission, I just add a new row directly below and keep recording actions.

Date. This column works hand in hand with the Action column. For each action, make note of the date on which it happened. Again, this column is repeatable.

Payment and compensation. For scholarly works, expect to be paid in complimentary copies and record those here. For essays and short stories written outside the scholarly world, record the dollar amount.

Notes. It may not sound like it, but this column is extremely important. Here record such comments as "Will hear back by January 15" or "Article due September 21." It's vital that you record when you'll hear back about a piece. You can find out this information from a publication's submission guidelines, which usually say something like "Responds in four to six weeks." If you submit an article on May 1, six weeks means that you should receive a reply by June 12. Highlight that date on the spreadsheet in an eye-catching color (yellow works well). If you haven't heard back by then, follow up.

FOLLOWING UP ON SUBMISSIONS

Because most publications don't accept simultaneous submissions (meaning you can submit a piece to only one place at a time), you need a response from one publication before you can move on to the next one on your list. Of course, if you're being paid for your work, it's very important to make sure you are paid on time. So what do you do if the expected date has passed without a check or a response?

Send a polite e-mail (or letter, if you submitted by snail mail) to the editor to whom you first submitted your story. Make it short and sweet:

Dear Mr./Ms. Editor's Last Name:

I submitted a short story, "Name of Story," on such-and-such a date. Because X amount of time has passed and I have not heard back, I am inquiring about the status of my submission. Please let me know when I might expect a decision.

Sincerely,

[your signature block with contact information]

Generally, this contact is enough to elicit a response. The editor will tell you when you can expect to hear back, will confirm the check is in the mail, or will give you a definite answer on whether your story has been accepted. Record this information on your spreadsheet, highlight any new hear-by date, and follow up as needed.

What happens if you still receive no response? You can wait an additional two weeks or so, and follow up again. If you still receive no response, it then falls to your professional judgment to decide how much effort you want to put into working with a particular publication. If you are submitting to a peer-reviewed journal, you may want to wait a little longer. Obviously, if you're waiting on a check, you'll want to follow through until you get it.

Once you've decided that you've waited long enough to hear whether a submission has been accepted, simply send the editor an e-mail stating that you're withdrawing your piece from consideration. Then send the story on to your next target publication. Create a new row on your spreadsheet, highlight the reply date, and prepare to follow up.

Publishing is a business that requires perseverance, patience, and knowledge of professional etiquette. Luckily for you, these are skills that librarians develop on the job. Just as you would go to bat to follow up on information for your patrons, so you must do the same for your submissions. Treat yourself as our own patron and ensure that your writing goals stay on track.

REFERENCE

Allen, Moira Anderson. 2003. *Starting Your Career as a Freelance Writer.* New York: Allworth Press.

INTERDISCIPLINARY PUBLICATION

Thinking beyond Library Journals to Write What Your Clients Read

MICHELYNN MCKNIGHT

What do your clients read? You know because you see those publications all the time. School librarians can and do write for journals that their teachers and administrators read. Public librarians may write for particular segments of their market, such as publications for teens or seniors. Some may write columns for local newspapers, like my biweekly "It's YOUR Library" column for the *Shawnee News Star.* (In my first job as a public librarian, I gave a new reporter help with backstory for her work, and she in turn helped me get the column.) Academic librarians sometimes write for the *Chronicle of Higher Education.* Subject specialists in large libraries or in special libraries write for the specialty publications their clients favor. For instance, there's Pam Sieving's (2007) explanation for nurses of Cochrane systematic reviews of medical research or Jim Henderson's (2005) insights on Google Scholar for doctors.

The key to breaking in to the literature in another field is to hook into something people want to know and explain it in their terms. (No librarians' jargon without explanation!) Our expert information needs analysis can go beyond the personal reference interview and the development of our own collections and services. As always, we can get some of our best ideas from listening to our clients.

COLLABORATE WITH YOUR CLIENTS

An important way to cross the discipline divide is to have a coauthor from the field. Such collaboration can start very informally. My first such experience started when I was a beginning hospital librarian eating lunch in the cafeteria. One day, I was explaining (again!) to a nurse that our library services and collection weren't just for doctors. We could help practicing nurses, and we had a good collection of print and online resources for them. The nurse wondered aloud whether nurses at hospitals without libraries could get such services. I explained that there were libraries in nursing schools and health sciences centers all over the state with collections and services they could use. After several casual conversations about the possibilities, we decided to try a small survey to discover libraries with nursing collections that were open to practicing nurses not affiliated with the library's parent institution. We started with two lists of libraries in our state: those affiliated with the National Network of Libraries of Medicine (NNLM) and those at schools with accredited nursing programs. We developed a telephone survey and called the directors of all the libraries on each list. Eventually, we had a 100 percent response rate. When we went through our results, we realized that, although not all counties in the state had a nursing school library and not all had a hospital library, each county had at least one or the other. We wrote a few paragraphs about how practicing nurses could get help for their daily work from these libraries and published it with the county-by-county list in the state nursing journal (McKnight and Patterson 1995). The article was such a hit that the same journal responded to requests and republished it the following year (McKnight and Patterson 1996).

The native call of the researcher and writer is not "Eureka! I've found it!" but rather, "Hmm, that's interesting." Noticing that the NNLM libraries (mostly hospital libraries and libraries affiliated with medical school) used the National Library of Medicine DOCLINE interlibrary loan system for journal articles, and that the nursing schools in universities without schools of medicine used OCLC for similar service, we wondered whether the availability of nursing literature varied significantly between the two systems. That led to a study of nursing journals available through the two systems in the state (McKnight and Patterson 1997) and later, with funding from a research grant from the South Central Academic Medical Libraries Consortium, to a study of the availability of nursing literature in five states (McKnight 2000).

REVIEWING SERVICE

Another way to write for other disciplines' journals is to provide a continuing service useful to both specialists and librarians. Some years ago, at a meeting of the Association of Academic Health Sciences Libraries, there was a conversation between the then president of the Medical Library Association and the editors of *JAMA* (the weekly journal of the American Medical Association) about how difficult it was to find evaluative reviews of the nearly two hundred new English-language medical journals that appear every year (Eldredge 1997). The result was the appointment of the volunteer *JAMA* review editor, who recruited medical librarians to work with clinician specialists to write reviews of new journals. The clinician did the disciplinary evaluation of the journal and the librarian gathered information about how the journal was published and indexed. With doctors from my hospital, I wrote two of these reviews (McKnight and Pickens 1997; McKnight and Bird 1998).

FOLLOW UP ON OPPORTUNITIES

If you are prepared to follow up on opportunities, you will find them. As Louis Pasteur (1854) admonished, "Chance favors only the prepared mind." Because I searched robust bibliographic databases for hours every day, I got the chance to teach online searching at the University of Oklahoma School of Library and Information Science as an adjunct instructor. Through personal connections, I encouraged some Ph.D. students in mathematics education to take the course to enhance their literature reviews for their dissertations. Soon such students were regularly taking the course; through them, I got to know what databases were most useful to their work. Their professors liked what they were doing and invited me to be a coauthor of a book for faculty mathematicians on how to find and use research in mathematics education—a field of research quite different from that in which they were trained but that they could use to enhance their own teaching. The result was *Mathematics Education Research: A Guide for the Research Mathematician* (McKnight, Magid, Murphy, and McKnight, 2000).

Working with people from other disciplines is rewarding and interesting. You can do it!

REFERENCES

Eldredge, Jonathan. 1997. "*JAMA* Journal Reviews: Analysis and Master Index 1992–1996." *Medical Library Association News* 292:22–24.

Henderson, Jim. 2005. "Google Scholar: A Source for Clinicians?" *Canadian Medical Association Journal* 172:1549–1550.

McKnight, Curtis C., Andy R. Magid, T. J. Murphy, and Michelynn McKnight. 2000. *Mathematics Education Research: A Guide for the Research Mathematician.* Providence, RI: American Mathematical Society.

McKnight, Michelynn. 2000. "Interlibrary Loan Availability of Nursing Journals through DOCLINE and OCLC: A Five-State Survey." *Bulletin of the Medical Library Association* 88:254–255.

McKnight, Michelynn, and Phillip C. Bird. 1998. "*Helicobacter.*" [Review.] *JAMA* 280:100.

McKnight, Michelynn, and Barbara Patterson. 1995. "Library Services for Oklahoma Nurses." *Oklahoma Nurse* 40:13–14. Reprinted in 1996: *Oklahoma Nurse* 41:17.

———. 1997. "Nursing Collections in DOCLINE and non-DOCLINE Libraries: An Oklahoma Survey." *National Network—Newsletter of the Hospital Libraries Section of the Medical Library Association* 21: 16, 23.

McKnight, Michelynn, and Bruce Pickens. 1997. "*Mind/Body Medicine: A Journal of Clinical Behavioral Medicine.*" [Review.] *JAMA* 278:1794–1795.

Pasteur, Louis. 1854. "Le hazard ne favorise que les esprits préparés." [Lecture.] University of Lille. (Cited in various places, including "Louis Pasteur," Wikiquote, http://en.wikiquote.org/wiki/Louis_Pasteur, accessed November 27, 2008, and H. Eves, *Return to Mathematical Circles* [Boston: Prindle, Wever, and Schmidt, 1998], 273.)

Sieving, Pam C. 2007. "Spotlight on Research: What Is a Cochrane Review?" *ORL-Head and Neck Nursing* 25:15.

THE END OR THE BEGINNING?

Learning from Rejection

ANIKA FAJARDO

My novel—like most first novels—was deeply personal. It was also—like most first novels—never published.

The V Word began as an in-class exercise in a beginning writing workshop. It was the story of a young woman named Stella who experiences healing and complete remission from an obscure disorder called vulvodynia. Women with this disorder endure chronic and embarrassing pain. There is no definitive cause, and there is no cure. As a sufferer myself, my vision was to use this novel to reach out to women with vulvodynia, to give them an average girl who was dealing with this strange disease, to let them see how this disorder could be a vehicle for growth and fulfillment and not just an obstacle to overcome. As I wrote, I kept those women in mind.

Five years and 320 pages later, I began querying literary agents—more than seventy agents.

About 10 percent of them responded favorably. Not bad for a first-time novelist with no formal training. Not bad for a novel that started as an in-class exercise. But of those 10 percent, all eventual reactions were the same: "just not compelling enough," "didn't keep me wanting to turn pages," "not my cup of tea," "didn't grab me." The responses were all similarly vague and unhelpful.

And then I ran out of stamina, faith, self-confidence, and agents. In other words, I quit.

Rejection and quitting aren't what you sign up for when you decide you want to write. I certainly didn't. But the experience, as painful as it was at times, taught me.

Writing a novel is an enormous undertaking, something I didn't, in my beginner's naïveté, realize. It gave me a crash course in grammar, word choice, pacing, and character development. I learned to rely on *The Elements of Style* and *Roget's Thesaurus*. I learned how to manage computer files and track changes in Word. I learned about query letters and partials, exclusives and rejections. I also learned about the publishing industry and the difficulties of a fickle market.

I discovered that writing is an almost visceral need, an addiction to creating something out of nothing, to filling a blank screen with black symbols. It is an obsession with language and imaginary worlds and the idea that my words can touch someone.

In all those megabytes of words and sentences, I strived to be true to myself and my goal for the novel. Despite a torrent of rejections, I kept in mind those women with vulvodynia. It was thinking of those women that helped me write query letter after query letter. It was also thinking of those women that made each rejection that much more painful. How would I reach them if I couldn't publish my novel?

And then, as I closed out my document for the last time and filed away my last rejection letters, I realized that I had reached someone. The thing is, the woman I reached wasn't a faceless sufferer—it was me.

In the end, the countless drafts and hours of work have laid the foundation for—if not a best seller—my own healing and growth as a writer. Even though I feel like a quitter for setting aside my novel, I'm not going to forget about Stella. When I'm ready, I'll be able to write more about this character I love. The advantage of spending five years with this cast of characters is that I now have an enormous amount of background knowledge that I can use in whatever else I write. I also have more than eighty thousand words of writing practice, practice that will help me write better articles, better short stories, and—perhaps someday—a better novel.

I've realized that the pile of rejection letters is a symbol not of failure but of effort. As painful as they are when they first arrive in the mail in my own self-addressed hand, they eventually become a part of my writing history.

My novel—like most first novels—may never make it to the bookstores. And because I didn't sign up for rejection and quitting, I'm going to keep writing and keep submitting. I owe it to myself.

SELF-PUBLISHING

BRUCE R. SCHUENEMAN

Self-publishing may have a faint aura of self-promotion and egotism, yet becoming a publisher, whether of one's own material or of material that supports a niche interest, can be a valuable service for both the publisher and the scholarly world generally.

My niche interests center on the French violin school, a group of violinist-composers active from about 1780 to 1830. I had published two articles on the French violin school, one in a little-known violin journal and the other in a popular magazine for string players. For several years, I worked on a translation of Arthur Pougin's nearly unknown work on Pierre Rode (a French school composer). Rode's obscurity made him attractive to me, but it was a handicap otherwise. I decided to publish my translation of Pougin's *Notice sur Rode* (1874) myself.

DECISIONS, DECISIONS

Self-publishing involves many decisions. Pougin's short book contained many footnotes, some extraordinarily important and informative, so I decided to eschew the execrable modern habit of using endnotes instead of footnotes—I wanted a book with Pougin's informative notes at the bottom of the page. I turned to a legal secretary (my sister Laura) for help in creating a professional textual look. Pougin's book also included images of the first few measures of all thirteen of Rode's concerti. I relied on our library's head of media services (Carol Tipton) to produce images of all thirteen concerti for insertion into the text. Pougin mentioned many names, and the value of adding an index seemed well worth the effort. I quickly discovered that constructing an index from scratch is a tedious business, but an index greatly enhances any book's accessibility.

Besides the thematic index images, I asked a local artist (and incidentally a library employee), Sylvia Martinez, to draw a black-and-white sketch of Rode, loosely based on one of the few known images of the great violinist. This image was converted to electronic format and used as a frontispiece.

After finding a suitable printer, I negotiated for hardback, sewn-in binding, title stamped on cover, and each volume shrink-wrapped. The shrink-wrapping is an excellent option if the expectation is that the book will sell in small quantities over a period of years.

PUBLISHING IS A BUSINESS

As a librarian I knew the value of having an imprimatur and an ISBN, so I decided to create a business. My first concern was to create a business name—a name that was both descriptive and perhaps a little intriguing. I eventually chose The Lyre of Orpheus Press, because of both its allusion to music (my niche interest) and its romantic flavor (at least to my mind). I applied for a business license with the state of Texas and registered with the local taxing authorities. In one sense, this was a costly move. I have never made more than approximately $200 income in any single year, so taxes on inventory and the occasional sales tax on Texas sales are excessive. The regular business footing is important, however, and is the basis for future growth.

A regular business foundation is also important for listing the book in directories and similar finding aids. Today, Lyre of Orpheus Press is listed in Global Books in Print, among other resources. Another consideration is the ISBN, an integral part of the book producing and selling world. Contacting Bowker (ISBN agent for the United States) in the 1990s, I invested in ISBNs for my foundling press. The original ten ISBN numbers have still not been exhausted, though that may happen in the near future.

The next step was advertising. The book is of most interest to two groups: libraries and violinists. To reach libraries, I sent a letter advertisement. To reach violinists, I placed an ad in *Strings* magazine and received orders from as far away as Australia.

Other published works from the Lyre of Orpheus Press have followed: two pieces of sheet music (one of them carried by a supplier in Arizona) and more books, though I have opted for perfect bindings done locally since the first book.

Small-press marketing becomes ever easier as the Internet age rolls along. Over the past three or four years, nearly all books from the Lyre of Orpheus Press have been sold through Amazon.com. Amazon is a marvelous means of distribution for the small press, as millions of people worldwide search Amazon's site, and Amazon welcomes small presses (though the price for the small publisher is the discounted cost that Amazon requires). In the past year or so, Amazon has issued its new Kindle electronic book reader, which (along with similar readers) offers another format for the small publisher and a means of continuing a title in print that may have gone out of print in paper format.

A PRESS OF ONE'S OWN

The Lyre of Orpheus Press has provided a platform for publishing certain materials that probably wouldn't have seen the light of day otherwise. A "press of one's own" provides a vital means of communication and can be part of one's authorial profile. Many of my subsequent publications on the French violin school have been based, to a greater or lesser extent, on Pougin's work, and my early efforts to translate and publish this work were a building block to the future.

My advice, based on my individual experience, may be encapsulated in the following points:

- Seriously consider self-publishing, but be sure to weigh pros and cons.

- If you decide to become a publisher, be as serious and intentional as possible, and know that some money will be required to do it right.

- Realize that proofreading, editorial tasks, printing, and marketing will be your responsibility.

- For most projects, don't expect to make money.

- Look for electronic format opportunities whenever possible.

- Integrate self-publishing into other authorial opportunities—don't neglect "regular" publishing.

- Most of all, be creative.

DIY PUBLISHING PROJECTS
Broadsides, Chapbooks, and Beyond

LISA A. FORREST

The do-it-yourself movement has led to a resurgence of handcrafted cool (pick up an issue of *ReadyMade* magazine and you'll see what I'm talking about)—but historically, poets have long experimented with DIY projects to distribute their work. Dating back to sixteenth-century Western European and North American history, the broadside (a single sheet with print on one side) was used to distribute descriptive narrative verse or song and was crucial to preserving traditional ballads and rhymed verse. When folded, the broadside was transformed into the chapbook, a small booklet named for the itinerant chapmen who pedaled the books. These small books once contained popular folklore, sensational tales, speeches, and hymns. Today, both broadsides and chapbooks are a perfect vehicle for the distribution of modern poetry. Whether publishing for yourself or publishing another's work, broadsides and chapbooks can be a simple, low-cost, and creative means of distributing printed poetry. Here's how to get started.

GET INSPIRED

If you've read this far, chances are that you are already feeling the glow of inspiration. The next step is to look around for ideas. Check out all of the bookmaking and journal-making books in your library. I'd highly recommend *How to Make Books* by Esther K. Smith (Potter Craft). Most independent and used bookstores carry chapbooks by local poets, so browse the shelves to see what other poets have done. If you're feeling really inspired, many community colleges offer bookmaking classes. If you're lucky, you might find bookmaking, screen-printing, and letterpress workshops sponsored by the local book arts collaborative. And of course, there are many online sources to investigate as well.

START SIMPLE

Once you look around a bit, you'll have a better idea of how simple or complicated you want your book to be. For example, will the book be handwritten, printed on a desk printer, or will you take it to a commercial copier? What about the binding—will the book pages be loose (stored in an envelope or box, perhaps), folded, stapled, or hand-stitched? Much of this will depend on how many copies you wish to create. For your first project, I'd suggest a simple folded book, which can be easily replicated on your desktop printer. A broadside of your favorite poem printed on card stock is also a really easy way to get started with DIY publishing. Accordion books or store-bought blank books (collaged or sketched with your own artwork) make great limited edition chapbooks!

CONSIDER COLLABORATING

Once you have an idea of the poetry you will be publishing, consider collaborating with a visual artist friend. Photographers, painters, collage artists—they all make terrific partners in poetry. Share your ideas and see what happens. If you're making a chapbook, you'll need an interesting cover design. If you're creating a broadside, you will probably want an image on it, too. Desktop publishing tools allow one to easily scan and insert images—or you might consider making each book or broadside an original. I've seen one-of-a-kind chapbooks, all using different sketches and paintings for each edition number. One of the more unusual designs I've admired used photos inserted into an opening in the cover design. The possibilities really are endless.

GATHER YOUR SUPPLIES, OLD AND NEW

Art supply and craft stores carry a wide variety of interesting papers and bookmaking supplies. There are many uses for recycled materials as well. Think cardboard covers wrapped with wire, or vintage postcards and photographs as pages for poetry. I've made limited edition books entirely out of discarded library resources, such as card catalog cards, book jackets, and 35 mm slides. Outdated topographical maps make intriguing canvas for poetry broadsides or pages for chapbooks. The world is full of bookmaking materials—sticks, feathers, cigar boxes, wallpaper, bingo cards—the only limit is your imagination. Don't forget basic things like a ruler, X-Acto knife, scissors, glue, and ink (whether stamp pad, laser jet, or lithography)!

GIVE YOURSELF TIME AND WORKSPACE

Set aside enough time to devote to your publishing project. Clear the desk and have all of your possible supplies ready to go. I would suggest making one copy of your prototype before printing off the entire edition. Sometimes, it takes a little problem solving to get it just right.

EXPERIMENT

Once you begin your project, don't be afraid to waver from your original plan of action. And it's OK if there are minor variations between copies. It's art—and art isn't supposed to be perfect.

CELEBRATE

Once you've completed your chapbook, throw a reading party to celebrate its publication. Invite your literary friends over for a house reading or find a community space to host a larger event. Local bookstores or libraries often rent out areas for poetry readings. Depending on your base cost for the book, you may wish to give your project away, trade with fellow poets, or sell the publication for a nominal fee. Don't forget to ask your local independent bookstore to carry a few copies on their shelf. It's also a nice gesture to donate your chapbook to any area libraries that host specialized contemporary poetry collections.

POETRY IS PRICELESS

I recommend that you get any ideas of making money off of the project completely out of your head. The point of the chapbook or broadside is to share your work and promote yourself as a writer—not to get rich. It's OK to charge a couple of bucks to cover your supplies, but don't be surprised if you end up giving or trading most of your copies to admiring friends and family.

VENTURE OUT

Good luck—and remember, chapbooks and broadsides aren't the only way to self-publish. Think creatively. Local copy centers and online services can put just about anything on a T-shirt, coffee mug, or greeting card. Why not your poetry? How about a whole calendar of poems? Your mother will love it.

SPREADING THE WORD

ROBERT S. NELSON

A herald is a person charged with the task of delivering information. In the medieval world, heralds were a very select group. Jumping ahead a few centuries, electronic discussion lists, online video, and podcasts have made the job of herald more egalitarian. A keyboard and access to the Internet allow the librarian-author to promote his or her work in a targeted and efficient manner. With a little technology and forethought, the librarian-author can proclaim the wonders of the written work to the world.

THE BUZZ

A press release is a static object awaiting something to set it in motion. This inertia is begun by what the industry refers to as buzz.

In the past, buzz relied heavily on publishers willing to spend their time generating interest about a particular work. If a publisher lacked a conduit to a particular audience, a published work might be introduced to a market with little fanfare. Things have changed. Instead of relying solely on publishers and their connections, in the twenty-first century, librarian-authors have more command over generating their own buzz.

There are numerous options available today that were unimaginable ten years ago. Electronic discussion lists with millions of subscribers are now commonplace. The proliferation of sites such as YouTube has completely changed the face of marketing. The ability to broadcast user-created MP3s, also known as podcasts, has opened new avenues for the librarian-author to develop a following. The best thing about capitalizing on these new media is that doing so does not require an advanced degree in computer science or a large marketing budget.

TOOLS OF THE TRADE

The press release is still useful, but its dissemination has changed drastically. Sending a press release to a local newspaper is helpful and strongly recommended, but how about sending a press release to millions of worldwide readers? Sites such as PRLOG (www.prlog.org) do just that and they do it for free. PRLOG will distribute your press release via the Web to no less than forty thousand RSS feeds (continuously updating web pages that an individual can subscribe to) and to sites such as Google News and other search engines. PRLOG is just one of hundreds of press release sites. An Internet search for "free press release" will yield helpful results.

Electronic discussion lists are similar in function but offer a more direct-marketing approach. A subscription to subject or genre-specific electronic discussion lists will provide access to interested parties with a simple click of the send button. Disseminating a press release via an electronic discussion list is an excellent way to reach a targeted audience, but finding the right list may require a little research.

Podcasts are a new medium to consider when promoting a published work. While there are a number of ways to generate podcast content, Audacity (http://audacity.sourceforge.net) is a great freeware editor. Once the podcast is recorded, it will need to be distributed. The options for distribution range from free to expensive. Pod Bean (www.podbean .com) will host and broadcast your podcast free. For a comprehensive tutorial, try www.how-to-podcast -tutorial.com.

YouTube has become synonymous with pratfalls and highlighting awful behavior. That notwithstanding, YouTube is also an excellent site for developing and distributing commercials for published works. Using digital video and basic video editing software, a dynamic and entertaining commercial can be created for little to no cost. Videos for YouTube need not be traditional either. Well-produced slides shows can be developed, saved as a digital video file, and posted to YouTube using software that most post-2004 computers have readily available free. For more information on creating digital video for YouTube, visit www.youtube.com and click on Help.

STRATEGIC USES OF NEW MEDIA

Once the various mediums are considered, the librarian-author should create a strategic plan to deliver promotional materials and maximize the effectiveness of these new tools. The following is a fictionalized account of how to use the new media.

A librarian recently had a collected work of poetry and essays accepted by a small publishing firm. This collection centers on the exploration of the natural world and its influence on human objects. The publisher plans to release the book in the next six months. To maximize her potential audience, the author created the following promotional materials and used several new mediums to deliver them.

She wrote a press release that detailed the scope, nature, and publication information of the book. In addition to this information, she included links and instructions to access her podcasts and YouTube video sites. This release was sent to a press release distribution site and posted on several electronic discussion lists that deal with literature and nature.

Over the course of the next several months, she broadcast podcasts of herself reading a poem from her book as well as reading works of other authors and poets who have inspired her. Each podcast concluded with a statement regarding the book, directions on preordering, and a reference to her YouTube posting.

Using photographs she took of manmade objects influenced by nature, she created a slide show that cycles through the images, interspersed with text from one of her essays, and set it to the sounds of nature. At the conclusion of the video, she provided information regarding her podcast as well as the publication and purchasing information regarding her book.

Once her book was published, she distributed yet another press release and continued to create podcasts. Now she requested audience participation.

She solicited readings and interpretations from listeners and then posted them to her podcast site. Her YouTube postings were updated to include video of local readings and interviews with other poets and naturalists. Each new creation included links to the appropriate vendor and information about new projects.

CONCLUSION

The new mediums of podcasting, electronic discussion lists, and YouTube have made marketing a publication an act of will. If an author is sufficiently motivated, it is not difficult to capitalize on these new avenues. It is important to note that these efforts will take time to master. With sufficient planning, a strong will, and some creativity, the librarian-author can become the twenty-first-century herald of his or her work.

TWENTY-FIVE YEARS AT BOOKEXPO
What I Learned about Librarian Authorship

ELIZABETH MORELLI

When I attended my first BookExpo (American Booksellers Association Conference) as a collection development librarian, I was asked why librarians wanted to attend a booksellers' conference. Because many library conferences concentrated on computer systems, BookExpo remained the largest national convention aimed at authors, publishers, publicists, agents, independent bookstore salespeople, and a few inquisitive librarians, that focused on the book.

I attend this very inexpensive three-day conference every year as a collection development librarian and a writer—and I am very comfortable with both careers on BookExpo's trade floor.

BookExpo, with a minimum of thirty-two authors signing their latest work every hour, gives all writers an up-close and personal experience with many writing giants as well as the smaller-press subject specialists. Many books are timed for release during this May and June conference event. Excitement, advance copies, and author readings fill the aisles, overlapping into conference rooms and publisher booths.

Compared to many writing conferences, artist retreats, workshops, and classes, BookExpo generates the most hands-on author information for the least cost year after year.

On registering, all conference-goers receive a thick guide with a floor plan. Because of the size of the floors, publisher booths are grouped by classi-

fication: international, audiovisual, children's, university, small presses. General publishers (not categorized) take up the largest area of the floor, though the children's space runs a close second. Specialty areas including African American, graphic novels, gay and lesbian, and magazines are also separated. Booths are numbered and content annotated in the guidebook, the conference attendee's bible. Some authors sign books in their publisher's booth as well as in the designated autograph area, so crowds are a common occurrence on the trade floor. Memorization of the layout becomes a first-day necessity.

A BookExpo experience may begin with a snaking line to a favorite author's table where the attendee receives a free book and autograph from the author (participants are asked to contribute one dollar per autograph to the city's literacy fund). An individual might have ten seconds to say something to the author, get a photo, or make a pitch for a library program. For all writers, this is the opportunity to think ahead, to strategize, and to "say the right thing" to engage the author in a brief dialogue (i.e., "You are so prolific. How do you do it?" Question asked of Joyce Carol Oates. "What author shaped your writing the most?" Tom Wolfe. "We grew up in the same city at the same time; do you ever get back there?" John Sayles).

Next to the autograph section, the BookExpo trade floor is daunting in its size and crowds but is the perfect place to find a publisher. Check out booths that spotlight similar genre or subject areas, then ask the right questions and leave a business card with all contacts, no matter how slim the connection. In some cases, the contact will call back the librarian but not always the author, so a follow-up phone call is helpful a few days after the conference.

Though it is energizing to wander the trade floor, the conference participant needs to compose a schedule. Writing a cookbook? Don't miss the Emeril demonstration at 2 p.m. at booth 4354. A fan of serial mysteries? Authors Sue Grafton and Janet Evanovich will lead a discussion in conference room 6 at 5 p.m. Keep author, agent, and publishing house appointments as key engagements.

Yes, literary agents are all over BookExpo, some with and some without badges. Often agents appear with their authors at the autograph tables and publisher booths. They attend the author breakfasts and lunches as well as many of the scheduled events and award ceremonies during the conference. (I made a verbal contract with an agent after I saved her place in an autograph line.)

Take a breather every couple of hours and leave the building or find a place to sit—probably on the floor—in the periphery of the halls. The adrenalin-driven conference is hard on the ears as well as the feet. *Library Journal* sponsors a lounge with free refreshments for all librarians (must state *librarian* on blue badge) on the trade floor.

Early on the first day, discover the shipping room (near the autograph area). Grab a free box, put a name on its flap, and place it in a space on a table. The box does not have to be used to ship books; it makes a great resting place for goods in between lugging the items back and forth to the hotel. Suggestion: wear a backpack—without wheels. Any wheeled device is strictly forbidden on the trade floor.

The American Booksellers Association releases a daily newspaper during the conference with the important news of the previous day. Arrive before the 9 a.m. opening to read this newspaper with a final cup of coffee. The early morning is a good time to pick up tickets (free) for the bigger authors' signings.

Some after-hour cocktail parties and events are by invitation only, but many are open to all or to a certain badge color. Attend as many activities as possible and touch base with all people who voice an interest.

Network, network, network. Keep business cards in hand, and learn to be assertive in illuminating your skills. Dress professionally but keep your feet in sensible shoes.

Understand that BookExpo is not for the meek of heart. While I always accomplish my goal of getting autographed books for our Friends of the Library to sell in the semiannual book sales, I sometimes don't speak up quickly enough to talk about my writing. Often I keep up with my morning schedule but slack off in the late afternoons to just enjoy spontaneous conversations with fellow librarians and writers. Do allow for some self-discovery time.

By the end of the three days of tired feet, I'm looking at the large banner hanging over the exit—"See You Next Year in . . ." and feel the excitement building for the next annual conference. It's then that I wonder why BookExpo remains a book and marketing best-kept secret.

For more information about the next BookExpo conference, see www.bookexpoamerica.com.

PART III
FINDING YOUR NICHE IN PRINT

NICHE

Writing about Diversity through Books

VANDELLA BROWN

Writing books about diversity, on such topics as heritage holidays and diverse cultures, ensures that there are many angles from which to look at diversity and reasons for self-publishing. A book about diverse holidays shares many observations, views, and experiences that enrich the personal perspective. There is an open market today related to reading and writing to explore heritage diversity. For example, African Americans spend about $365 million a year on books by and about themselves. Hispanics need more written books, as 65 percent of children's literature is written in English and only 35 percent is written in Spanish. There are languages other than English in which little or nothing is published in the American book marketplace, such as French, Italian, Yiddish, Russian, Polish, Armenian, Vietnamese, and Native American and African languages (White and Cox 2004).

The need to write in the children's diversity market is great, and it is fed by the continuous growth of immigrant populations and multicultural immersion in the United States. I wanted to enter this immersion market because of my interest in celebrating cultural holidays.

I had several reasons for entering the diversity writing market, none of which dealt with being competitive. Conveying my opinion and perspective about celebrating Kwanzaa to the reading community seemed important and was influenced by my workshops on celebrating Kwanzaa at home. Kwanzaa is an African American cultural holiday celebrated for seven days, from December 26 to January 1 of each year. More than 12 million people celebrate Kwanzaa. With the original concept of celebrating Kwanzaa, from the founder Maulana Karenga, came family versions and public events to celebrate the cultural holiday. As I shared my family's additions to the holiday, I felt that Kwanzaa was a necessary medium for sharing cultural writings with the reading community. In the process of writing about this celebration, I discovered a niche; I explored a reading audience and went from royalty publishing to self-publishing and then to subsidized publishing.

My first book, *Celebrating the Family: Steps to Planning Family Reunions* (1991), derived from my workshops on reunion planning at genealogical conferences. It was a workbook to assist planners in organizing family reunions from any cultural perspective, but it encouraged determining holidays and special traditions that might inspire a reunion. I had a contract with a publishing company for the book, a simple contract in which I received a percentage from the sales, or royalty. In our contract, the publisher filed and held the copyright for an agreed-on number of years. After that period, the publisher submitted a letter returning all copyright pledges back to me. Of course, as the author, I was given the rights to reproduce and copy the book at anytime. It worked out smoothly. At the same time, I also was presenting workshops related to Kwanzaa, and I decided to self-publish a quick, handy guide for my workshop, *Celebrating Kwanzaa at Home* (1998). The booklet sold for $2 to $3 and made enough to cover the cost of its production. I developed the booklet by assembling my own design and format and using an office services company to duplicate copies.

Because the booklet sold so well, I discovered that I had tapped into an audience that enjoyed imaginative and basic ways to reflect on Kwanzaa at home. This was an audience that attended my workshops and used libraries as a source of information. I had uncovered a cultural reading and writing niche. A niche in the publishing market refers to writing on a specific subject or genre.

As I continued to do the workshops on celebrating Kwanzaa at home, I included an activity for gift giving that made Kwanzaa a lot of fun. This led to the subsidiary publication of my book *What Is a Zawadi to We? A Poetic Story Celebrating Kwanzaa and Gift Giving. Zawadi* is a Swahili word for "gift." The book, with colorful paper-craft illustrations, is one that you read aloud while passing around gifts to guests. It's designed for Kwanzaa, but it can be used at any gift-giving event. I developed an author-subsidy arrangement with a colleague who had opened her own publishing house. A subsidy publisher may not be for everyone. You have to provide much or all of the financial cost yourself, so you become the sole copyright owner, but a subsidy publisher may provide distribution, advertisement, and contacts with other market promotions. Subsidy publishing, sometimes called cooperative publishing, can work well in the cultural writing market. The subsidy publisher created a contract description, the format—the size, number of pages, number of photos or illustrations—and the cost for publishing and a suggested price in order to make a profit from the book's sales. A selection of bookstores and book jobbers were also included in the agreement. My subsidy publisher operated on a time line and assisted in designing the layout, proofreading, and providing galleys and finally the finished product. Financial expense is paid directly to the subsidy publisher, usually in three to four installments, following each completion of the book's printing activity. Of course, that may vary among publishers.

As Americans continue to be more inclusive in their diversity, there will be a need to write about diversity and how the mainstream absorbs culture. Writing and publishing books about different people, traditions, and holidays can strengthen libraries' ability to serve the cultural community and our nation of learners.

REFERENCES

Brown, Vandella. 1991. *Celebrating the Family: Steps to Planning Family Reunions.* N.p.: Ancestry.com.

———. 1998. *Celebrating Kwanzaa at Home.* N.p.: Vandella Brown.

———. 2007. *What Is a Zawadi to We? A Poetic Story Celebrating Kwanzaa and Gift Giving.* Park Forest, IL: Lumen-Us Publications.

White, Maureen, and Ruth Cox. 2004. "A Longitudinal Study of Recommended Translated Children's Books Published in the United States between 1990 and 2000." *Teacher Librarian* 31 (4): 25–29. www .teacherlibrarian.com/tlmag/v_31/v_31_4_ feature.html.

PUBLISHING MYSTERY FICTION

KRIS SWANK

If ever there was a genre invented solely for the pleasure of librarians, it would be the mystery. Mysteries have much in common with librarianship, such as fact gathering, detail orientation, and puzzle solving. So, it's no wonder that the ranks of successful mystery writers include several librarians: Miriam Grace Monfredo, Dean James, and Marcia Talley, to name a few. If you'd like to join that list, writing your mystery may be the easy part. It's getting published that's tricky. Publishers prefer a sure thing, like Janet Evanovich's next mega–best seller. But even novice writers with good stories can find outlets for their work.

WHAT EDITORS WANT

Although there's no magic formula for selling your novel, the noted editor Ruth Cavin, in *Writing Mysteries: A Handbook by the Mystery Writers of America,* identifies three critical elements of a good mystery: believable characters, a realistic and interesting atmosphere, and writing that is smooth and accurate.

Cavin says, "The most important element of the mystery novel, to my mind, is *character.*" Avoid cardboard stereotypes. Your characters should be complex, interesting individuals with dreams, fears, and foibles. Settings should have widespread appeal and be recognizable to readers. However, editors don't want a rehash of the same old territory. In 2003, C. J. Sansom entered the crowded field of Renaissance-era mysteries with his book *Dissolution.* But Sansom's protagonist, the hunchbacked lawyer Matthew Shardlake, was a completely original and compelling character.

But even fascinating characters and colorful settings can't make up for poor writing. Like any other craft, writing improves with practice. Establish a routine and write regularly. Also, consider taking writing classes or workshops to gain valuable insight and criticism.

PERSEVERANCE MAKES PERFECT

Jeri Westerson calls herself the poster child for perseverance. After writing a dozen novels in as many years, she finally sold *Veil of Lies* to St. Martin's Press in 2008. It was actually the second mystery she'd penned featuring the disgraced medieval knight Crispin Guest. But as Westerson learned through her writers' group, Sisters in Crime, many authors of series don't sell their first title. The difference between published and unpublished authors is often the determination to keep writing despite initial rejection.

Once you've written your mystery, it's time to submit it to an editor. Kathy Lynn Emerson, in *How to Write Killer Historical Mysteries,* recommends that you first send a one-page query letter, not e-mail, to a specific editor at a publishing house. (Use the resource guide at the end of this article to locate addresses.) Simply inquire whether the editor would be interested in reading your work. Include a mini-synopsis and author biography.

If an editor asks to read your manuscript, Emerson advises submitting a hard copy on white paper, double-spaced with at least one-inch margins all around, in an easy-to-read black font of at least ten-point size. Submit your story to only one editor at a time, as publishers frown on multiple submissions. And if at first you don't succeed—well, you know.

SHORT STORY AND ONLINE MARKETS CAN GET YOU NOTICED

Writing short mystery stories is a good way to break into publishing, and it may serve as a springboard to novel writing. Several popular series detectives began their literary lives in short stories. Peter Tremayne's Sister Fidelma and Mary Reed and Eric Mayer's Byzantine sleuth John, Lord Chamberlain, were introduced in story anthologies. I. J. Parker's Japanese detective Akitada first appeared in *Alfred Hitchcock's Mystery Magazine.*

Online e-zines can get you noticed, too. Kelli Stanley sold her first mystery novel, *Nox Dormienda,* to Five Star Press. Then, while awaiting its publication, she wrote a mystery short for the e-zine *Hardluck Stories* featuring the same sleuth, the Roman-British physician Arcturus. Stanley gained valuable prepublication buzz for *Nox* when her short story "Convivium" earned a 2007 Spinetingler Awards nomination.

Although e-zines are considered less prestigious, rarely pay, and disappear with regularity, they still expose novice authors to a wide audience. E-zines are often free, and the response time from their editors is typically shorter. While *Alfred Hitchcock's Mystery Magazine* and other print magazines can take up to three months to respond to submissions, a story I submitted to the e-zine *Orchard Press Mysteries* was accepted in a week.

Amazon.com's digital Shorts and its e-book reader Kindle are raising the bar in electronic publishing, but Amazon currently accepts only published authors. However, print-on-demand (POD) services like Blurb.com and Lulu.com put digital publishing within reach of even new authors. Unfortunately, bookstores and book reviewers are, as yet, not generally interested in POD works. That might change as successful mystery writers like Simon Levack and Clayton Emery take full advantage of the digital revolution. Both authors published their latest novels in digital formats.

Whether you are submitting your story for print or electronic publishing, follow submission guidelines carefully. They're typically available on the publisher's website.

NETWORKING IS KEY

Both Stanley and Westerson recommend that new authors join professional writers' groups for advice and support. Westerson says Sisters in Crime "prepared me for a whole new outlook on marketing and provided me with a fantastic critique group." Stanley joined CrimeThruTime, an online discussion group for historical mystery buffs, only after navigating the publishing maze on her own. "Not a strategy I recommend!" she warns.

Mystery conferences and conventions, such as Malice Domestic and Bouchercon, are also good places to network. Conventions allow authors to rub shoulders with booksellers, editors, literary agents, and fans. Check convention websites for more information.

SELECTED RESOURCES FOR MYSTERY WRITERS
BOOKS ON WRITING AND SELLING MYSTERIES

Emerson, Kathy Lynn. 2008. *How to Write Killer Historical Mysteries.* McKinleyville, CA: Perseverance Press.

Ephron, Hallie. 2005. *Writing and Selling Your Mystery Novel: How to Knock 'Em Dead with Style.* Cincinnati, OH: Writer's Digest Books.

Grafton, Sue, ed. 2002. *Writing Mysteries: A Handbook by the Mystery Writers of America,* 2nd ed. Cincinnati, OH: Writer's Digest Books.

Hayden, G. Miki. 2001. *Writing the Mystery: A Start-to-Finish Guide for Both Novice and Professional.* Philadelphia: Intrigue Press.

FINDING MYSTERY PUBLISHERS

"Crime Fiction Publishers," www.overbooked .org/genres/mystery/links/mystpub.html

Literary Market Place. Medford, NJ: Information Today, annual.

"Mystery Book Publishers," http://publishers .omnimystery.com/index.html

Novel and Short Story Writer's Market. Cincinnati, OH: Writer's Digest Books, annual.

Writer's Market. Cincinnati, OH: Writer's Digest Books, annual.

SHORT STORY MARKETS

Alfred Hitchcock's Mystery Magazine. Accepts unsolicited manuscripts up to twelve thousand words; paying.

Ellery Queen's Mystery Magazine. Accepts unsolicited manuscripts, 2,500–8,000 words; First Stories department for new authors; paying.

Short Mystery Fiction Society. Lists print and online, paying and nonpaying markets for short mysteries.

WRITERS' GROUPS AND CONVENTIONS

Bouchercon World Mystery Convention

Malice Domestic Convention

Mystery Writers of America

Sisters in Crime

Yahoo! Groups lists more than 350 groups under "mystery writers," including CrimeThruTime, DorothyL, Historical Mystery Fiction Writers, and Shortmystery.

WRITING FOR REFERENCE BOOKS

SIGRID KELSEY

Librarians, especially those working at reference desks or selecting books, have professional job duties that require them to learn about a variety of subjects. For them, writing reference book entries is a natural extension of their daily work. Authoring articles on topics such as women who served in the American Civil War, Eleanor Roosevelt, lyric poetry, and persons from the Middle Ages has been interesting and rewarding for me professionally. Writing short reference articles does not necessarily require prior expertise in the subject, as long as one has an interest in the topic and the ability to learn about it, qualities usually found in librarians. In addition, reference books offer opportunities for librarians seeking topics more closely related to librarianship. Books in disciplines including business, computer science, popular culture, history, literature, and others include articles pertaining to librarianship. For example, a psychology reference book might include an article on bibliotherapy, while a reference book on emergency management might contain an article on disaster planning for libraries. Reference books covering almost any topic have the potential to include a library-related article.

Reference book entries, editors, and scope vary widely. Some articles, like academic journal articles, are peer-reviewed and intended for a scholarly audience, requiring authors to have a background in the area. Others are intended for K–12 readers or a general audience and are shorter, requiring less research on the author's part. Regardless of the length and audience of a book entry, writers should pay close attention to style, accuracy, deadlines, and other guidelines that the editor provides.

Before deciding to write for a reference book, authors should consider the differences between writing for reference books and writing for journals. Scholars often write a journal article before identifying a publication venue or submitting a proposal. Reference book editors, however, usually have a contract with a publisher and a list of entries required before they recruit authors. Thus, the authors have a deadline and topic assigned to them before starting to write. Because of this, authors committing to write for a reference book should understand that, unlike a scholarly journal, a variety of authors and an editor are relying on them to meet their obligations before the book can be published. An editor can replace authors who fail to do so, and in some cases, tardy authors can stall the production schedule of the entire book. If a book is late, a publisher can cancel the contract and publication of the book. Unfortunately, situations like this are not uncommon and can be disastrous for a librarian who is depending on the publication to earn tenure. Before choosing a writing project, tenure-track librarians should keep this potential hazard in mind and find out whether their library prefers peer-reviewed articles in professional journals to earn tenure. Finally, most reference books are not widely indexed in the library literature, so other faculty may be less likely to read and cite articles in reference books, even scholarly ones, than in journals.

There are also advantages to writing for reference books over submitting work to scholarly journals. Editors with a list of topical entries normally assign them to only one writer, so that writers do not compete for the entry. Thus, if the article is well researched and written, it is likely to be published. Knowing a publication date, and having security about the likelihood of seeing one's work in print, can be a strong motivator. In addition, calls for papers in reference books can provide ideas to authors who have difficulty thinking of a topic on which to write. The number of calls for papers in reference books offers countless choices in topics, audience, and article length. Entries in reference books are often shorter than journal articles, and therefore can be less daunting to write than a lengthy article.

STEPS OF WRITING FOR A REFERENCE BOOK

1. Identify a book (see the list of resources at the end of this chapter). Read the call for papers closely to determine the scope, audience, and deadline. Writing for a reference book that does not already have a publisher may decrease the likelihood of publication and increase the time it takes to see one's work in print.

2. E-mail the book editor expressing interest, and include your résumé or CV. If a call for papers has specific instructions, follow them. Aspiring authors without previous publications should consider submitting a writing sample with their query or expect to be asked for a sample.

3. Editors may assign authors a topic or ask them to choose one and provide a deadline. Authors should not assume that deadlines come with padding. Authors may sign a contract, including a copyright agreement, either at this step or later.

4. Once submitted, an article may be peer-reviewed or reviewed by the editor(s). Authors may be asked to make revisions.

5. Final submissions may be in paper format or by e-mail. Some books send page proof with a deadline as short as a few days for making changes and corrections.

6. The book is published if all parties fulfill their obligations. If applicable, an honorarium or payment comes after the book is in print, but not all authors are paid for their work. Many, but not all, publishers provide authors with a copy of the book.

WEBSITES WITH CALLS FOR REFERENCE BOOK ENTRIES

The websites here include calls for reference book entries, conference presentations, journal articles, book reviews, and more. Search the Internet for phrases such as "call for papers" or "call for proposals" to find more resources.

ABC-CLIO Become an Author Page. www.abc-clio.com/publishing/authors/prospects_zip .aspx. Includes a form for prospective authors and contributors for ABC-CLIO. The editors review the registrants and contact authors who are matches for books.

A Library Writer's Blog. http://librarywriting .blogspot.com. Identifies publishing and presentation opportunities in library and information science and related fields.

Beyond the Job. www.beyondthejob.org. Features articles, calls for papers, job-hunting advice, professional development opportunities, and other news and ideas.

Encyclopedia Website. www.encyclopediaweb site.com. Features information for contributors and prospective contributors to M. E. Sharpe's encyclopedia projects.

Humanities and Social Sciences Net Online. www.h-net.org/announce/. Has a searchable database of writing opportunities under the link Announcements.

IGI Global's Web Page. www.igi-global.com/ requests/author_encyclopedias.asp. Lists calls for short articles for upcoming Information Science Reference encyclopedia and handbook titles.

University of Pennsylvania Calls for Papers List. http://cfp.english.upenn.edu. Lists calls for papers, mostly related to English literature, but including crossover topics like education, history of the book, popular culture, and libraries.

WRITING SEQUELS

JANET HUSBAND

THE IDEA

As the adult-book selector for a medium-sized public library system, I was the person whom branch librarians and others turned to for miscellaneous bookish information. Naturally, they all wanted to know when the new Sue Grafton or Robert Parker was coming out. But some of the questions were trickier:

- Who wrote the mysteries starring the Prince of Wales?

- Which books by Agatha Christie feature Miss Marple?

- Who was the first hard-boiled detective?

I knew the answer to some of the questions but had to research others. In doing so, I discovered that there was no single reference source that could answer all of these questions. What to do? Start a card file, of course—this was way before personal computers came to libraries.

Like a true librarian, I loved my handy and increasingly useful little card file. Not surprisingly, it took me a long time to realize that I was building the foundation of a reference book. When the idea finally struck, I feared I was suffering from delusions of grandeur. After all, I was just a librarian toiling away in my basement office. Who was I to think that I could write a book? Or get one published?

I suspect that many books are born and evolve this way: slowly from a professional interest and a perceived need. And many die at this point, too. Projects with real potential can easily languish without outside support. I was fortunate that my librarian-husband and my always-supportive sister encouraged me to continue. Potential authors should tell friends and colleagues about their ideas for an article or book. The interest, support, and suggestions of others in the field will validate your project and give you that boost of energy necessary to proceed.

THE FORM

Michelangelo may have said, and others certainly have paraphrased, "I saw the angel in the marble and carved until I set him free." It was immediately apparent to me that my tentative book about novels in series would turn into a monster if I did not set limits at the outset. I had to answer questions such as

- Will it contain children's books? Young adult books?

- How many books make a series? Three books? Two?

- Will it include out-of-print series?

So I was forced to define the scope of my project early in the process. Later I realized what an advantage that was. A clear mission is essential to a smooth creative process. It helped me avoid unnecessary work and focus on the important stuff. It is all too easy for authors to be lured into unproductive side streets—in my case, an example is those series composed of short stories rather than novels. The Father Brown mysteries by G. K. Chesterton might seem to warrant inclusion, but because they are all short stories, I excluded them.

Granted, there was still some indecision, but nothing paralyzing: is Louisa May Alcott's *Little Women* series for children or adults?

It also helps to have a firm idea of the book's virtual shape; the old beginning, middle, and end problem. I thought I was home free on that because the obvious arrangement for this material was alphabetical. But wait: Alphabetical by what? By author or series? Will titles be listed alphabetically? Or chronologically? Decisions had to be made. I suspect that these decisions are never easy. Even with straightforward narrative or exposition, authors must decide on chapter and heading divisions. Establishing guidelines at the outset does not mean that they are written in stone, but it creates boundaries—and probably improves your character.

THE TITLE

Now I know what my book is about. And you know what yours is about. But getting that across to the public may not be as easy as you think. The working title of my book was *What to Read Next* and I didn't realize how bad that was until quite late in the game. As a librarian, I do my share of bemoaning bad titles. My personal nominee for the all-time worst title is *Why Are We in Vietnam?* which is a novel by Norman Mailer.

Eventually I realized that my title was in fact downright misleading. *What to Read Next* sounded like a general readers' advisory book. And beginning with *What* was almost as bad as beginning with *Why* or *How*. Who would remember it correctly?

I thought I should have the word *Series* in the title, because that is what librarians call a set of books. But to most people the word means baseball games or a group of events, as in "a series of tornados." Finally I hit on *Sequels*—a wonderful, shiny word that everyone understands and likes thanks to all the *Rocky* movies. It would need a subtitle, but I'd known that all along. My book became *Sequels: An Annotated Guide to Novels in Series.*

THE PROPOSAL

The next step—writing the proposal—is easier than you might think. A proposal is the standard way of asking publishers whether they would be interested in your book. A good proposal summarizes your topic in a concise but detailed manner and includes a scope statement, that is, what is covered and what is not. It helps to be a logical thinker here. Fortunately, most librarians are. Another important feature is a brief professional biography that makes clear how you have gained enough knowledge to write about the subject. You send the proposal to one publisher at a time, so start at the top.

Choosing the right publisher was easy for me: the obvious first choice was the American Library Association. The ALA is not only a professional organization but also a major library publishing house, perhaps the biggest. As a librarian, you will already be familiar with the major publishers and will know how to research the others. Just pick the top one for your subject and mail the publisher your proposal.

The entries in a compilation such as *Sequels* have so many variables that describing them all would have been extremely tedious. So I supplemented my proposal with a significant number of examples. In fact, I wrote up the "A" and "B" sections (the book is arranged alphabetically by author)—starting as I meant to go on—and sent that along with my proposal.

THE ACCEPTANCE

The joy of opening that letter of acceptance is indescribable. Enjoy it while you can. Perhaps you will be as lucky as I was and the long, hard road to the finished work will include frequent bumps of discovery and exhilaration along the way.

TIPS FOR COMPILING A PUBLISHABLE BIBLIOGRAPHY

JOHN R. BURCH JR.

During the spring publishing season of 2009, McFarland and Company published a bibliography that I compiled titled *The Bibliography of Appalachia: More Than 4,700 Books, Articles, Monographs and Dissertations, Topically Arranged and Indexed*. The following steps are the ones that I undertook as I compiled my bibliography.

The first step in the process was the selection of a topic. In my case, I blundered into the topic while working on my Ph.D. dissertation. I was conduct-ing research on an Appalachian county in Kentucky and was having a difficult time identifying sources for background information. I eventually found the information that I needed and documented the sources of the data in the bibliography for my dissertation. Once the dissertation was completed, I decided that there was a real need in the reference literature for a bibliography on Appalachia, and I determined to address the problem.

Once I had the topic, I had to answer the question, Who am I compiling the bibliography for? The answer to this question helped determine the types of materials that I chose to include in the bibliography. I determined that I was writing for an audience that included both lay readers and individuals conducting scholarly research. Thus, I opted to include books, articles, research reports, chapters in edited works, and doctoral dissertations. I included doctoral dissertations because they can be obtained through interlibrary loan. Although there were a few websites included in the bibliography, I did make a conscious effort to generally exclude Internet sites. The reason for this decision is that Internet addresses constantly change, as does content. While this decision worked for me, it is not one that I would recommend to others, as I know that many publishers favor websites for inclusion in bibliographies.

An important consideration is the publication period that the bibliography will address. Because my bibliography focused on a discipline that had been emerging since the late 1960s and thus did not have an unmanageable number of publications, I chose to include materials published from the beginning. If I had been working on a bibliography on the history of the United States, I would have chosen to focus on materials published within a much more narrowly defined number of years. The inclusion of works published in a shorter period of time will also help you cover the topic more comprehensively. Bibliographies covering works published over decades tend to become a sampling of representative works. For example, my bibliography provides a representative sample. I simply did not have enough easy access to published materials to even attempt comprehensive coverage of the interdisciplinary field of Appalachian studies.

If you wish to publish a bibliography, you need to consult potential publishers early in the process for several reasons. First, you need to gauge whether there is even one publisher interested in potentially publishing your bibliography. This may sound harsh but is unfortunately true. Although you may know that your work fills an obvious void in the reference literature, that does not mean that a publisher feels an obligation to fill that hole. Your bibliography will be evaluated strictly on whether the publisher feels that the company can make enough money on the work to make at least a small profit. Apparently, many publishers do not believe that they can easily make money on bibliographies; thus, few bibliographies are published relative to other types of reference works. Also, a publisher that is interested in publishing the work may want to set parameters on your bibliography to make your work more marketable. The publisher may want to expand the scope of your bibliography or determine the types of materials you choose for inclusion, the number of entries, and so on. You may have to make concessions for your bibliography to ever get published. Don't necessarily reject a publisher's suggestions, because the publisher takes a financial risk when choosing to publish a bibliography and tries to ensure that the final product will market well enough to at least break even. That said, be sure that you do not make concessions that cause you to feel a loss of ownership over your own work.

Once I knew I had a publisher, I turned to constructing an alphabetical, by author, list of publications that I would include in the bibliography. I chose this method to help ensure that I did not include the same work multiple times. At this point, I also determined what style of entries I would use to ensure uniformity throughout the work.

During the compilation of entries, one must decide whether the entries will be annotated. If the entries will be annotated, will the annotations be descriptive or evaluative? I initially opted to annotate but changed my mind very quickly. My reason for abandoning the annotation process was that I did not have easy access to a significant number of the works I was including in the bibliography.

With any project of this type, one must set a date to cut off data inclusion. This is especially true for bibliographies, because new materials that could be included are published on what seems like a daily basis. Once the cutoff point is reached, then the compiler can begin the finishing stages in the work. For me, the finishing stage began with the conversion of my one alphabetical list into twenty-four chapters arranged by subject. The chapter titles I settled on were bluntly obvious, such as "Agriculture" and "Women and Gender." I did this because chapter titles are now included in MARC records and are thus searchable in library catalogs.

Once all of the entries had been placed into a chapter, I began the painstaking process of numbering each entry. I assigned each entry a unique number that was used during the indexing process. Numbering was a monotonous process, and despite my best efforts, I made errors. Unfortunately, by the time I noticed the errors, I was already finished with the indexing. Rather than starting over, I just noted

BEING AN ALA NEWSLETTER EDITOR

STACY RUSSO

Are you interested in writing and helping other librarians get published? Do you want to become more active within the profession? Would you like to attend programs and discussion groups at conferences as a reporter? Do you want to learn more about how a particular division or roundtable of ALA works? If you answered yes to some or all of these questions, then editing an ALA newsletter may be the job for you.

At the time of this writing, ALA has eleven divisions and seventeen roundtables. Within the divisions, there are often sections, committees, roundtables, or other groups. The focus of these various subgroups is eclectic and shows the strengths and diversity of our profession. For example, the Association of College and Research Libraries (ACRL) has seventeen sections. A few examples are African American Studies Librarians, Arts, Literatures in English, and Rare Books and Manuscripts. Because most of these sections have newsletters, opportunities for getting involved in writing and reporting on topics that interest you are numerous. I served as the assistant editor and then editor for the ACRL Women's Studies Section (WSS). My appointment was an excellent way to be actively engaged in the profession. Editing an association newsletter provides opportunities that are often open for both seasoned writers and editors and beginners.

HOW TO BEGIN?

Some professional groups have several applicants for newsletter editor positions when they become available, which makes it competitive to secure the job; others may struggle to find someone willing to be the editor. This can also change from year to year. If you are not sure you want to sit in the editor's chair or if you just joined the section and know there will likely be competition to be appointed, you can always get a start by contributing short pieces to the newsletter. I contributed a piece to the WSS newsletter as a newer section member before receiving the editorship the following year.

It is almost always true that editors are on the lookout for articles and need members to contribute for the newsletter to stay afloat and be dynamic. If you are on the electronic discussion list for your association, you will likely see calls for contributions. You do not have to wait for these calls; many editors welcome story ideas at any time. Being published in the newsletter will give you name recognition within the association. Also, the current editor or coeditor will naturally be involved with accepting, editing, and formatting your work. If these individuals make the decision on who to appoint as the new editor or assistant editor, which is the present case with the WSS newsletter, then they will already know you as someone with an interest in the publication.

WELCOME TO EDITING

Depending on the history of the newsletter, once you are appointed editor, there may be specific guidelines to follow. For example, you may be required to use certain logos, format the newsletter in a standard way, and report only on association news. This does not mean that your creativity is stifled, but it is important to review previous issues of the newsletter and ask questions of the former editor. Before making significant changes, it is also wise to first check with the group's executive board and, if necessary, association leadership.

Knowing the history of the newsletter well is also helpful for a new editor, because it provides a template. Having a framework to work within may make your job easier than beginning entirely from scratch. If you are in the position of starting a brand new newsletter or if you have been given the charge to completely refashion an existing one, the good news is that many ideas are readily available. Most associations publish their newsletters online, providing new editors with ideas for design and content.

PUTTING OUT CALLS

A good editor will ensure that the voice of the association is heard in the publication, not just the editor's voice. One way to solicit contributions is to put out calls. Good calls

- are brief but include as many specifics as possible (e.g., deadlines, word-count requirements, editor's contact information, submission specifications)
- provide ideas for topics, if applicable
- give contributors ample time to write
- give editors ample time to compile, edit, and format (it is a good idea to always provide yourself a cushion of time to extend a call and/or deal with unforeseen obstacles.)
- are followed up by a deadline reminder as the date nears

Another thing to consider with calls is that you may put out a general or specific call. With a general call, you are open to members' ideas on possible topics. You should do this only if you know you will likely have room to fit some unique pieces.

Often, however, you have specific assignments that you need others to cover. In this situation, be direct about what must be written. You may discover that no one responds to a specific call for an article that needs to appear. In this case, you may need to write the article yourself. This is another reason why providing ample time between the initial call and the deadline is a necessity.

WHAT TO INCLUDE?

The content of your newsletter will vary, of course, depending on how many submissions you receive and the history and guidelines of your group. There are some standards that often appear. If your newsletter does not have any of the following, these are ideas to consider:

- chair's (or president's) column
- names of new members (including all who joined since the last issue)
- member profiles
- member news
- committee and/or task force reports
- photographs from the group's programs or events
- announcements for the group's upcoming programs or events
- book and media reviews

ESTABLISH COHESIVENESS

On a final note, it is important, as stated earlier, to represent the voice of an association, but the newsletter needs to also be cohesive. This is a challenge for editors. Spelling is one part of this. Although it may sound obvious, when you are dealing with many writers, you will understand the mechanical difficulties that arise. Scan articles for problematic words. Will you require *Website* as the spelling or must it be written as *Web site*? Is it *academic librarian* or *Academic Librarian*? What about *e-mail* or *email* or *E-mail* or *Email*? Standards should also apply for bylines, citations, and footnotes. If you produce a cohesive newsletter with relevant and informative content that succeeds at representing members' voices, you will have performed well as an editor!

PARTNERS

Helping Your Hometown Paper Promote the Local Library

BETH NIEMAN

Writing for the local newspaper about books, library events, and local history gives you exposure as a writer while keeping your library in the public eye.

Libraries, with their notoriously small budgets, must often settle for running one- or two-line announcements in the local newspaper when a special event is coming up, or perhaps they forgo the newspaper altogether in favor of putting up some fliers on the library bulletin boards. By writing a regular library feature for your local newspaper, you can raise the visibility of the library in your community and provide a valuable service for your readers.

When contacting an editor to propose your idea of writing for the newspaper, be sure to treat your meeting just as you would a job interview. Dress professionally and come prepared to discuss several ideas. Bring a couple of polished writing samples showing the kind of thing you'd like to do for the newspaper. Listen carefully to what the editor needs from you.

Newspaper editors know their subscribers like to read local news that isn't readily available elsewhere. As a librarian who writes, you are uniquely situated to provide local historical information about your area and to highlight library resources of interest to your community. If you're not particularly knowledgeable about local history, interview someone who is, and write an article tying together local history with specific books and reference materials in your library collection.

Many newspapers have an arts and entertainment section, which is an excellent location for an occasional library feature article or even a regular column highlighting new books and other library materials. Beware of committing to a weekly schedule unless you're reasonably sure you can keep up with it. Whatever the frequency of your contribution, never miss a deadline! Missing your deadline means the editor has to scramble to find something else to fill the space reserved for you.

One way to avoid missing deadlines is to work ahead. Have several backup articles ready to submit when you want to take a vacation or in case of illness or a family emergency. Also, if you know that you want to write about something seasonal (maybe reviewing some gardening books for spring or barbecue cookbooks around the Fourth of July), you can prepare those articles any time of year and they'll be ready when you need them.

You might find a monthly format easier to manage. You might even prefer to publish articles in special sections, which newspapers often run periodically to tie with seasons or events. For example, there may be an annual "best-of" section run by your paper in which readers vote on the best pizza place in town, the best car wash, and so on. You could tie your library into that section with an article about the best new books to read for different age groups or in various genres.

Make sure your community knows that the library is a place full of great information where interesting things happen, by promoting special events. If your library hosts a summer reading program, alert the newspaper. Don't settle for a little announcement, though. Make sure you let a reporter know when you'll have a photo opportunity, such as a special guest speaker, a storytelling performance, or a fun activity. Your library just might end up on the front page!

If there's no reporter available to cover your event, don't let that stop you. Newspapers also accept submissions. You can take a couple of photos, write a short article, and send it in. (Be sure to get the names of the people you photograph and permission to submit their photos to the newspaper.)

Submit a digital copy of your work rather than a typed copy. Newspaper publishing has undergone many changes in the past thirty years. While they were once painstakingly assembled by hand using lead type, newspapers are now produced on computers using publishing software. Keep in mind that the less work the newspaper staff has to do to get your article into print, the more receptive they'll be to working with you. If you've already put your article together on a word processor, the editor will likely prefer that you e-mail it rather than send a paper copy that has to be retyped by a staff member.

Can you charge a fee for providing material to your local newspaper? For onetime feature articles, probably not. If you are doing some of your writing and research while on the clock at your library job, in a sense, you are already getting paid for this work. For a regular contribution such as a weekly column or a monthly feature, you may be able to negotiate something with your newspaper editor. But then you might not feel right about working on your articles while you're working at the library.

Whether or not you collect payment from the newspaper, you are receiving valuable exposure in print and a byline. You'll build a portfolio of published writing that you can show an editor when you're ready to submit a magazine article idea or a have a book proposal you want to sell. Your portfolio is proof that you can write publishable material, that you're a responsible author who meets deadlines, and it will give editors an idea of what kind of assignments you can handle.

Writing about books and your library for the local newspaper benefits both you and your community. Not only will your articles provide information to the public and publicize the library, but you'll also gain valuable writing experience and build your credentials as an author.

PRESS KITS AND NEWS RELEASES

FAYE C. ROBERTS

Although only the largest libraries might employ public relations professionals, even small libraries can develop professional press kits and craft effective news releases. These tools create a positive image and help communicate the library's message.

PRESS KITS

A press kit is a folder of information about your organization prepared in advance of a news event. The kit is designed to provide a reporter with supplemental information that can be used to flesh out a current story or to inspire ideas for future stories. A well-organized press kit includes basic facts about the library, its leadership, and its programs and services.

When a reporter on deadline contacts you, having a press kit can save valuable time and reduce stress. Whether the inquiry is about your own library or the local implications of a national issue, advanced preparation is the key to telling your library's story effectively.

Standard press kits include a "backgrounder" that provides essential details about the library, a fact sheet, and recent press releases. The kit can be customized for special events by including promotional materials such as bookmarks or giveaways for a summer reading program. For complex stories, an additional question-and-answer sheet can provide further details that a reporter might want to address. It's critical that every item in the kit be factual, spelled correctly, and up to date.

Backgrounder. The backgrounder, or background document, is usually one or two pages in length. It includes the library's mission statement and an overview of its facilities, programs, and services with related web links. This information may be presented in a bulleted list. The names of library leadership should also be included: board members, directors, and key staff. List the URL for the library's web page and include press contact information.

Fact sheet. The fact sheet is one page in length and may include the library's mission statement. It should list the library's address, URL, and main phone number, along with the locations and hours of branches and other outlets. Press contact information should include a name, title, direct phone line, and e-mail address.

Leadership biographies. While profiles are an optional component, having profiles of board members and the library director can be a great time saver. Biographies should be no more than fifty to a hundred words and limited to topics relevant to the individual's library role. List the board chair first, then officers, followed by other board members and the library director.

Although corporate press kits sometimes contain flashy materials with lots of glitz, libraries are advised to take a simpler, less expensive approach. You don't want the cost of your press kit to become the focus of the news story.

A simple two-pocket folder from a stationery supplier is sufficient. Add an attractive label with the library's name and logo for a customized touch. The number of press kits needed depends on the number of media outlets that you plan to contact. It's best to prepare kits only for the near future. Review the contents before each use and update any data that has changed.

NEWS RELEASES

News releases or press releases are a fundamental way to communicate with the media. The release is a concise, focused announcement of a news event. Library press releases might be about a new program or service, a grant or honor awarded, or progress made on a major project. Press releases can announce special events, describe new equipment, introduce new staff, or give new information on an existing program. The key to the news release is always what's new.

To have your stories appear in the media, give the newspaper or other media outlet what it wants. Before writing the first press release, study each outlet to learn the stories they run. A major metropolitan newspaper may not be interested in the activities of a single-branch library, but a neighborhood newspaper may be hungry for local news. A release that appeals to a newspaper's readership is more likely to be used.

Contact reporters and editors to find out their publication schedule and deadlines. Ask about formats for news releases and whether they prefer to have them submitted by e-mail or hand-delivered.

In general, a news release should be double-spaced on standard 8½-by-11-inch white paper, either letterhead or plain. List the name, phone number, and e-mail address of the person to be contacted for additional information. A release date or "for immediate release" tells the editor when to use the story.

A headline, in all caps, describes the story and hooks the editor's attention. Each release should focus on one news event. Rather than combine two or three news items, prepare separate releases and submit them at different times.

The body of the release is written in the inverted-pyramid style, with the most important information given first. The first or lead paragraph should contain all the basic facts: who, what, when, where, why, and how. These should be concisely stated in one hundred words or less.

The remaining text provides additional background and helps put the story in context. It's a good idea to also include a brief description of the library, its mission, major services, and web address. Avoid jargon and abbreviations. The entire press release should be double-spaced and no more than 250 words. If the release extends more than one page, type "MORE" at the end of the first page. On the last page, type "###" or "-30-" to designate the end.

Check all details carefully, especially dates, times, locations, and budget information. Quotations can enliven a story but make sure your quotes are accurate.

In addition to using a spell-checker, proofread the release carefully and ask someone else to review it as well.

REACH OUT

If you're having difficulty obtaining media coverage, become proactive. Invite a panel of media representatives to discuss news coverage for nonprofit groups. This exciting new library program for community organizations would certainly deserve its own press release—and you're just the one to write it.

WRITING A NEWSPAPER COLUMN

FAYE C. ROBERTS

Is it right for you?

"Would you like to write a newspaper column about the public library?" This surprising phone call came when I had been a library director for four years. The caller was managing editor of the local newspaper in our community of fifty thousand people. She explained that the paper was experimenting with a weekly book section and wanted to include a library-focused column each Friday. I jumped at the chance.

Even in this age of blogs, web pages, and other electronic communications, the local newspaper is still a significant source of local news. Newspaper readers may also be library users and supporters, now or in the future.

The opportunity to write a newspaper column brings a host of potential benefits to the reader, the newspaper, the library, and to you, the author.

Every librarian realizes the enormity of the library's backstory, the myriad tasks that support the library's programs and services. Few of these details are ever seen by the general public. Because libraries serve the entire community, everything about a library is of potential interest to someone. Sharing this information with local residents acquaints them with the public library's contributions to the community's quality of life and to their lives in particular.

The newspaper benefits from the addition of interesting, no-cost copy, dependably submitted, that's appealing to its readers. The library benefits from regular publicity shaped by a knowledgeable advocate.

You, the author, benefit from community exposure as a spokesperson for the library and from the satisfaction of being a published writer.

Committing to a regular writing schedule is not for everyone. Writing takes time. For those who add writing to an already-full range of duties, finding time to write may be a challenge. Writing a weekly column means finding this time every week, regardless of vacation schedules, illness, or a pressing workload.

The commitment to writing and the process of doing so are easier for those with interest and skill. With practice, skills may be sharpened and the time required may be reduced. The big challenge for me was coming up with an interesting topic week after week.

GETTING STARTED

While you, too, may receive an unexpected invitation to write a column, more likely you will need to sell your local newspaper on the idea. Study the paper to determine what style and column length are most appropriate. Write three or four sample columns on different subjects. These illustrate both the range of possible topics and consistent writing skill.

If a weekly column is not the most desirable arrangement for you or the paper, explore the possibility of biweekly, monthly, quarterly, or just occasional columns. Even a trial period can provide a chance to get established.

TIPS FOR SUCCESS

Keep your promises. To maintain credibility and a good working relationship with your editor, you must honor deadlines. If the newspaper agrees to reserve space, you must fill it with something worthwhile. Make every effort to consistently submit your material even before the deadline.

Look for stories everywhere. Public libraries offer a wide range of column topics and all those topics have a human side.

Consider the reader. Look at the library from the user's standpoint instead of the staff's. Users care about solutions to their problems. Rather than just describe the local history collection, explain what it offers for the amateur genealogist. Use anecdotes to add a personal element. A column outlining interlibrary loan procedures may be deadly dull. A more engaging story describes how library staff tracked down an article that a parent (or businessperson or teacher) needed to solve a problem.

Make it easy for the editor. Write from the top down. Put the most important points of your column at the beginning. In this way, if the column must be shortened, essential information will be retained.

Suggest a headline. Many regular columns run under a standard caption. A well-written headline expands the caption, summarizes the content to follow, and draws the reader's attention. An engaging first sentence pulls the reader into the story.

Maintain the pace. For me, the pattern of writing a column each week was best. If I tried to get ahead by writing several columns at a time, it broke the rhythm of weekly writing. When it was time to write again, it could be difficult to get back into the habit.

Keep it fresh. Rather than stockpile columns for future use, I found it more productive to keep a list of ideas that I could use at any time. When inspiration was elusive, I could expand these ideas to fit the occasion. For example, I'd relate a list of health and exercise titles to New Year's resolutions. I used parenting titles in a column on helping kids adjust to school. A discussion of library lending practices or meeting-room use could appear in any season.

Share the joy. Give others the opportunity to write guest columns. Highlight specific departments, programs, or events and those who work with them. Encourage staff members to research and write about topics that interest them. If they're reluctant to write, interview them and tell the story yourself.

MAKING A DIFFERENCE

When a library user brings in your column torn from the newspaper asking to learn more about its content, you know you've found a great way to connect the public library to the community it serves.

BOOK REVIEWS

SIGRID KELSEY

ook reviews help librarians obtain information when selecting library books, compare potential titles to those already owned, and justify purchases of library material. In addition to selecting books, typical job duties for librarians include cataloging books, recommending books to patrons, and creating bibliographies and displays of library material. Book reviews can help librarians learn about recent and forthcoming material and provide information to assist with many of their job duties. Given that their jobs require them to be aware of the scope and availability of literature in a variety of disciplines, librarians have the appropriate breadth of knowledge to write the book reviews as well. Writing book reviews offers an opportunity for librarians to become even more familiar with the literature and publishers available to their libraries, and because their colleagues use book reviews in their work, it provides a valuable service to the library profession. Reviewing books also serves as a vehicle to develop writing skills and to practice working with editors and meeting deadlines, expertise needed for both professional work and larger writing projects.

The length and types of book reviews vary widely. For example, journals dedicated to publishing lengthy reviews of books, like the *New York Times Review of Books* and the *Women's Review of Books,* are highly competitive to review for and comparable to writing a scholarly article. English faculty members specializing in literature typically write for these journals. Society journals in every field publish reviews of books of interest to their readership, and experts in the respective fields usually write these as well. Reviewing for this type of journal, therefore, is more competitive than reviewing for journals publishing shorter or less specialized reviews.

Other journals publish book reviews read widely by librarians who use the reviews to learn about potential library purchases. The American Library Association (ALA) publishes several journals with pages dedicated to book reviews, mostly written by librarians, and read by librarians. *Choice: Current Reviews for Academic Libraries,* for example, is a magazine of book reviews published by the Association of Research and College Libraries, a division of the ALA. *Choice* reviews are less than two hundred words, and reviewers are required to be faculty members or librarians at academic institutions in the United States or Canada. *Reference and User Services Quarterly (RUSQ)* publishes longer reviews (three hundred to six hundred words). Most other library science journals publish book reviews written by librarians and read by librarians. *School Library Journal (SLJ)* and *The Lion and the Unicorn* publish book reviews of children's and young adult literature and are essential tools for public and school librarians. Public and school librarians write many of the book reviews published in *SLJ* and *The Lion and the Unicorn.*

BECOMING A BOOK REVIEWER

To become a book reviewer for a journal, first identify a journal to review for. Most journals have websites with contact information and directions for submitting work or applying to review books. Reviewers should choose topics and journals appropriate to their background and be able to understand how the reviewed book fits in with the related literature.

STEPS TO REVIEWING A BOOK

1. A book review editor contacts the reviewer by e-mail, with a title and deadline, asking whether the reviewer is interested in reviewing the title.

2. Once the reviewer agrees to review a book, the journal editor or book publisher sends a review copy to the reviewer. The review copy is for the reviewer to keep. Sometimes, the review copy of the book is a prepublication copy, and in these cases, the binding or other parts of the book may be incomplete.

3. The reviewer carefully reviews the book, using the guidelines, deadline, and other instructions given from the editor or publisher. Often, book reviews have a quick turnaround time.

ELEMENTS OF A BOOK REVIEW

The length of book reviews varies, depending on the venue. Reviewers for children's books review the illustrations as well as the text. Other book reviews typically include the following:

- the complete bibliographic information of the book

- a brief description of the scope of book, including the length and purpose

- the qualifications of author or editor of the book

- the audience for whom the book is intended

- a comparison to similar books

- a recommendation of who should buy the book

- the name, job title, and workplace of the reviewer

Book reviewers should not attempt to seek out every typographical error in a book, but they should mention obvious omissions or errors that affect the meaning of the book. Reviewers need not describe how to use the book or provide information that readers are able to obtain from the publisher's website or advertisements. Because book reviews have a limited length, it is important that reviewers use concise and descriptive language.

SOURCES FOR PUBLISHING YOUR REVIEWS

To apply to be a reviewer, you can e-mail the book review editor of a journal expressing interest and including your qualifications. Here is a list of a few journals that publish book reviews:

Choice: Current Reviews for Academic Libraries. www.choicemag.org. Reviewers for *Choice* must work at an academic institution of higher education as a faculty member or a librarian. The website has a form for potential reviewers to submit.

RUSQ. www.rusq.org/contact/. The contact page lists the book review editor, whom interested reviewers can contact by e-mail or mail.

portal: Libraries and the Academy. http://muse.jhu.edu/journals/portal_libraries_and_the_academy/info/1.4.editorial.html. The editorial board web page has e-mail addresses for the review editors.

The Lion and the Unicorn. www.press.jhu.edu/journals/lion_and_the_unicorn/guidelines.html. The Instructions to Authors web page states where to send inquiries about reviewing books.

School Library Journal. www.schoollibraryjournal.com/info/CA6409017.html?q=contact+us. The Contact Us page lists the e-mail address and phone number for the book review editor.

REVIEWING BOOKS FOR A NEWSPAPER

TOM COOPER

I have been writing book reviews for the *St. Louis Post-Dispatch* since 1996. It doesn't pay much, but I get free copies of books and a nice feeling when I see my name in print once in a while. It also lends a bit of prestige to whatever library I'm working for when people see that someone on the staff has the credentials or the professionalism (let's not say the pure dumb luck) to write book reviews for a major newspaper. It wasn't easy getting a break, and it hasn't been easy keeping my name in the pool of available reviewers, but I've learned a few things along the way.

Most librarians know that simply having a love of books doesn't guarantee that you'll be a good librarian. The same applies to reviewing books. Librarians come from many academic disciplines, and if you didn't study English, or at least pay attention in a course on literary criticism, you may not have the education necessary to review literature. Newspaper reviewers don't pepper reviews with too many literary terms; but if you don't recognize that an entire work is allegorical, or that a book's climax is a contrived use of deus ex machina, you're not likely to say anything instructive or meaningful to intelligent readers, regardless of whether you use the technical terms for those things.

BECOMING A REVIEWER

If you expect to become a reviewer, you must find a niche or two in which you can honestly claim to specialize. My specialties are Japanese fiction in translation and Eastern European fiction in translation—both of which I studied in my undergraduate years and have kept up with ever since—and books about food and food history: I cooked professionally for nearly ten years before becoming a librarian. Because I have established my credentials with these few subjects, my editor now sends me books from a much broader spectrum.

Breaking in is the hardest part. You are not going to break into reviewing at papers such as the *New York Times, Los Angeles Times,* or *USA Today,* which maintain staffs of professional reviewers and often have reviews written for them by the likes of Joan Didion or John Updike. But many papers have a book review editor who oversees a group of people who review on assignment. If your hometown has a decent newspaper with good circulation, and you believe that you could do a good job of reviewing, there's no reason you couldn't be one of those people.

Check to see whether the reviews in the paper are always credited to staff writers, or if many of them come from people who are listed as "special to" the paper. The credit might also say something like, "So-and-so is a freelance writer," or "So-and-so is a professor of American history," or many other things. If that's the case, you have an opening. Find out who the book review editor is and send that person a brief, professionally written letter (not an e-mail) stating your credentials and the niche in which you are interested and offering your services. If you don't get a response after several weeks, try again.

I hate to beat the same drum you've heard so many people thump on before, but it often comes down to who you know. I did study English in college and graduated magna cum laude. I worked in libraries for years, most notably in the Office of Collection Development at St. Louis Public Library, where I read hundreds of book reviews every week. Although I thought this was the perfect background for someone hoping to become a reviewer, my letters to the book review editor at the *Post-Dispatch* all went unanswered. I even sent in a review I had written of a new book, to prove my ability to write: again, no response.

Then one day my wife called me to say that at her place of employment she had gotten a new client who happened to be the book review editor at the *Post-Dispatch.* Within a few months, I had my first review in the paper. Yes, I pushed it, but that's what you have to do. If you are not prepared to take advantage of any little chance you get, you probably won't make it into print. Anybody you meet who is even remotely connected to the paper you are hoping to write for can be a valuable connection.

At one point several years ago, my editor at the *Post-Dispatch* became angry about something and ceased sending me books for review. It was a personal matter not even connected to my reviewing, and I won't go into it here; but I will caution you to expect some degree of unprofessionalism in dealing with newspaper editors—they are, alas, all too human. I sent a few letters hoping to patch things up, with no effect.

Then one day I was teaching a computer class at the library where I was then working, and I met a very nice older gentleman whom I got to know quite well. His wife, it turned out, was the features editor at the *Post-Dispatch*—the book review editor's boss. I mentioned my quandary, he suggested I send a letter to his wife, and before you know it, I was reviewing books again. The book review editor wasn't too happy about it, but if you expect to do anything in the competitive world of newspapers, you can't worry too much about making people happy.

Your motivation should be getting your name out there as a recognized expert and a professional whose words carry weight: doing so should benefit the library you represent and the profession we serve.

HOW TO WRITE REVIEWS

A librarian writing book reviews has a few advantages to play to, as well as a few problems to avoid. One advantage is our skill at getting people interested in books. In book discussion groups, book talks, readers' advisory interviews, or day-to-day transactions at the circulation desk, we're in touch with people and what they're reading, what they respond to, what makes them want to read a book. All of this can inform your reviews and help you to express yourself in ways that resonate with readers.

But don't rely too heavily on what people say. If three or four patrons have returned a book by the author you are about to review, each one telling you he's too wordy, or hard to understand, you may approach the assigned book with these comments in mind. Clear your head, start from page 1, and form your own opinion. Perhaps the author's verbosity is really a great flair for description, or for characterization, and these are strengths you will highlight—despite what patrons have said about him.

If you are assigned a book by an author whose work you've never read, you should read an earlier book by the same author before reading the assigned one. Then you can comment intelligently on how this book fits in with that author's work. Perhaps both books are astonishingly similar, perhaps astonishingly different. Perhaps characters or settings recur. If an author sets all of his or her books in the same fictional city, and you don't know that, your opinions will carry little weight with readers who do. Here again a librarian has an advantage over other reviewers—you can get the books at work, and you know how to use interlibrary loan for those that aren't in your collection.

Most books for review come with public relations fliers that will note the publication date; if not, check *Publishers Weekly, Library Journal, Kirkus Reviews,* or another source to find the date. Read the book and get your review written by that date, if not earlier. The PR material usually includes biographical information about the author. If there is none, make an effort to find some—another advantage for the librarian reviewer. Showing that you are aware of the author's background helps establish your credibility as a reviewer.

While doing your homework, avoid the temptation to read other reviews of the same book. They affect your objectivity and color what you write, especially if you disagree with an earlier reviewer. Your review should be a cogent and concise essay about the qualities of a book, and why those qualities make the book worth reading or not worth reading. It should not be your side in an argument somebody else started. Leave that sort of thing for Amazon and the blogosphere.

A book review is not a book report: don't spend several paragraphs on a synopsis of the plot. Only tell enough of the story to help readers understand the points you will make, and avoid extraneous detail. For instance, if a book is a love story, and the man is an accountant and the woman is a lab technician, but no point of your critique hinges on their jobs, then don't talk about them. Don't talk about minor characters, unless you need to discuss the author's use of them. Skip names wherever possible. Readers will learn that the lovers' names are Mack and Sadie when they read the book.

Too many reviewers use the same terminology: books are *compelling,* the writing is *luminous,* and the climax is *stunning* or *revelatory.* They refer to authors as *stylists* who write *spare and elegant prose.* It is especially bothersome when reviewers use flighty synonyms for the word *write,* like *pen* and *limn*. Express your thoughts in simple, straightforward style, and use special literary terms only when nothing else will work.

Above all, avoid spoilers. Many reviewers these days give away the ending of a book or movie as a means of denigrating the work. But it is a smarmy and smug technique best left to smarmy and smug journalists. It is often important to point out that "revelations in the final chapter" resolve the plot, or "one last clue leads the detective to an unexpected conclusion"—and these things will pique readers' interest when you use them wisely. Just don't tell readers the revelations or the clue.

Find out exactly how your editor wants submissions to come in. Mine likes the whole text submitted in the body of an e-mail: editors are increasingly averse to opening attachments. Very few still receive hard copy.

Don't submit 1200 words when you are asked for 800 just because you think you have important points to make. Learn to edit, or you will get edited, and you will seldom like what someone else chooses to cut out of your review. However, don't begin by planning to write eight hundred words. Begin by writing down the thoughts you have about the book,

and edit back from there if you need to. If everything you have to say about the book takes only five hundred words, don't try to stretch by adding new thoughts. Brief but meaningful beats long and rambling any day, and this is a fact newspaper editors know in their bones.

Remember the things your editor says about your reviews and continue to improve on the basis of them. My editor often compliments a well-placed quote from the book, so I know she likes to see quotes and I use them where I can. She dislikes long paragraphs, so I try to break my text up into manageable bits. This is a good style for newspaper work: any paragraph that doesn't quickly make a key point is asking to be pared down—or edited out.

Finally, decide how you want to be credited in the paper for your reviews. Mine currently read, "Tom Cooper is the Director of Webster Groves Public Library." If you are not the director, you should check with your supervisor to see whether you need permission to use your library's name. Most libraries are happy to get their name in print in a newspaper for something as relevant to what they do as a book review—but many libraries have policies in place that require employees to get permission first.

LEARN HOW TO REVIEW BOOKS

JOHN R. BURCH JR.

The most practical advice I received as a student at the University of Kentucky's School of Library and Information Science during the early 1990s was to become a book reviewer for *Library Journal, American Reference Books Annual (ARBA),* or *Choice: Current Reviews for Academic Libraries.* The professor who gave this advice claimed that this was the easiest way for young librarians to begin publishing in a way that would advance one's career. To ensure we learned how to write reviews, this professor gave all of her students plenty of practice through graded assignments. I took the professor's advice to heart and became a reviewer for all three publications at the first possible opportunity. I discovered that the reviewing skills needed for each publication differed, which forced me to develop my skills to meet the needs of each one.

I first became a reviewer for *Library Journal* when it was seeking individuals to review books about Native Americans. Although my undergraduate major was in U.S. history, I really did not have an academic background in Native American history. My expertise in the subject was developed over a lifetime of reading about Native Americans and visiting museums and archaeological sites. Because *Library Journal* was seeking librarians to make informed recommendations to other librarians, it appeared that my supposed expertise was acceptable and they started sending me books to review. I quickly discovered that I needed to learn how to write succinct sentences because the reviews tended to be very short. Despite the limited number of words one has to work with, the reviewer is expected to describe the book's content, identify comparable works, and make a recommendation as to what type of library would be interested in acquiring the work. I learned that to be an effective reviewer for *Library Journal,* one does not need to have an encyclopedic knowledge of all the works published on a given topic, but one does need to have a working knowledge of the monographs that are available for sale to make pertinent comparisons and recommendations.

Once I grew comfortable writing reviews for *Library Journal,* I decided to apply to review for *ARBA.* Once accepted to contribute to *ARBA,* I quickly discovered that Libraries Unlimited was not all that interested in my subject specialty. Instead, it valued my experience as a reference librarian. I often received books to review on topics that I barely knew anything about and was expected to write detailed, descriptive reviews on them. At first, I struggled with reviewing reference works about subjects that were foreign to me. It did not seem to be fair to the people that constructed the reference works to be evaluated by a complete novice. Then it dawned on me that in my everyday work I often grabbed reference books off the shelf that I knew nothing about and presented that data to patrons as factual. My knowledge of the subject had little to do with the utility of a reference work, and it was that utility that I was to primarily determine as a reviewer for *ARBA.* Once I had determined the utility of a reference tool, then I could make as much of an educated decision as I could as to the quality of the information contained therein.

Because I worked in an academic library and wanted to bolster my promotion potential, I decided to review reference books for *Choice.* The reason that *Choice* was particularly valuable for promotion was that faculty members around campus were familiar with *Choice* cards and used them to help develop the campus library's book collection. Through their use of *Choice* cards, they had already acknowledged in a sense the academic gravitas of *Choice.* For most of my tenure with *Choice,* I have reviewed only reference books about Native Americans because I did not have, in *Choice*'s view, the subject expertise to review regular monographs. My subject expertise was appropriate only for reference books, because that type of reviewing also required the ability to evaluate the usefulness of a reference tool. This was not a slight at me: most *Choice* reviewers are subject specialists holding advanced degrees in the fields that they review. Since earning a Ph.D., my reviewing opportunities with *Choice* have expanded.

Although I have reached the point in my career that book reviews have virtually nothing to do with my professional advancement, I continue to review for all three publications. I still find reviewing as enjoyable and challenging as I did the first time I wrote a review for *Library Journal.* Like my professor, I also recommend to librarians that they seek out opportunities to review books for professional publications. Book reviewing not only will hone their writing skills but also will allow them to affect libraries all over the country as they assist colleagues in selecting appropriate books for their respective collections.

KEYS TO A HEALTHY REVIEWER-EDITOR RELATIONSHIP

DOUGLAS KING

As a frequent book and video reviewer for a variety of publications, as well as the current book review editor for the *Online Audiovisual Catalogers Newsletter,* I have been on both sides of the reviewing fence. I wrote reviews for several years before deciding to try my hand at editing reviews, and I have found both tasks to be professionally challenging and personally rewarding. Being involved in the reviewing process as a reviewer or editor is an excellent way to learn about the publication process, to develop and hone your writing and critical-thinking skills, and to contribute to the library profession.

Book and video reviewing can be an extremely positive experience if you, as a reviewer, build and maintain healthy relationships with your editors. As a reviewer, I learned how to do this, and as an editor, I have tried to apply the same techniques in dealing with my contributing reviewers. I have found all the editors with whom I have worked to be extremely personable, helpful, and dedicated to the craft of reviewing, and I have tried to follow suit.

Once you have a few reviews under your belt and discover you enjoy reviewing and have a knack for it, I hope you will consider serving librarianship as a review editor. I have come up with a few pointers I hope will help reviewers develop positive relationships with editors.

Do not take criticism personally. Your editor has a job to do—to make your review, and thus the publication, as well written and useful to the profession as possible. So be thankful, not resentful, for the improvements your editors make to your reviews.

Learn from your editor's edits. It is important to read a good number of reviews within your publication before you start contributing your own, but it is still likely that your first couple of reviews will need a good amount of editing. Analyze the changes your editor makes, and apply this knowledge to your next review. Typically, the changes will involve clarification and concision, but they also might include grammar, diction, and syntax. Ask how you can improve your future reviews.

Follow the basic rules of good writing. Take advantage of spell-checkers and grammar-checkers so that your contributed reviews will be as polished as possible before your editor even considers their content. Your editor works hard, so make his or her job as easy as possible by eliminating common but easily avoidable mistakes such as misspellings.

Stick to deadlines. Your editors are not giving you a deadline to make your life difficult. They are doing their job. Without deadlines, there would be no publication schedules. Submit your review as early as possible (without rushing through it and doing a sloppy job). If you can't meet your deadline, let your editor know as soon as possible. Extensions are sometimes possible, but ask early, not late. Once you receive an item to review, mark your calendar and start thinking about how you will manage your time so you can easily and definitely meet your deadline. When will you watch the video or read the book? When will you write, revise, and rewrite your review?

Follow the publication's rules. This goes for deadlines, word counts, citation styles, means of submission, and so on. Every publication is different, so take the time to learn its policies and guidelines. If you are unsure of something, promptly ask your editor. He or she would prefer that you ask before submitting your review rather than contribute something that is unsuitable or needs a lot of editing.

Be prompt, polite, and professional in all correspondence. All of the editors I have worked with conduct business in this way, and it is of paramount importance that you communicate in the same manner. This will keep communication open and constructive. Your editors deserve to be treated with courtesy and respect. Trust me—they will treat you in kind.

As with any relationship, the key to success is communication. In the world of reviewing, much, if not all, of the communication will be conducted via e-mail. It is important that you check your e-mail often, especially around deadlines, because it is possible that your editor will contact you asking for clarification or changed content. As a reviewer, I diligently check my e-mail, always looking for messages from my various editors, and I am very quick to respond. If I can answer questions immediately, I do so. If I need some time to make my edits or fully answer questions, I quickly let the editor know that I have received the message and am working on a solution. Editors will appreciate your quick response. And as an editor, I like to know my reviewers are attentive, responsive, and care about the quality of their reviews. Editors' messages may grow increasingly brusque as deadline time approaches, but it is important not to take this personally. Editors are just trying to get their work done and provide their publications with the best possible reviews. Sometimes phone calls will be required to solve particularly sticky issues, but this is rare.

Building and maintaining positive relationships with review editors are not difficult, and the rewards are manifold. For instance, by getting on good terms with your editors and staying there, you are more likely to receive items to review that they think you will enjoy. For instance, because our strong relationship and her understanding of my interests, my *Library Journal* video review editor knows that I am a Bob Dylan and Beatles fanatic, so she is quick to send me Dylan documentaries and Beatles films. Also, she alerts me of upcoming Dylan and Beatles books so I can make review requests to the popular arts book review editor. Yes, in many cases you can request items to review. Review editors are glad to know of reviewers' expertise and enthusiasm.

Finally, I have learned that the world of publishing is fast paced, hectic, and sometimes stressful.

Review editors rely on their reviewers to provide well-written reviews that adhere to the publication's policies and require minimal revision. Also, they count on their reviewers to meet their deadlines or at least be honest and forthcoming when deadlines cannot be met. Clearly symbiotic, the reviewer-editor relationship is important to build and nurture, but doing so is easy and well worth the effort.

PEER-REVIEWING

ROBERT P. HOLLEY

Peer-reviewing appears to some as a mysterious process in which hidden executioners slice and dice, accept or reject, and finally spit out the eager author's manuscript with no reasons for the decisions except irrational whims. I see a glimmer of truth in this exaggeration because peer-reviewing is a secret process to allow reviewers to give honest opinions without fear of reprisals. Most reviewing forms have two sections—"comments to be shared with the author" and "comments for the editor"—with the expectation that the reviewer, even if the criticisms are constructive, will be kinder to the author. Data-driven research studies on the comments, contents, and changes from the peer-review process are thus about as unlikely to appear as a scholarly analysis of the taped tenure discussions at a major university.

To help understand the process, I will share my experiences as a peer reviewer. As a senior scholar who can pick his activities, I find peer-reviewing one of the most rewarding tasks in my professional life. I get a large number of manuscripts to review, about five to ten each year, because I never say no, turn the manuscripts around quickly, and am told by the editors of the journals that authors find my suggestions helpful. I have additional insights from the comments that I've received on my own publications. I doubt that you can be an excellent peer reviewer without a substantive publishing record of your own.

I approach the task as a puzzle in communication. Most of the time, the editor has weeded out the totally dreadful manuscripts. My method is to read the manuscript as if I had downloaded an electronic version of a published article. I make comments within the article and have a second document open to make notes for my final evaluation. I assume that the article should make sense on the first reading without having to backtrack and that the author has included enough information to make the article self-contained. I don't expect to have to track down the references to understand what the author's text is trying to communicate. The author should also have an understanding of the general level of expertise of the readers of the journal and not write an article that only the five other specialists in the world on the topic will understand.

I pay special attention to the title and the abstract because many potential readers decide whether the article interests them from its brief information in the various indexing and abstracting services. I suggest changes if the contents of the article differ significantly from what the title and the abstract promise. I also pay special attention to the conclusion as a key part of the document. Does the conclusion accurately represent the article as a whole, especially if the author presents counterevidence in the body of the manuscript against the preferred conclusion?

I comment most frequently about a lack of context. The author, who is close to the situation, often assumes knowledge on the part of the reader that the reader can't be expected to have. If the author is talking about a library, I want to know the basic facts about it. Sometimes, I suggest that this type of material appear in an appendix if including it within the body would break the narrative flow. The author should also be able to understand what is local practice and not assume that all libraries do things the same way.

On a substantive level, I expect the evidence to support the author's conclusion. Is there an alternative hypothesis that would explain the phenomenon? Does the author explicitly tell the reader about the assumptions behind the methodology, and do these assumptions appear reasonable for the conclusions that the author makes? I take care to let editors know that I have no statistical training because my doctorate is in French literature and assume that another reviewer will verify the statistical analysis. I nonetheless can still spot obvious potential problems such as poor response rates, small samples, and a limited number of cases in the data set.

I expect the author to report any statistical results in an understandable format that does not require me to input the data into a spreadsheet. The author should calculate the percentages for the reader rather than provide only the raw numbers. Similarly, the author should accurately label the columns so that they are understandable without reading the accompanying text. Sometimes a graphic is the best way to present complex data, but the author should make sure to choose the right type of graphic, because a poorly rendered graph is more confusing than none at all. Just because the spreadsheet offers the option doesn't mean that the graph will present the results clearly.

To complete the peer-reviewing process, I list my concerns in priority order and indicate which prob-lems are deal breakers in my opinion and which changes would help but are not critical to the manu-script's publication. I sometimes but rarely suggest additional research because I understand that the author has most likely moved on to anther project. I often propose small tweaks that will make the paper better with little effort. The editor has final say in transmitting my comments to the author. From my own experience as an author, editors normally tell me that I must make some changes while others are at my discretion. I appreciate when the comments include suggestions on how to make the change, because I am often aware of my paper's faults when I send it to the editor but unsure of how to correct them.

My final comment is to say how rewarding it is to see a paper published in a final format that is vastly improved from the first manuscript version. Perhaps some peer reviewers suggest irrational changes, but most aren't executioners out to torture the author but instead focus on helping create a better pub-lished article.

TEN TIPS FOR BECOMING A SUCCESSFUL RESTAURANT REVIEWER

RUTH PENNINGTON PAGET

For two years, I reviewed ethnic restaurants in Monterey, California, for the *Monterey County Weekly* newspaper, whose circulation num-bered more than two hundred thousand. I used my librarian's search skills to ferret out elusive ingredi-ents, cooking methods, and cultural and historical details. This research made readers feel as if they had traveled abroad whether or not they would go to the restaurant.

The following tips share advice that I wish I had received prior to my restaurant reviewing stint.

1. KNOW HOW TO COOK

Showing readers that you know how to prepare eggplant parmesan or egg-drop soup, for instance, inspires their confidence in your ability to judge a restaurant's offerings. Experimenting in the kitchen with the ingredients and cooking procedures of sev-eral cultures gives you the basic knowledge you need to be a competent reviewer.

2. TELL A STORY

The best tip an editor ever gave me was to tell a story even if writing a restaurant review. The beginning can be as simple as how the owner or host greets you. Use time waiting at your table to describe the decorations, comfort, and professionalism of the wait staff. The substance of your review revolves around describing the meal. The ending should contain your recommendation along with a quote or anecdote that sums up the experience.

3. WRITE WITH YOUR FIVE SENSES

A statement such as "The eel tasted great" fails to convey what the eel tastes like. What tastes great for the reviewer may taste like mud to the reader. Instead a sentence such as "The eel had an earthy, mushroomlike taste and a smooth texture" gives the reader a clearer idea of what the eel in a particular dish tastes like and feels like on the tongue.

In the same vein, a sentence such as "The sizzling rice soup crackled and looked like puffed rice" appeals to our sense of sight and sound. This sentence conjures a sensory image in the reader's mind.

The sense of smell follows the same pattern. Saying "The couscous smelled heavenly" evokes different sense sensations for different people. A better way to describe couscous would be, for example, "The couscous's aroma of cinnamon and ginger wafted toward me." Reading this sentence gives the reader a better idea of what to expect.

You can find a good list of culinary adjectives in Dianne Jacobs's book *Will Write for Food: The Complete Guide to Restaurant Reviews, Articles, Memoir, Fiction and More.*

4. PITCH RESTAURANTS YOU LIKE TO EDITORS

Even the restaurants you like have flaws. Readers appreciate knowing about bad restaurants, but they love hearing about great ones. Get known for your great picks, and your readers will learn to interpret your silences about other restaurants.

Reviewing a bad restaurant ranks right up there with getting a flat tire as far as experiences go. Not only do you have to eat a bad meal, but you also have to relive it when writing up the review.

5. DISCUSS FINANCES WITH THE EDITOR

Publications serious about hiring an anonymous reviewer typically pay the reviewer a flat fee to spend on a meal for two, followed by payment for your review after it is published.

People dream of the food reviewer's life. Mimi Sheraton described in her memoir *Eating My Words* that the *New York Times* paid her restaurant bills of $100,000 per year. Closer to the freelancer's reality is Dianne Jacob's quip in *Will Write for Food* that it helps to have a rich spouse to be a food writer.

6. INVESTIGATE THE RESTAURANT BEFORE YOU GO

Obtain a menu discreetly or get it from the Web. Having a menu handy will give you the prices, which makes the review write-up easier.

Knowing what the menu items are allows you to look up how to make the dishes in cookbooks or on websites such as Epicurious.com. This research helps you identify herbs you might not be familiar with such as galangal or fenugreek.

Call ahead or check the restaurant's website for the address, days and hours of operation, methods of payment, and reservation policy.

7. RESEARCH IDEAL BEVERAGE ACCOMPANIMENTS

Showing your wine and other beverage knowledge helps establish your credibility with readers. Jancis Robinson's *The Oxford Companion to Wine* provides detailed information on wine regions that will help you add pizzazz to your wine comments. For wine-tasting vocabulary and insight, I recommend Michael Broadbent's *Pocket Vintage Wine Companion.*

8. FOLLOW UP WITH THE OWNER(S)

The usual practice for anonymous reviewers is to call the restaurant the next business day to interview the owner and verify prices, hours of operation, and spellings.

Because I specialized in ethnic restaurants, language barriers often precluded telephone follow-ups. Often after I had paid for my meal, I would introduce myself to the owners and do my interviews on the spot.

9. UNDERSTAND THE RESTAURANT WORLD

If you have never worked in a restaurant, try to learn about what is happening in the kitchen. An amusing way to get a glimpse into the restaurant world is to read Anthony Bourdain's book *Kitchen Confidential.* This books details his life as a chef in almost every kind of restaurant establishment, from beachfront fish houses to chic bistros and gastronomical temples.

10. SEIZE THE DAY

Don't wait for a spot at a newspaper to become vacant. You can begin reviewing restaurants on blogs or create you own newsletter. These venues may even lead to newspaper opportunities.

Creating your own luck is not a far-fetched idea in the food and wine world. Jancis Robinson writes in her memoir *Tasting Pleasure: Confessions of a Wine Lover* about how her entrepreneurship created her dream job. In the beginning, she purchased her own wine, critiqued it, published a newsletter at her own expense, and self-delivered the newsletter in London's exclusive neighborhoods. The newsletter became a hit, with the result that the *Financial Times* asked her to become its wine columnist. Now she has wineries sending her free cases of wine in the hopes that she will write about it.

To conclude, I would say that I obtained my restaurant reviewing work with a traditional query letter and published clips. Getting published clips is the stumbling block for many would-be writers, which is why I suggest first doing your own online reviews on blogs or in online columns.

WRITING VIDEO REVIEWS

DOUGLAS KING

As much as I enjoy reading and reviewing books for publications such as *Library Journal, Online Audiovisual Catalogers Newsletter, portal,* and *Journal of Electronic Resources Librarianship,* I get a special thrill from contributing video reviews to *Library Journal.* My day is always brightened by the mailed arrival of a DVD for review, no matter how busy I am with other personal and professional responsibilities. Not only do I personally enjoy the task of reviewing, but I also recognize how important it is to the profession to inform public, academic, and special libraries' decisions on what to add to their collections and what to avoid.

Writing video reviews can be as challenging, and thus rewarding, as writing book reviews. The one advantage reviewing videos has over reviewing books is that, in almost all cases, it takes a lot less time to watch a film than it does to read a book. However, I have found that, in many cases, writing video reviews takes substantially longer than writing book reviews.

No fewer than three weeks before the deadline, I watch the video, including all bonus footage, occasionally pausing the film to take notes and jot down potentially usable phrases as they pop into my head. I give the video my full attention, just as I would a book for review. Later that day, or more commonly the next day, I compose the first draft. A day or two later, I revisit my initial draft and commence the revision process. I revise heavily, with the final version typically bearing little resemblance to the initial one, and for some reason, this is truer for my video reviews than my book reviews. Somehow, my initial drafts of video reviews almost always extend far beyond the allowed word count, requiring a good amount of revision and concision. I add, delete, rephrase, move sentences around, weed out unnecessary words, and do whatever else it takes to come up with a suitable review that satisfies both my editor and myself.

As with all reviewing, writing video reviews requires analytical thinking, clear and concise writing, a mature and thoughtful approach to the craft of filmmaking, and an understanding of how visual media fits into library collection management. I have come up with a few pointers to help writers new to video reviewing.

Read other video reviews in the publication. This will give you a good feel for the desired tone, content, and length.

Watch the entire film, including bonus footage. This may seem like a no-brainer, but nonetheless it is worth mentioning and emphasizing this point, just in case certain reviewers are tempted to avoid plowing through a particularly boring or pointless film or are considering skipping seemingly trivial bonus features such as participant interviews, trailers, and so on. You would not, I hope, write a book review without reading the entire work. The same principle holds true for videos. As for bonus features, these are frequently the reason a library would want to add a particular video to its collection. All bonus footage worth watching should be mentioned in your review. Libraries do care about content added to new releases and reissues of older titles.

Summarize and evaluate. Finding the right mix of summary and evaluation while telling the reader what he or she should know about a work is one of the most challenging aspects of writing any review. In general, your review should be more summary than evaluation, because you are a reviewer and not a critic, but both elements are important. If reviewing a feature film, do not reveal too much plot (a sentence or two will usually suffice for short, two-hundred-word reviews) or give away the ending. You should comment on the film's strengths and weaknesses and evaluate its overall quality and effectiveness.

Suggest who the potential audience might be. In other words, consider who may benefit most from viewing the film. Is its most fitting audience informed laypeople, the general adult population, young adults, or perhaps scholars and researchers? Is it appropriate for both classrooms and living rooms, or just one of those? This is an important consideration when reviewing both fiction and nonfiction films.

Trust your opinions. As an information professional who cares about both librarianship and the power of film, your opinions matter. State them confidently, but back them up.

Eliminate personal biases. If you carry a bias into the viewing, you should avoid reviewing that particular title. Reviews should be fair, unprejudiced assessments of the film as a whole, devoid of any personal, political, religious, or other bias.

Use plain, readable language. Your review should be well written and articulate, but avoid drawing attention to your astonishing linguistic virtuosity and mastery of arcane multisyllabic words, and keep the focus on the reviewed work. Readers should not need a dictionary to comprehend your review.

Rely on your editor. Your editor is your friend. The editor is there to help make your review as good as it can be, so be thankful for his or her editing skills and be as polite, prompt, and professional in your communications as possible (see my other chapter, "Keys to a Healthy Reviewer-Editor Relationship," for more advice on this topic).

As with all professional writing, read your work aloud, and find someone forthright and forthcoming to read your reviews before submitting anything. Reading your work aloud provides you with a strong sense of the review's flow, consistency, clarity, and overall quality. A trusted personal editor can spot errors and suggest helpful edits before submitting your review. Try to find an experienced reviewer to read your work and offer candid comments and suggestions.

Finally, always remember the importance of your task as a video reviewer. Film plays a vital role in enhancing education and enriching lives, which is reflected in libraries' judicious acquisition of videos. A glut of DVDs is released, and it is important for library managers, acquisitions librarians, and others charged with spending their institutions' money to know what is worth buying and what they can skip.

ADVICE FROM AN EDITOR

Writing for a State Library Journal

ELIZABETH A. STEPHAN

Writing and publishing at a professional level can be intimidating, and the world of academic publishing can be even more intimidating. Before taking the leap into peer-reviewed publishing, consider submitting materials to a state library association publication. State library association publications are professional publications that highlight the work of local and regional libraries and librarians. Working with a local publication and editor is a way to publish in a less intimidating setting. It is a way to get your name in print, to get some recognition for what you have accomplished as a librarian, and to become familiar with the publishing process. In addition to an introduction to publishing, it is also a way a new librarian can network with their peers.

State associations produce trade publications that are sent out to their members. I edited *Mississippi Libraries,* the publication for the Mississippi Library Association, for three years. During that time, I worked with a lot of first-time authors. I would like share the advice and guidance I gave to the writers I worked with.

Mississippi Libraries often had theme issues— library as place, technical services, and grant writing, to name a few. We tried to focus on topics that would appeal to everyone. I often worked with librarians who thought that no one would be interested in what they had to say or that what they did wasn't worth writing about. Don't make these assumptions. Remember, this is your chance to talk about you, your ideas, and the things you and your library have done. Many librarians face the same issues and challenges, and knowing how someone else has faced them can be helpful and inspiring.

Every publication has its own unique submission issues, but some issues are universal. The most commonly asked questions I heard as editor of *Mississippi Libraries* were about length of article, photographs, and topic. In my experience, both as a librarian and as an editor, these three things can scare many new librarians away from publishing. In addressing these common questions, I hope to demystify the publishing process.

SUBMITTING AN ARTICLE: WHAT TO ASK

There are a few things to ask about when submitting an article: word count, images, and contract. Length is often defined by number of words. The actual length of an article can be hard to determine because the length in print will depend on the font type, font size, images, and several other factors. A good rule of thumb is that one thousand words equal about one page in an 8½-by-11-inch publication. An article of two to two-and-a-half pages in a magazine will be about 2000 to 2500 words, which is about a four-page, single-spaced Word document. Ask the editor how many words were in a previously published article. I would often refer to an earlier article as an example for length and word count and tell writers how many pages it was in Word. Word count is used to determine length. Remember, though, word count is only a guide. It helps give the author an idea of how long an article needs to be. If you have 2300 words instead of 2500 words, don't use wordier sentences just to meet the word count. Most editors would rather have a well-written article over a wordier one.

There are two main issues to consider with images: copyright and image size. Both can cause delays and headaches when publishing an article. Whenever you submit an image for print, always include a photo credit even if you shot the photo yourself. If you don't know or can't find out who took the image, don't submit it. Photo copyright can cause all kinds of legal headaches for authors and publishers. It is best to be absolutely sure who took the image and to give that person credit. For an image to be used in a print publication, it needs to be at least 300 DPI (dots per inch). The higher the DPI, the better is the resolution and the larger the image can be printed. Most digital cameras will take images with this resolution or higher. If you are scanning the image (or having someone scan it for you), you can set the DPI. Images taken off of a website often have a DPI as low as 78 to accommodate slower Internet connections. An image like that could be used in print, but it would be about the size of a postage stamp. When in doubt about image size, the larger the image—and the higher the DPI—the better. A large image can always be decreased in size, while a small image cannot be increased in size.

When it comes to the contract, the best advice is to ask the editor who retains the rights to the article. What does it mean to obtain the rights? In a very simple, nonlegal way, if the author maintains the rights, the author can republish or distribute the article. If the magazine or journal retains the rights, that publication can reprint it and must approve any other reprints of the material. There are other rights issues that would fill an entire book. It's a complicated topic. The best thing is to ask questions and be aware of your options and rights as an author.

SUBMITTING AN ARTICLE: THE PROCESS

When an article is submitted, it goes through a process. That process varies from publication to publication. It may be edited several times: once for style and another for readability. In addition to editing an

article, the editorial staff may also apply the publication style, captions, subheads, and write an abstract. Because of this, once an article is submitted, consider it submitted. Do not submit it until you have the final version. Many publications have a streamlined process that is difficult to interrupt. If changes are absolutely necessary, contact the editor. Some editors will review articles before the final submission, but don't expect it. I did it on a case-by-case basis. Some writers want to see the article before it is published. If you must see it, ask, because not all editors will send back an article for review. If I had to rewrite or reorganize an article for clarity, I would send it back to make sure I had everything correct.

The editor of a publication is the readers' advocate. It is the editor's job to review the article for style and clarity. In rare cases, the article may be rewritten, but a common rule for editors is to not change the voice of the author. It is not uncommon for an editor to contact the author with questions or clarifications. It isn't a judgment on your writing or your style—it is merely the editor looking at your article with a fresh eye.

EDITING A PUBLICATION

Editing a state publication is both rewarding and time consuming. It is an excellent networking and service opportunity, but taking on the responsibility of managing a publication should not be taken lightly. It is a lot of work and a major commitment. Editing a publication is incredibly fulfilling, but I can't stress this enough: do not take on the task if you are not willing or able to give it the time that is needed. While editing a publication requires writing skills and a basic understanding of grammar, project management and networking skills are just as important—if not more so. If you are unfamiliar with the territory—both in a geographic and a political sense, start as an assistant editor or copy editor. You can learn the process and become familiar with the people before taking on the publication yourself.

Editing an article is a skill, usually a learned one. Not all writers are good editors, and not all editors are good writers. An editor needs to be able to see the big picture of the publication and make sure the articles work together as a whole. One of the key points to remember as an editor is to not change the author's voice. It is much easier to rewrite an article than it is to edit it. Being able to do that takes time and patience, but once you learn it, it becomes second nature. My last piece of advice to any new editor: find a good assistant editor. If you are allowed to find or hire an assistant, do. Because project management is such a large part in managing a magazine, finding someone to help with the editing is crucial.

Publishing in a state association journal is a logical start to publishing in library and information science literature. Using it as a way to learn a little about the publishing world can build confidence and demystify the process of getting an article published in a national journal.

FIND YOUR NICHE IN MAGAZINE WRITING

KAY MARNER

For years I was a wannabe writer, unpublished and without a genre. Then I joined the staff at Ames Public Library and found inspiration at my fingertips. Today, I freelance regularly for two magazines and blog professionally for a magazine's website.

It all started with a picture book.

My husband and I adopted our daughter, Natalie, from an orphanage in Russia. When her preschool teacher announced an upcoming unit on families, I searched frantically for a picture book to recommend that would reflect the diversity of today's families. I fell in love—hard—with Todd Parr's *The Family Book* (and with Parr himself, whom I later interviewed for *Adoptive Families* magazine). I fell so hard, in fact, that I just had to write about it. I wrote a book review and e-mailed it to *Adoptive Families* magazine. A reply came: "Please provide a brief bio to accompany your byline." A few months later, the editor e-mailed to ask whether I'd review a poetry collection. I'd found my genre.

FROM A TO Z, OR ADOPTION TO ZOOLOGY—WHAT'S YOUR NICHE?

If you're a librarian, chances are you love to read. Convert your reading interests into writing opportunities. Write book reviews.

Writers are often told: write about what you know; what you're passionate about. I write about books, libraries, and my children. Make a list of your personal interests, hobbies, and life experiences. Write about these topics.

Don't limit yourself to publications aimed at librarians and booksellers. Why put your writing up against that of hundreds other librarians? Instead, use your library skills to compete with other writers.

Use your skills as a librarian to search for consumer and trade publications related to the topics on your list. Don't limit your search to *Writer's Market*.

Read several issues of the periodicals you identify from your search. Do they feature book reviews in each issue? Who writes them? Can you approximate their style?

In the past five years I've reviewed dozens of books for *Adoptive Families* and *ADDitude* magazine. Although these were unpaid assignments, I was satisfied. I enjoy discovering new books and the process of writing about them. I also take pleasure in the online relationship I've developed with the magazine's editor. "Have you seen (fill in the blank with the latest adoption book)? What do you think of it?" Most of all, I love seeing my name in print!

MAKE YOURSELF INDISPENSABLE TO YOUR EDITOR

Approach him or her routinely with titles you recommend.

Use your library skills and access to find those titles. Subscribe to personalized recommendation services from e-booksellers, read pre-publication alerts in library journals, and scan new arrivals in your library's receiving and processing area for titles related to your areas of interest.

Meet every deadline. Accompany every submission with an offer to rewrite if necessary.

Be loyal. Don't offer your services to competing publications.

When I was offered my first paid assignment, an interview with acclaimed children's book author Robert Munsch, I certainly didn't say no. Other paid assignments—interviews and feature articles—followed.

The clips I accumulated and the relationships I formed came in handy when I saw that *ADDitude* magazine was looking for bloggers. On the strength of those clips, I was offered a contract to blog professionally for the website. I post to my blog *My Picture-Perfect Life* three to seven times per week.

As a working library paraprofessional, I now have all the writing assignments I can handle. After all, I have no plans to quit my day job—yet!

WORKING WRITER OR WRITER WHO WORKS?

When I was a child, and dreamed of becoming a writer, I didn't picture myself becoming rich and famous. I didn't picture my book on display at a bookstore. I pictured my name in a library's card catalog!

What are your goals when it comes to writing? Are you building up clips and contacts in hopes of writing full time? Or, like me, are you satisfying a desire to write while working in the library world?

If you want to earn a living, book reviews will provide clips, but they won't replace a paycheck. Move on to bigger projects as soon as possible.

FREELANCE MAGAZINE WRITING FOR LIBRARIANS

NANCY KALIKOW MAXWELL

Have you ever read a magazine article, shook your head in disgust, and thought, "I could have written something better than that?"

If so, then you are perfectly positioned to become a magazine freelance writer. All it takes to successfully publish magazine articles is motivation and perseverance. As the inane article you just read reveals, writing ability is helpful but not necessary.

The need for magazine articles by freelancers—writer's parlance for anyone not on the magazine staff—is great. Freelancers produce up to 75 percent of the content of many periodicals. Some publications, especially new titles, are 100 percent freelance written. Because so many magazines rely heavily on outside writers, opportunities abound to have your work published.

BIG WRITING DREAMS START HERE

If you plan to write that great American novel or publish the magnum opus on tree squirrels, instead of contacting a book publisher or literary agent directly, you may have better luck getting a few magazine articles published first. A literary agent once told me that having an unpublished author pitch a book idea directly to a publisher or agent is like proposing marriage to someone you just met on the Internet. A better approach is to get a few literary first dates by publishing an article or short story in a magazine. Because literary agents and book publishers sometimes scour magazines in search of new writing talent, you could be the one who receives the writer's equivalent of a marriage proposal.

FINDING THE MAGAZINE AND TOPIC

Write what you read. One of the biggest obstacles new writers face is deciding on the magazine to write for. The first place you should look is in your bathroom—or your living room, bedroom, or wherever you stash piles of magazines you have read (or want to read one of these days when you get the time). You will already have gained an advantage because you are familiar with the publication. "Study the magazine" is the freelance equivalent of "Location, location, location." Knowing the audience, writing style, article length, tone, and format are all essential elements for successful freelance article production.

Head to the shelves. If you don't regularly read magazines (shame on you!), visit a major bookstore or public or academic library and browse the magazine racks for a publication that captivates you. Keep looking until you find one that passes the five-minute test: one that you find yourself reading for at least five minutes.

Another source to consult for magazine titles is *Writer's Market,* an annual publication that lists magazine titles by subject. This must-have item for magazine writers provides the aforementioned percentage of titles written by freelancers, as well as information about the types of submissions accepted, how much they pay, and details about submitting your work. Most public libraries and major bookstore outlets have the publication.

Librarian's edge for topic selection. Once you have selected your target publication, you need to decide on the topic to write about. Here librarians have an automatic advantage. No matter what publication you are targeting, you can always find a library angle to write about. Every genre of publication—from sports to teens to gardening—could carry a library piece.

I demonstrate this point at writing workshops for librarians by distributing randomly selected magazines. Each participant is asked to describe an article that could appear in a future issue about libraries. Among the ideas generated have been an article in *Camping Today* about the library's travel books and camping directories, a piece in *Bridal Guide* about the reference etiquette books, or a *Pet Age* piece with recommended children's books about caring for your new puppy. Simply mentioning that you are a librarian in the cover letter automatically qualifies you to write any of these pieces.

Nonlibrary topics. If you want to write about a topic other than libraries, you need to look inside—deep inside your mind, your heart, and your soul—to find a subject that you are preoccupied with, fixated on, passionate about. What topic of conversation compels you to step up on that soapbox and pontificate endlessly, or at least it seems endless to those who hear you? What issue makes those nearest and dearest to you roll their eyes and say, "Oh, boy. There she goes again about *that*?"

That should be the subject of your freelance article. Consult the publication's author's guidelines, which are usually available on the magazine's website for further submission details and start writing. Keep working at your article until it is publication perfect, or at least as good as you can possibly make it. Don't stop when it is half finished, assuming that others at the magazine will fix any problems, or exceed the word count limit.

ARTICLE SUBMISSION

Once your manuscript is ready, you need to prepare a one-page cover letter summarizing what the article is about and why you are qualified to write it. Some sources suggest sending a query letter before sending the magazine article, but most beginning writers have better luck sending the finished piece because they lack a prior publication record. Address the letter to the appropriate magazine staff member, whose name can be found either in the publication or on the website. A self-addressed, stamped envelope should be enclosed to facilitate learning the fate of the submission.

IF AT FIRST…

Expect bad news. Although your topic could be exactly on target and your piece perfect, it may be rejected. Chances are it will be rejected. Prepare yourself for a "thanks, but no thanks" response. When it comes, let yourself have a good cry, but don't get your manuscript wet because you will be sending it out again. Actually, you will need to rework the piece to fit the needs of the next target publication, so go ahead and cry directly on it. Then write a revised manuscript and cover letter, throw that package in the mail, and wait for the next rejection. Try not to get discouraged if it takes several attempts to place your piece. To stay motivated during the process, go find that magazine with the stupid article. Pick it up and repeat to yourself: "I could have written that." Stay with it; sooner or later, you will.

MAGAZINE ARTICLE SUBMISSION INGREDIENTS

- Cover letter—one-page, flawlessly written
- Article manuscript—double-spaced with your name and article title, flawlessly written
- SASE (self-addressed, stamped envelope)
- Crying towel for rejections

Repeat as needed.

WRITING WHAT YOU KNOW FOR SERVICE TO OTHERS
Professional Journals

ELAINE SANCHEZ

A major reason to write articles for professional journals is to share experiences. The "how we did it right at our institution" article is not really a self-aggrandizing piece of writing. Instead, its intent is to advance the work of any organization that might use your methods, so that other organizations' processes can improve more quickly than if they had to go it alone. Reporting your work in a professional journal brings your successful ideas to everyone and offers them the chance to use easily obtained work-flow improvements that they didn't have to struggle to create.

After you have created a more efficient work flow, provided a new service, or whatever your success or breakthrough is, the typical response is to feel gratified with the experience and pleased with its success. The second response should be the desire to share it with others to advance the profession. An article in a professional journal achieves this second, higher purpose. When an article is written with this aim, readers invariably understand that the article is a well-intentioned effort to improve their work or professional lives. Promotion of self or organization hinders the message and decreases reader confidence in the content of the article.

To benefit the largest audience, and to have a stronger chance of getting the article published, select work processes or ideas that have characteristics that guarantee their usefulness and interest to readers.

The ideas should be unique, not well represented in current literature, and reflect current issues or hot topics in your area of expertise.

The work presented must be something you know about.

Workflows or ideas that have a wide audience of interest, or that can be expanded for use in many areas, have better success at being published, are useful to more readers, and can be built on and expanded.

Work processes that include an aspect of information technology usage are usually of more interest to readers, as many have organizational pressure to streamline work flow with new technologies.

Literature research is crucial to identify how, or if, your particular article content has already been addressed.

Review professional library and other electronic discussion lists and their archives (e.g., blogs, wikis) related to your ideas, to determine how your topic has been treated over time and whether your article will fill a need or address unanswered questions.

Consider a short survey of electronic discussion lists to determine others' treatment of your ideas, and further identify any unaddressed needs.

Modify your article content on the basis of the results of your literature research and electronic discussion list (blog, wiki) analysis to highlight your new ideas. Always include the summarized results of the literature search for the benefit of your readers.

Finally, your article topics must be useful, thought provoking, and explained clearly so that they are fairly easy to understand and implement. Clear and concise instructions and graphic examples are critical to reader comprehension and idea utilization.

After you have selected and refined the ideas for the article, figure out how to write the article so that readers will be intrigued and personally involved. The writer must engage readers' imagination and directly connect with them, so that they can see how the ideas presented worked for you and could work for them. The aim is to educate readers, help them assimilate your ideas, and help them generate their own.

Thoughtful, brief accounts of your organization and its work environment before and after the change create the initial connection to start readers imagining their work flow compared to yours. Outline the thought process and actions you went through so that readers benefit from your experiences without having to go through the same.

Articles should include your organization's steps with the following:

- description of your organization before the problem or required change that generated the new ideas or work flows

- statement of the problem or required change

- explanation of what group was organized and why members were selected to investigate

- description of research performed and analysis results

- identification of possible solutions and the pros and cons of each

- identification of limitations and exceptions

- description of successes, obstacles, and failures in attempts to determine the best solution or idea

- description of the final solutions, with graphic examples, tables, and personally thoughtful narrative to connect with the reader textually and visually

- culmination of your organization's story with the description of how this change has affected your work flows, staff, services, or whatever has benefited from the change

- engagement of readers' imaginations as you present open-ended or untested ideas that arose in the process of change for their consideration or additional research.

- provision of links to procedures and any bibliography or literature research summary

- assistance for readers' questions or ideas to solidify your relationship with readers and to provide active support for the success of their organizations as well their own professional growth

Once you've completed your article outline, or written your story, there are a few practical actions to take to pursue publication.

- Identify journals whose scope encompasses the content and purpose of your article and consider whether they are ones in which you wish to see your article published.

- Read articles in the journals to better understand what kinds and styles of work they tend to publish.

- Consider whether the journal is refereed and whether this is necessary for you; who the audience is; whether you want local, regional, or national presentation; and whether the scope matches your professional or organizational philosophy.

- Look at the publication schedule to determine any necessary writing or submission deadlines.

- Read author instructions carefully and write or modify your article to comply.

- Once you have your article written or outlined, write a presubmission letter to the editors of the journals you have selected that is geared toward their particular scope. A presubmission letter contains a summary of your article, notes any research, includes the article length or word count, explains in an engaging way why your article is of interest to their readers, and is one page long.

That's all it takes to write what you know for service to others and to send it for publication in a professional journal: a problem, working through it, a solution, a desire to help others through what you have learned, confidence in your ability to write your story, and doing it with the help of the steps found herein.

THE HERO'S JOURNEY TO AN ACADEMIC PAPER

DAWN LOWE-WINCENTSEN

In every story there is a beginning, a middle, and an end. How to get to those places can be unique, but no matter the subject, no matter the scene, these pieces are always there. Fiction writers talk about a story arc, the way that you get from beginning to end with the peak of the action some place in the center. John Barth (1999, 129) discusses a story arc as a "stylized profile of Gibraltar viewed from the west." There is a slope up to a peak, then a steep drop back down. This chapter takes you through the pieces of this arc and demonstrates how to place them in an academic paper.

A BEGINNING

Introduce the characters, settings, and the details needed to tell the story. Shakespeare does this with monologues, such as in the opening of *Richard III* (act 1, scene 1, lines 29–32):

> And therefore, since I cannot prove a
>   lover,
> To entertain these fair well-spoken days,
> I am determined to prove a villain
> And hate the idle pleasures of these
>   days.

In just four lines we learn that Richard is not happy that the wars for the throne are seemingly over and forgotten. He goes on to give us a more in-depth picture of the time leading up to the beginning of the play, of his deformed body and motivations for villainy, and of his plans therefore. There are more details throughout the play, but this is enough to get the audience going.

In research, this is the introduction and literature review. Start with the purpose, a theory, and why the research was conducted. Build on that with a literature review. Give enough detail so that the audience can follow the story once they reach the middle, but do not overload them with so much background that they forget what the introduction said the purpose was.

THE MIDDLE

As a story progresses, action happens to ratchet up the tension. The hero's journey is a classic model for this. The character starts a journey and is faced with increasingly difficult obstacles along the way. One example of this is the classic fantasy trilogy *The Lord of the Rings,* by J. R. R. Tolkien. In the beginning, the purpose is set forth that the One Ring must be destroyed. Frodo Baggins then begins his journey, first across the Shire, then to Rivendell, then to Mount Doom in Mordor. The story is more complex than this, but at each stop in the journey, the tension is taken higher and more details provided, pushing the reader along to the climax.

The journey model of storytelling is closest to research. Think about the journey a researcher goes on as he or she composes a thesis, plots a project, applies for funds, and performs experiments. Each of these steps is a stop along the journey. The thesis is covered in the beginning, but the method and the experiments are all part of the middle. Organization is key to the story arc. Use each piece to build up to the next, creating a story and tension as the article progresses.

The language used also creates the dramatic tension that helps the readers stay engaged. Use action phrases to describe the process. Describe the process in enough detail that the readers understand the process. Similar descriptions are good to use when graphs are present. Some people may read the caption, but more will read the in-text descriptions.

Frodo is the research topic. He travels through the Shire and the Old Forest as the research method is explored or credit is given to the funding agency. As the hobbits reach Rivendell, problems in the research come to the reader's attention; as the Fellowship splits up, make recommendations for where research offshoots can go. As Frodo faces Shelob and the final rise to the climax begins, start to share the hints of the results. Crossing Mordor is where you begin to really delve into the results. Eventually there is a climax; the hero or thesis emerges, victorious or not, and there is a wrap-up.

AN END

The end is nigh! The readers can feel the home stretch. They are at the top of the arc or peak, looking down into the abyss. Give them something meaningful to land on. This is more than a few line breaks and the word fin.

In Homer's *Odyssey,* Odysseus returns home at the climax. He must kick out his wife's suitors and return his home to its peaceful prewar state. There is more action involved, but not at the same level as the battles he has fought to get to this point.

The research has been stated and the results given, but there is still action that should be taken, and everything needs to be wrapped up and packaged for the article to succeed. Take this opportunity to remind the readers of the original purpose, and briefly touch on the steps taken to get here. Write some final thoughts, give some direction to go if someone wants to base a new story on this research, and then the paper is ready for a few line breaks.

There is a myth among writers that all writing flows from a muse through their fingertips and keyboards then on to the screen. This method can create a story zigzag or a curlicue. Research with an arc, a stylized Gibraltar to climb, is easier to follow for the audience and easier to follow for the author. The pieces are well organized and laid out so readers know that each stop along the way is leading to the final climactic result: a beginning, a middle, and a end, in that order. This can be accomplished through outlining and preparing each piece of the story before writing begins. It is not intuitive to everyone, and it does not flow from a muse to the page. Organizing before the beginning is the way to create a story arc.

REFERENCES

Barth, John. 1999. "Incremental Perturbation: How to Know Whether You've Got a Plot or Not." In *Creating Fiction,* ed. Julie Checkoway, 126–134. Cincinnati, OH: Story Press.

Shakespeare, William. *Richard III.* East Lansing: The Literature Network. www.online-literature.com/shakespeare/richardIII/.

RESEARCH EVIDENCE IN QUALITATIVE DATA

Finding Out Why and How, Not Just How Many

MICHELYNN MCKNIGHT

Einstein once said, "Not everything that counts can be counted and not everything that can be counted counts" (Calaprice 2000, 318).

Any good reference librarian knows that the kind of information that answers a question must fit the question. For instance, the answer to "Why do students wait until the last minute to start their term papers?" will be expressed in words representing concepts, while the answer to "What percentage of students wait until the last minute to start their term papers?" will be expressed in numbers. The answer to the first is expressed in qualitative data (words, concepts, or narratives), while the answer to the second is in quantitative data (measurement). Forcing the expression of the answer to the first question into an artificial quantitative answer doesn't improve the evidence, yet too many librarians believe that they can answer that question with only a number derived from a forced-answer survey. We've all been handed surveys with a list of answers from which we have to choose and have known that our real belief isn't expressed in any of the available answers (McKnight 2001).

Good research, like a good reference interview, begins with defining the question. Only after it has been defined can we move on to thinking about the kind of evidence that would best answer the question. Next, we consider where that kind of evidence might be found and choose a method of searching for it. In scientific research, we consider what methods are best for gathering and analyzing data to produce valid and significant evidence. When we have chosen the best method for this question, we carry out the research ethically and with scholarly care to eliminate as much bias as possible. We analyze and evaluate the results, then we consider what further research is appropriate.

In any case, the nature of the question—not the researcher's preferred method—determines whether the researcher uses qualitative, quantitative, or mixed methods. The good reference librarian knows that not all questions can or even should be answered from a handful of favorite or at least familiar sources. As Barbara Wildemuth (1993, 451) puts it, "There is no such thing as the one correct scientific method." And just as the good reference librarians know that some questions require responses from multiple kinds of sources, some research questions require mixed quantitative and qualitative methods.

For most librarians, the research methods with which they are most familiar are those used most in their prelibrary education or in the disciplines of their clients. Thus, it's natural that librarians most familiar with social sciences may be more familiar with case studies, histories, biography, ethnography, or phenomenology, while those most familiar with other sciences are well acquainted with experimental research, randomized samples, control groups, and statistical analysis. The former may be used to finding evidence inductively by building grounded theory based on observation, while the latter may be used to finding evidence deductively by posing and testing an experimental hypothesis based on a preexisting theory. One is more likely to use narrative data analysis tools like NVIVO, while the other is more adept with statistical tools like SAS. Librarians do both kinds of research, and both kinds are publishable if the appropriate methods are followed with high standards of rigor and ethics.

In any case, the librarians who want to publish research in a peer-reviewed journal must use appropriate methods. They would be wise to study methods with which they are not so familiar, both so that they understand methods for answering their own questions and so that they have a better understanding of others' research. While all ALA-accredited schools of library and information science offer research methods courses, only about half of them require such courses (McKnight and Hagy 2009).

Even those librarians who have had research methods courses probably will continue to refresh and update their skills throughout their careers. The following books (which are the most frequently used texts currently used in such courses) are good both for introduction to and for review of research methods:

Babbie, E. R. 2007. *The Practice of Social Research,* 11th ed. Belmont, CA: Thomson Wadsworth.

Creswell, John W. 2007. *Qualitative Inquiry and Research Design: Choosing among Five Approaches,* 2nd ed. Thousand Oaks, CA: Sage.

Creswell, John W. 2009. *Research Design: Qualitative, Quantitative and Mixed Methods Approaches,* 3rd ed. Thousand Oaks, CA: Sage.

Creswell, John W., and Vicki L. Plano Clark. 2007. *Designing and Conducting Mixed Methods Research.* Thousand Oaks, CA: Sage.

Leedy, P. D., and J. E. Ormrod. 2005. *Practical Research: Planning and Design,* 8th ed. Upper Saddle River, NJ: Prentice Hall.

Powell, Ronald R., and Lynn Silipigni Connaway. 2004. *Basic Research Methods for Librarians,* 4th ed. Westport, CT: Libraries Unlimited.

REFERENCES

Calaprice, Alice, ed. 2000. *The Expanded Quotable Einstein.* Princeton, NJ: Princeton University Press.

McKnight, Michelynn. 2001. "Beyond Surveys: Finding Out Why." *Journal of Hospital Librarianship* 1:31–40.

McKnight, Michelynn, and Carol R. Hagy. 2009. "The Research Imperative: MLA Policy and the Curricula of Schools of Library and Information Science." *Journal of the Medical Library Association* 97 (2): 134–136.

Wildemuth, Barbara M. 1993. "Post-Positivist Research: Two Examples of Methodological Pluralism." *Library Quarterly* 63:450–468.

TEAM WRITING
Professional Journals

ELAINE SANCHEZ

Working as a team to come up with ideas for a manuscript, and then writing and editing them to create an article worthy of publication in a professional journal, is an invigorating and enlightening exercise in the practices of tolerance, patience, compromise, humor, creativity, and synergy. The resulting article is always better than originally envisioned, and the creative process unleashes benefits to the writing team well beyond the finished article. It is less daunting to work with a team if it is your first attempt to write for publication.

To successfully write as a team there are several practices that simplify the writing and editing processes. They are simple to understand, sometimes harder to follow, but always helpful in finally getting that article written. The writing project requires a unique and useful idea, work flow, or service that generates the concept for the article. Typically, a manuscript written by a team arises from a group effort. Others that were not initially part of this team could be included for various areas of expertise, but it is the creators of the new idea or service that generally have the best information to share. The group should brainstorm all aspects of the idea to see whether an article outline can be generated. This provides the initial support of and confidence in the idea to write for publication.

To support and develop the writing project, after the idea is conceived, there are several conceptual and organizational decisions that must be reached. The team should do the following:

Discuss and determine whether the content in the article outline is beneficial to share with other colleagues through publication in a professional journal.

Discuss the time commitment for the project and accept responsibility for adhering to the eventual writing schedule.

Ensure that everyone who participates in the writing process buys into the idea of writing for publication and into seeing the process through to its completion.

Address the issues of confidence in the writing process, such as editorial and writing support, direction, authority, and coauthorship credit.

Secure administrative approval for the writing project and establish a time line, both of which are important to the project's eventual success.

With these decisions made, team members should feel secure and successful in their writing efforts, know that authorship will be fairly established, and be assured that the article will have consistent style. These conceptual and organizational decisions must be reached to the satisfaction of everyone on the team.

Once the ideas and content of the article are determined, the project is approved, and the group is formed, the remaining practices listed here provide the structure that moves the article from conception to creation.

Establish (and stick with) writing meeting frequency, duration, agendas, ground rules, and time line.

Engage in participative and positive methods to add ideas, change content, and modify article structure throughout the process, striving for consensus.

Remember to incorporate tolerance, patience, compromise, humor, creativity, and synergy and to keep your ego in check in everything that you do individually and on the team.

As writing evolves, read the text out loud for fun and to improve readability.

Experience, discuss, and acknowledge that there is little value in perfection. Instead, meaning and clarity rule, with compromise and consensus employed to keep the writing going.

Avoid grammar policing, and resolve conflicting styles by consulting reference tools, reviewing author instructions, and remembering the audience.

Celebrate each and every milestone to keep the team encouraged and motivated.

Decide to finish! Stop worrying about punctuation and small things, as the editor will eventually provide his or her own standards for your work.

When you decide to finish, do so with a last team read-through to ensure clarity, consistency, and simplicity of style.

Identify journals for your article, noting the scope and author instruction.

Use a model presubmission letter, editing as a group to intrigue the journal editor.

Send the presubmission letter out and celebrate your success!

Share your manuscript and your successful process with your bosses and others to encourage them to consider future writing projects.

Keep the door open for other future team writing opportunities for yourself.

The intellectual process and product of team writing serve both the profession and team members through the creation of new ideas, increased understanding, and strengthened networking and relationships. The other benefit of team writing comes from the writing process itself. Through this joint intellectual effort, team members discover newfound confidence in their writing abilities and a real-life demonstration of the extent and value of their expert knowledge, used for the good of their colleagues in the profession.

What are the criteria of success for team-writing projects? It is important to realize that not all team-writing projects will be accepted for publication. However, publication in a professional journal is not the most important criteria of success for team writing. Success is achieved, and must be recognized, when the article is completed to everyone's satisfaction and when team members realize and value their writing skills and knowledge, as well as those of their coauthors. Team writing is a journey, not necessarily a destination. The goal is to get there, together.

CRAFTING A COMPELLING BIBLIOGRAPHIC ESSAY

BETH M. SHEPPARD

DIAMONDS IN THE ROUGH

What is a bibliographic essay? It is a piece of writing that blends the main features of the book review, annotated bibliography, and full-length article into one document. Further, authors use it to introduce readers to the best resources available on a given subject or topic. The key to crafting a strong bibliographic essay is to create full-length paragraphs of text in which several books are compared with one another. For such an essay, annotated bibliographies, works cited, and even subject guides serve as the raw materials from which a compelling bibliographic essay might emerge. So, don't hesitate! Scroll through the documents on your hard drive. You may have a list of resources that is a diamond in the rough.

SEVEN STEPS MAKE YOUR WORK SHINE

There are seven handy steps to use to transform existing works cited lists into a publishable bibliographic essay.

1. Separate the gold from the dross. When looking at any list of resources, cull what is truly valuable from what is filler. Works that are incidental to the main topic, texts that are out of date, and those that are very hard to find should generally be eliminated. Of course, the older book that is a true classic in the field may be retained. Let your knowledge of the subject guide your choices.

2. Sort the various precious ores. Once you have pared down the list of resources, arrange them in groups with common characteristics. Classification might be made on the basis of subject matter, time periods, approaches or methodologies, particular trends in the field, or other criteria. At this stage, you should discard any title that does not neatly fit one of the broader categories. Likewise, any group with fewer than three items may not be necessary. These collections of materials will form the basis for the sections of your essay.

3. Assess the results. Once you have clearly delineated the individual groups, write a summary sentence or two to explain the basic organizational principles that you used during sorting. This summary will become the first draft of a strong thesis statement.

4. Learn the trends. Just as with fashion, it is vital to know one's target audience to encourage the best match between your work and those most likely to receive it. Knowing the age bracket, reading level, and background of the anticipated readers helps determine the language, style, and content of the essay. To assist with this process, it is good to view the sample bibliographic essays that have been published in a journal to which you are thinking of submitting your work. With this new information in mind, the astute author will revise the summary from step 3 so that it appeals to the intended audience.

5. *Create the facets.* A diamond doesn't really reveal its beauty until it is cut into facets. The equivalent procedure in shaping the body of a bibliographic essay involves describing the individual resources in each of the groups created in step 2. The strongest essays are ones in which the author highlights each resource's important features. Authors of outstanding essays also compare the various texts with one another, comment on a book's intended audience, or discuss the qualifications of the person who created the resource. But be cautious. An item that is so flawed that it cannot be warmly recommended to the readers of the bibliographic essay does not deserve to be part of the setting that you are about to create. Eliminate it from the essay. Only items that sparkle despite small blemishes should be included.

6. *Form a stunning setting.* Even the most brilliant gem will lack luster if placed in an inferior mounting. In the case of the bibliographic essay, the discussion of individual titles is enhanced by the structure of the essay as a whole. The summary written at step 3, for instance, may be expanded to form a full-fledged introduction. Another aspect of the setting involves making certain that each paragraph flows from the previous one and relates to the thesis. The easiest way to do this is to use transition words. Lists of such words are readily available on the Internet. Finally, an integral part of the setting is the conclusion. No essay is complete without one!

7. *Polish it up.* The draft must now be transformed into a work of high quality. Sometimes this stage is called revision. During revision, you add descriptive words and adjectives to change bland prose into exciting text; insert alliteration, metaphors, and other elements of style to engage the reader; spice up vocabulary by using a thesaurus to eliminate frequently repeated words; and eliminate redundant sentences and thoughts. And don't forget that running a spell-check program is not the same as proofreading! If the piece has your byline, it is your responsibility to make it as clean as possible.

FINDING A HOME FOR YOUR ESSAY

Having completed the seven steps, the next trick is to find a home for the essay in a publication that is a good match for what you have written. Most journals like *Publishers Weekly* and *Choice* have online sites that detail requirements for formatting and submission.

THE DIAMOND IS READY TO GLEAM

A compelling, well-written bibliographic essay originally crafted from the raw materials of an existing list of resources and structured according to the basic steps outlined here is sure to shine as brightly as a precious jewel!

ADDITIONAL RESOURCES

American Library Association. 2006. "*Choice* Bibliographic Essays." August 29. www.ala.org/ala/mgrps/divs/acrl/publications/choice/bibliographic/essays.cfm.

Sheppard, Beth M. 2008. "The Art of the Bibliographic Essay." *Theological Librarianship: An Online Journal of the American Theological Library Association* 1, no. 1 (June): 46–48. http://journal.atla.com/ojs/index.php/theolib/article/view/29/44.

U.S. Army Warrant Officer Career College. 2008. "Writing Guide #7: Transition Markers." July 15. http://usawocc.army.mil/IMI/wg7.htm.

THE LIBRARIAN AS ESSAY WRITER

ELIZABETH MORELLI

In third grade, we wrote stories. While most students maneuvered their dogs and cats through neighborhood fantasies, my prose concentrated on issues such as, "Why are only sixth graders allowed to be safety patrols?" My thesis sentence was usually the title, and my main body, the argument. The summary included ways to correct the situation.

Years later my passions ignited around books and libraries. As a librarian who enjoyed writing, every book that I touched became a potential subject. What I yearned for was a way to channel these writings into more than straightforward book reviews.

Fortunately, James Frey entered the literary world with his very controversial book *A Million Little Pieces.* Here was a book problem screaming for a librarian-writer to turn it into an essay. I discovered *Style Weekly* (Richmond, Virginia), a local newspaper heavily involved in the arts and sold the article quickly under the title "When a Memoir Isn't." The essay contained the stuff of librarianship: an analogy between fiction and nonfiction, explanation of a memoir, definition of literary license, and examples of autobiographical novels. The essay was in the third person from a librarian's point of view. First person would make the article too personal, I felt.

Because *Style Weekly* spotlights the essay of the week on its back cover, complete with cover art, many readers saw and commented positively on the article. Their comments helped cement my relationship with the newspaper as a freelance essay writer. Now I broadened my subject base: local late-night news (first person), baby boomers' retirement destinations (third person), and a web essay on buying a car on the basis of backseat capacity (first person). My librarian self, as an authority on memoir classification, had opened the door. Once established, readers accepted a variety of subject articles, not always relating to libraries.

The librarian was behind the writer; the writer needed the librarian. The two careers began to align closely in a symbiotic relationship.

When it came time to choose writing conferences, I skimmed the listings of *Poets and Writers Magazine.* In 2007, Writing the Region: A Writer's Workshop Honoring Margaret Kinnan Rawlings caught my eye. Located in Gainesville, Florida, the workshop was aimed at the general writer but used the roots, writing practices, and area to pay tribute to *The Yearling* author. An essay contest on Rawlings was an offshoot of the workshop and was backed by the Gainesville Association for the Creative Arts.

Although I had read Rawlings's more famous works, I didn't have a Floridian past or much knowledge of Rawlings's life in her Cross Creek hamlet. What I did remember was that Richmond's famous daughter, Ellen Glasgow, had that connection. Rawlings had admired Glasgow's work and was chosen, after Glasgow's death, to be Glasgow's biographer. (Rawlings died before completing the first draft.) The Glasgow House was a block from the library, and books and writings on Glasgow were plentiful at our library. I wrote a historical essay detailing the unusual relationship between the two women and connected the article to Richmond and the present-day Ellen Glasgow House. "The Unwritten Life" won first place in the contest. Again, my librarian self provided the information for the essay.

In entering writing contests or submitting articles for publication, the librarian-writer will not find essays as a category in *Writer's Market* or *Poets and Writers Magazine.* However, essays can be found in every subject category throughout the book under nonfiction headings. In the Contest and Awards section of *Writer's Market,* the writer with library experience may want to check out the contests boasting an author's name: Annie Dillard Award in Creative Nonfiction, the Elie Wiesel Prize in Ethics Essay Contest, the Ralph Waldo Emerson Award. Familiarity with an author shortens the planning process for any writer.

Writers need to read authors who write in an essay style. The best-known informal essayist today is undoubtedly David Sedaris, whose books are routinely best sellers. He shapes his past into humorous vignettes in a very informal essay manner. If he decided to write short stories, his present style would create excellent coming-of-age fiction. The fiction writer has the capacity to narrate in exactly the same manner as the casual essayist.

For examples of formal essayists, read the following authors: Edgar Allan Poe, Ernest Hemingway, Ralph Waldo Emerson, Charles Dickens, Jane Austen, Mark Twain, Willa Cather, Jack London, Kurt Vonnegut Jr., Noam Chomsky, Joan Didion, and Susan Sontag. The formal essayist uses the literary form to introduce an idea, opinion, or viewpoint by creating a thesis statement and supporting examples, unlike the informal piece.

Ultimately, to be a definitive essayist, the writer must bring a passion and sense of authority to the topic—often pulled from career and life. The writer must be well read to write by example. The writer's approach needs to be fresh and the voice authentic. For the topic to shine, the writer's research must include precise comparisons and examples. And he must have the knowledge to step back from his model at the right time and write, and then rewrite.

Most librarians do not set out to be writers; most writers do not set out to be essayists. If librarians choose to be writers, the very fact that they select essays as their writing style is characteristic of their library career. The formal essay is one of the more structured literary styles, from a limited or personal point of view, that may incorporate a thesis statement, a discourse, and a conclusion. Librarians tend toward organization, accuracy, research, and of course reading. They can pull repeated examples of books and content to make the literary essay flow. From the first written word, they have the ability to write from a subject and a classification perspective.

TEXTBOOK WRITING

Locating and Working with Textbook Publishers

ANN MARLOW RIEDLING

First, it might be wise to define a textbook as a book used in schools, colleges, and universities as a standard work for instruction on a particular course or subject. Traditionally, textbooks are published only in printed format. However, many publishers are allowing textbooks to be made available as electronic books (or e-books).

Textbook writing is immensely rewarding for the depth of knowledge you gain in the area, and the reward of actually paving the way for others to teach, and for giving voice to new ideas and knowledge. It's just something you have to want to do for reasons other than career or finances because it doesn't really help either these days. Another gratifying part of writing a textbook is receiving compliments from complete strangers. Positive comments make you realize that you're touching lives out there that you'll never know about.

For authors, the key to success is self-discipline, not brilliance. Authors must have the drive, perseverance, determination, ambition—whatever you want to call it—to sit and write: day after day, week after week, month after month.

If you are passionate about your subject, know your market, and don't mind hard work, writing a textbook could bring you much satisfaction in a job well done. Textbooks are often perceived as dry, boring, and a chore to write. But they are essential reading for tens of thousands of students, and the rewards for successful authors can be substantial.

The trick is to be informative and comprehensible while imparting a sense of excitement in the subject area; know your market. Assume that your readership will be small; that's why you have to make sure you love the subject. Small or not, it is vital to know whether your readership exists. It is essential to research the market and find out about potential readers and competitors.

Most people believe that you need a great idea for a textbook to put your mark on the discipline. Nothing could be further from the truth! Original ideas are few and far between. My suggestion: simply blend a smidgeon of originality into a tub of the same old thing. Make the idea fresh and current and interesting for the reader.

To date, I have written several textbooks, including *An Educator's Guide to Information Literacy: What Every High School Senior Needs to Know, Learning to Learn: A Guide to Becoming Information Literate in the 21st Century, Information Literacy: What Does It Look Like in the School Library Media Center, Catalog It! A Guide to Cataloging School Library Materials, Helping Teachers Teach: A School Library Media Specialist's Role,* and *Reference Skills for the School Library Media Specialist: Tools and Tips.* Two more textbooks are forthcoming: *Extreme Searching for Teens: Curricular Tools* and *Reference Skills for the School Library Media Specialist: Tools and Tips.*

One attraction of writing a textbook is being able to do things your way. It is enjoyable to incorporate your own way of explaining concepts and your own bag of examples and nifty metaphors. It's fun to share your clever examples with a wider audience than the classroom. Another plus is the self-education that you get from having to organize the material. In addition, class testing the book can be loads of fun and helpful at the same time.

As you draft sample chapters, you'll face every textbook writer's dilemma: do I write for students or for the professors who order the copies? Students want simplified, clear, and entertaining texts; to reach an average student, your style must compete with Facebook and MySpace. In contrast, many professors want intellectual complexity and vocabulary that announces, "This is higher education, deal with it!" From my observation, most textbook writers figure out which group butters their royalty checks. I, however, took the path less traveled and wrote directly for students. Today it gratifies me greatly when students say my book talks to them and that they really use it when they land a job.

To locate a publisher, jump online and search for similar textbooks in your area of expertise. Often, the guidelines for submitting a proposal to that publisher can be found on the publisher's website. If not, find a contact name and e-mail that person. Follow the proposal guidelines to a T. All guidelines will have some variation of the following: tentative title, approximate number of pages, basic or general description, purpose and scope, table of contents, draft preface, books with similar content, length of final text, tentative deadline, and a copy of your vita. Occasionally (especially if this is the first book you have written) they may ask for a sample chapter.

Now, to win a contract, you must create a dazzling book proposal that demonstrates your expertise, your ability to write simultaneously to Einstein and an unmotivated nineteen-year-old. At the same time, you must show that the textbook will enhance the publisher's reputation as a leading-edge moneymaker. The proposal must explain how your textbook is unique, what makes you the only person in the world who can write it, and why it will quell competitors. In general, create the impression that you are enthusiastic, creative, and energetic but professional and experienced.

Your proposal has been accepted—hallelujah! Your publisher will then provide you with an editor who will simultaneously make your life simpler and create tons more work. Your editor is your lifeline, but he or she also has an agenda and you must be wary of it at times. In other words, stick to your guns, but choose your battles carefully! Ultimately, you will love your editor and he or she will love you, too! It can be a love-hate relationship!

A copy editor will polish your book to perfection. Copy editors are fastidious—trust them! The copy editor polices spelling, grammar, and punctuation—even the minutest of mistakes—and looks at other issues such as word usage and political correctness. A copy editor is the cherry on top of the whipped cream!

Finally, the big day. A FedEx box arrives with ten copies of your new book inside. You smile with pride, sniff the book's newness, and crack the spine.

Most textbooks die in the first edition. But if you say the old ideas in a new-wave style, you may be asked to work on a second edition.

WRITING NEW EDITIONS OF YOUR TEXTBOOKS

ANN MARLOW RIEDLING

An urban legend is that textbook revisions are merely cosmetic. Actually, the investment needed to bring out a revision is only slightly less than that for a first edition. Much more is involved, therefore, than slapping on new covers. Your contracts must be renegotiated, you may be brought onto the team and others retired, editors apply new market research and competition analyses to develop a revision plan, and usually the book is at least partly redesigned. The degree of similarity in appearance between a revision and its previous edition depends almost exclusively on market considerations. Do people love this book and remain loyal to it? Then make it look much the same. Are people dissatisfied with it or iffy? Or is there simultaneously a major new challenge from a competitor? Then make it look different.

Industry standards dictate that a revised edition of a textbook should be approximately one-third changed from the previous edition or substantively different in some other way. This extends to replacing a third or more of the photos and figures. The real reasons for revising are to correct, update, improve, or adapt a work. However, there are other reasons. For example, teacher education texts had to be revised after enactment of the No Child Left Behind Act. Most publishers made rapid and costly revisions in selected titles after September 11, 2001. Sometimes textbooks are revised because customers object to certain content or because certain content is outdated or wrong. While some of these changes do not add up to a third of the book, they necessitate a revision.

Although it is easy to think (and not unheard of) that publishers put out new editions as often as they can get away with to reap more profits, this usually is not the case. For one thing, textbooks, especially first editions, normally need at least two years of sales just to pay for themselves, much less to pay the authors their royalties and the publisher its margin. For another, the market readily punishes publishers (justly or not) who put an older edition out of print by bringing out a new higher-priced edition after only a year. While this may look like corporate greed, it's usually just a desperate effort to save a book with insufficient sales that otherwise would be taken off the market entirely. Such a book might even be revised heavily enough (half changed) to be brought out as a new first edition. Older textbooks often are recycled in this way, through mix-and-match cannibalizations.

Unless it is in a series designed as annual editions, therefore, a book that is revised after one year is in trouble. Maybe it had something in it (or not in it) that was killing sales. Maybe it was late coming out and missed its sales for the first semester of its copyright year (in which case a revision can justify permitting it to continue to exist at all). In any event, the publisher risks double shortfalls by bringing out a revision before the previous edition has paid for the cost of publishing it. In light of these facts, we may wish to reexamine our prejudices and assumptions regarding textbook revisions.

There no doubt are other myths about textbook publishing. Now, however, we come to the baffling matters of how a textbook revision is built.

The worst is over, but much yet is to be done! Not necessarily! Research, data, and references must all be updated. Regardless of how long you expect the preparation of the next edition to take, it will probably take longer. The good news is that it may take less time than the first edition.

Know your (perhaps new) editor. Editors seem to come and go. If you have a new editor since your first edition was published, talk to the editor about what she or he thinks about the first edition and would like to see in the next edition. Also be sure to have a clear idea about the editor's plan and schedule for the revision.

Your publisher may have changed since the first edition of your textbook was printed. The integration of lists after acquisitions can be difficult, as the (now-larger) publisher may have books that compete with one another. This might affect the enthusiasm that your editor will have for having your book come out in a new edition. Be aware of what makes your book different from, and better than, competing books by the same publisher, and be ready to communicate that to your editor.

Obtain (or hopefully you have kept) a workable electronic file of the publisher's copyedited version of the previous edition. This may be less of a problem now than in years past, but your life will be a lot easier if your publisher can give you a workable electronic file of the previous edition or if you kept one handy on your flash drive.

Don't start writing too soon (especially regarding data and statistics), but don't start too late either. If you start writing too soon, your material will be that much more out of date by the time the book is printed, which can be as much as a year after you finish your manuscript and thus more than a year since you wrote a chapter containing the material. If you start writing too late, you won't make the deadline for the completion of your revision.

Keep track of instructors who wrote to you, especially those who wondered when the next edition was coming out. Respond promptly to any instructors who wrote you, and let them know when the new edition is about to be published. Make clear to them that you appreciate any comments or suggestions they might have about your book.

It's difficult to predict accurately whether a textbook will sell well or poorly. Even if your first edition did well, the next edition might not. The odds are, though, that it will do well if the first edition succeeded.

CHILDREN'S LIBRARIANS!

Use Your Skills to Fill Your Collection Gaps

MARGARET READ MACDONALD

How many times have you gone to the shelves and muttered, "Someone needs to write a good book on ant farms"—or some other as-yet-unresearched topic. Or perhaps the current book you need hasn't been written yet to replace out-of-date materials. We all bump into collection gaps. But most of us never do anything about it—other than perhaps mentioning it to a publisher at a conference.

But there is something we can do. And as resourceful librarians, we are in a unique position to do this. We can research and write the book we need.

As children's librarian at Bothell Public Library, I was constantly approached by parents who had been asked to handle Skit Night for outdoor education week. They felt they needed a good book of skits. And they needed it desperately. I tried to explain: "You don't need a book of skits. Someone who has been to camp before will say 'At Camp Lakewood we did this great skit last summer.' And another child will chime in with 'At Camp Seabeck we did *this* skit.' Then you simply choose the skit your cabin wants to do." Of course this did not reassure anyone at all. There were only a couple of skit books left in our library system, both so worn out that they had long ago been withdrawn from branch circulation.

While chatting with publishers at ALA, I proposed the notion of a new skit book. The idea took hold and I started work on the project. Of course, as a librarian, my first approach was to order up all the skit books available in any library anywhere. But after reading through those, I realized that this was not the approach I needed. What I needed to do was to ask kids for skits.

Collecting skits proved easy. I had two teenage daughters, so I planned slumber parties and coaxed out of the girls every skit they could remember. I tackled Boy Scouts in the library, and I queried every teen that I met. When I had 101 skits, I stopped, typed up the manuscript, and sent in the book. That was the easiest book I ever wrote—er, compiled.

A few years later, my family was sitting around the kitchen table at our Guemes Island summer home singing rounds. Then we came to a stop. Surely there were more rounds out there. But none of us could think of one. Time to research a round book! A search showed not many round collections. I began to collect rounds from young singers I knew. Our family tried out rounds in collections I ordered up on interlibrary loan, searching for good rounds that might be lying fallow and just needing a new crop of singers to bring them to life.

Because this project involved music, in which I was less expert, I asked a friend to help. When I mentioned rounds, Winnie Jaeger ran to her closet and lugged out a box full of rounds. She and her partner, Mary Whittington, are avid recorder instructors and had a houseful of music. Now I had a whole new lot of rounds to select from. And because Winnie had been born and raised in Germany, we ended up including some German rounds as well. One thing led to another and soon we were hosting a round sing at their home. Their recorder-playing friends arrived and we passed out rounds and sang and played an evening away just to make sure the rounds in the book were as much fun as they looked to be on paper. So *The Skit Book* received a companion: *The Round Book.*

Finding a press for this type of book is not as difficult as trying to find a publisher for your novel or picture book. Consult publishers' catalogs to see who might be interested in the nonfiction topic you think needs treatment. Check your shelves to see which publishers produce books similar to the one you would like to write. Do your research well, and approach only publishers who might be able to use your book in their line. You won't want to write the whole book before you find a publisher, but you will need to do enough work to show them exactly what such a book would include. Explain in your proposal why such a book is needed. The publisher will expect you to have researched and be able to show what books already exist on this topic. These books may be out of date or may not cover the topic as extensively as you plan to do. In what way will your book appeal to the library buyer? If libraries already have five books on frogs, why would they buy yours?

Sometimes, you have an idea for a book that just must be written. So you go ahead and write it, on the faith that it will eventually see the light of day. This was the case with my eight-hundred-page tome, *The Storyteller's Sourcebook: A Subject, Title, and Motif-Index to Folk-Literature.* When studying anthropology at Indiana University, I had used the Stith Thompson *Motif-Index of Folk-Literature.* I remember sitting on the floor in the closed stacks of the old library poring over the descriptions of world folktales in amazement. I could look up a topic—frogs—and find tales about frogs from all over the world. Later, as a children's librarian, I needed such a tool. But the massive Stith Thompson work wouldn't help. It indexed scholarly sources available in research libraries. I needed the same sort of index, but one that would index the folktale collections in my children's library. "That could be a fun project," I thought. So I began to compile just such an index. After a couple of months, I began to realize the enormity of the project I was tiptoeing toward. I wrote to a colleague, Anne Pellowski, for advice. Was I really foolish to attempt this? Would my index be different enough from the Faxon indexes? Those included subject indexes but not motif indexes. And they did not describe tales in the way my motif index would do. Anne encouraged me. So I plunged forward. Anne wrote a letter to the ALA publishing division encouraging them to publish the work. They turned it down. But I was hooked by now. I worked on the project for eleven years—and wept through ten rejections by publishers who gave me great encouragement for a while and then got cold feet on the project. But I did not give up. And eventually Gale Research published the book in 1982.

What can you learn from my experience?

- Look around at your collection. Spot gaps that need filling and go fill them!

- Ask for the advice of fellow librarians. They can help you formulate your project. And they might be able to help point you to publishers who would be interested in your work.

- If you truly believe in a project, never give up.

FROM STORYTIME TO PICTURE BOOK

A Path for the Children's Librarian

MARGARET READ MACDONALD

Who better to write fine picture books for children than those who use them daily? As children's librarians, we have accumulated years of experience in the use of picture books with children. Reading aloud over and over, we come to have a sixth sense of what works and what does not flow off the tongue quite so well. Letting this sense guide us, we are in a position to create picture books that will prove themselves truly worthy of storytime.

My own method is based on oral sharing with multiple audiences. This might not work for everyone, but it is one way to hone a text. I begin with a folktale that I think would be great fun to share with the children. You could also begin with an original story you have created that you think has good child appeal. Be sure that the story really excites you. You are going to be sharing this story again and again for many years. So choose a tale with staying power.

Now that you have your story idea, the work begins. Tell this story to many, many groups of children. It helps if you can tell the story rather than read it at this point. The oral telling allows the words to shift and flow and settle themselves into their most listener-friendly patterns. Minor plot points may shift, too, as you respond to your audiences. Seek out diverse audiences to practice your tale on. Each audience will respond in a different way; each will draw something new from you and from your story.

Once the story has settled itself into a predictable form—one that is fairly stable and has stopped morphing radically, it is time to get it down on paper. You can just sit down and type it out, or you can tape your own performance of the tale and transcribe that, to make sure you get it down just as you are telling it.

Now that you have fixed the text in print, another round of editing begins. Is this really the way you want your tale to appear in print? Are there different word choices you would make? Will the tale sound as fine in the voice of another reader as it does in your practiced presentation?

The proof in the pudding is in the speaking in this case. Give your text to a friend and listen as he or she reads aloud. Keep a copy of the text in your hand and mark any spots where the reader stumbles or where the sound of the language seems awkward. Rewrite and try it on another friend. I finalize my editing by asking young men who are family friends to read the texts aloud. They know nothing of the skills of story reading. I want my picture books to sound just as well in the voice of a father reading to his child as they do in the library storytime. So I test them on people who are unskilled reading aloud.

OK, the story is working well, even in unpracticed readings. It is ready to send off to a publisher—probably again and again and again. You will have a better chance with publishers if you have a personal contact, so don't be shy about asking the editors met at conferences if you can send your story to them personally. But be sure your manuscript is worthy of their time before you ask this favor.

The work of a children's author is just that—work. It is a full-time job, not an avocation. To hope for success in the field, one must do all the things that are required of any other field. The first step is to join the professional organizations: the Society of Children's Writers and Illustrators (www.scbwi.org) is a must. Attend their meetings and conferences. Find a writer's support group. Organize your time so that you have regular periods to write. And create more than one manuscript worthy of submission. Publishers want to publish authors, not accidental onetime picture book creators.

Once the picture book is accepted and given to an illustrator, you will have a final chance to hone that book. You will receive the black-and-white illustrations from the illustrator. At this time, you get to see the vision of another person for this story. The illustrations will not be quite what you had expected. Paste up a dummy using your text and the illustrations and read it to groups again. You may need to do slight rewrites to make sure that your words truly match what the illustrations are showing. Watch the page turns and make sure the language is flowing beautifully as the book moves from page to page. I always read the dummy to many groups at this stage, making minor alterations to the text after every reading. This is the fine-tuning that makes the book truly speakable for the end user.

Now you have a picture book to be proud of—one that has been created, shaped, honed, and fine-tuned through use of your skills as a children's librarian, one from which other children's librarians will benefit for years to come or at least until the book goes out of print (sigh). But that is another story.

THE PUBLIC LIBRARY AS PICTURE BOOK PUBLISHER

KAY MARNER

My first picture book, *Dog Tales: The Adventures of Smyles,* debuted at a book-release party hosted by my publisher. More than two hundred people joined the celebration, and I inscribed books for attendees for nearly two hours.

Even though I was a first-time author, the publisher was so confident in my main character Smyles's viability that it produced a plush toy to merchandise with the book.

Today, nearly every child under the age of seven in Ames, Iowa, and surrounding areas owns a copy of my book, as does virtually every day-care site and preschool classroom.

How many first-time authors can say all that?

My publisher is Ames Public Library, where I'm a library assistant in Outreach Services. Smyles, the book's main character, is the library's mascot. *Dog Tales* was published in conjunction with Project Smyles, Ames Public Library's early literacy outreach program.

What better promotional tool could a library hope for than a book? Yet, to my knowledge, *Dog Tales* is the only book of its kind in existence: a book written about a specific public library, for that library's youngest customers. If you're a librarian who writes, you're uniquely suited to express your love of reading and libraries by writing a similar book.

IMPETUS

Several years ago, Ames Public Library retired its road-weary bookmobile and replaced it with a new one. Because we had hoped the new bookmobile would perform a promotional role in addition to serving as a mobile library, we took special care in designing its exterior vinyl graphics. The graphics portray a neighborhood scene, populated by people

of various ages and featuring local landmarks. The focal point of the neighborhood is a large tree. A sign touting the bookmobile as "Your Neighborhood Branch" hangs from one branch. Under the tree, a blue dog listens as his human companion reads to him from a book titled *Dog Tales.*

The new bookmobile evolved, as envisioned, into the library's premier promotional vehicle. Soon, a custom-made mascot, Smyles, a two-legged incarnation of the blue dog from the bookmobile's graphics, joined the bookmobile to further its promotional role.

FIND YOUR MAIN CHARACTER

Chances are that your main character won't be as obvious as mine. Search your library carefully. The perfect protagonist will find you.

- What is the theme of the decor and furnishings in your library's children's area?
- Does a puppet greet storytime attendees?
- What graphics grace your newsletter or programming calendar?
- Are there mice in the storage room?
- Does a friendly ghost roam the biography section?

To connect readers to your library, your main character must be organic rather than stemming purely from your imagination.

INSPIRATION

Around the time that the new bookmobile debuted, I began three new seemingly unrelated projects at work. One was to develop a proposal for a new outreach initiative, whereby the library would serve children in day-care and preschool settings.

Another was to develop a branding campaign. Through regular appearances, Smyles was achieving excellent brand recognition. The public recognized Smyles as the library dog, and they clearly loved him. We'd brand Ames Public Library with Smyles and his print image. Think Smyles; think Ames Public Library. Love Smyles; love your library.

The third project was to write a book. If the blue dog on the bookmobile's side could come to life in the form of our mascot, Smyles, I reasoned, his book, *Dog Tales,* could become an actual book. We'd discussed creating a coloring book. This is a library, I thought. Why not publish a picture book?

Think of all the stuff libraries sell or give away to promote or fund-raise or as incentives for reading: bookmarks, book bags, coffee mugs, pens, magnets, and so on. None of these says "library" like a book.

INTERMINGLING

As I worked on these projects, their objectives, once distinct, began to coalesce in my mind. I realized that a custom picture book was the key both to a one-of-a-kind early literacy program and to branding and promoting the library.

By sending librarians to day-care centers and preschools to provide storytimes and deposit collections, we'd create lifelong readers. If we ensured that the children connect this service to the library, we'd create lifelong library users.

We planned to give each child a free book through Project Smyles to expand children's home libraries. That book could be one of any number of popular picture books, or it could be *Dog Tales.* Home libraries would grow, as would good feelings about Ames Public Library.

At Ames Public Library, we had Project Smyles. When you're looking for a hook, consider tying your book into a bigger, already-sanctioned project:

- Is your library or community approaching a major anniversary?
- Is the area of town your library is located in undergoing revitalization?
- Does your community sponsor an annual festival?

By piggybacking with another project and identifying shared goals, you may discover a potential source of funding.

DOES YOUR LIBRARY HAVE A STORY TO TELL?

In *Dog Tales,* Miss June, a bookmobile librarian, goes out of her way to welcome Smyles and his dog friends to her outdoor storytime, portraying libraries as inclusive and welcoming and librarians as approachable and friendly. Because I envisioned the book's illustrations featuring likenesses of the Ames Public Library and bookmobile and, of course, Smyles, the book was a perfect branding tool. Who would argue against a book that would accomplish so many objectives?

IMPLEMENTATION

I developed a comprehensive work plan for implementing Project Smyles. I prepared a plan for systematically branding Ames Public Library, using the Smyles character and his image. I positioned *Dog Tales* as the cornerstone of both projects. When I presented the plan to the library's board of trustees they applauded. Two months later, they approved a funding package, giving me the go ahead on all three projects.

When you are working on the nuts and bolts of your work plan, be sure to delineate each step in the publishing process and target completion dates, the person responsible, and detailed cost estimates. Key steps include

- writing text
- contracting with the illustrator
- receiving completed illustrations
- contracting for design, printing, and binding
- editing and approving layout
- arranging for printing, binding, and delivery
- planning, publicizing, and executing the release party

LET'S TALK MONEY

- Ames Public Library spent about $10,000 to publish 5,500 8½-by-11-inch soft cover, perfect-bound books.
- I wrote the story on my personal time and donated the rights to the library. We contracted with the publisher for a flat fee. The layout, printing, and binding

- were awarded through a request-for-proposals process.

- We built the cost into Project Smyles's first-year budget, which relied on grants, a bequest, and funds from our library's foundation.

- We sell the books for $7.99 each, at the library and at two local retail outlets.

- All proceeds from sales return to Project Smyles's operating budget, and because funding to publish *Dog Tales* was provided up front, with no provision to repay publishing costs, all proceeds are profit.

Funding exists for virtually any worthy project. First, identify specific, valuable, realistic outcomes. For example, Project Smyles receives grant funding related to school readiness and early literacy development. Here are some ideas for finding funding for your project:

- Check the website of every business in your area. Nearly every national company provides grants.

- Investigate funding for the arts. Funds may be available to pay an illustrator.

- Hold a contest. A first-time illustrator may donate his or her work for the thrill of being published.

- Ask businesses to sponsor your book in exchange for acknowledgment on the book's cover.

I learned the basics of producing a picture book from books about self-publishing in our library's collection.

Project Smyles and *Dog Tales* have exceeded all expectations. Smyles is well known and well loved. And I'm a published author. Picture yourself reading your new book to a smiling, supportive crowd at your book release party. Now make it happen. I did!

WRITING FOR CHILDREN'S MAGAZINES

MARY NORTHRUP

For many, writing for children means writing a book. But there is a whole world of writing for children in children's magazines. Articles are satisfying and rewarding to research and write, and they can lead to publishing credits that can help in getting your book published, if that is your goal.

No matter what you like to write, a market exists for it in a children's magazine. This includes

- Fiction of all types for all ages

- Nonfiction, including informational pieces, features, and profiles or interviews

- Puzzles, activities, and other filler material

TYPES OF MAGAZINES

Do you like history and doing research in that field? Then you may want to write for *Calliope, Cobblestone,* or *Dig.* Is health and fitness your passion? Then try the magazines in the Children's Better Health Institute group, such as *Turtle* or *Jack and Jill.* How about articles on timeless and traditional activities? Look into *Hopscotch* or *Boys' Quest.* If you like to write about religious themes, many children's magazines for a variety of faiths are looking for writers.

In addition, if you have the background or experience, you may be well qualified to write for specialty magazines that cover such wide-ranging topics as science, horses, dance, cheerleading, and more.

Editors look positively on librarians who write (because they know how to research) and teachers who write (because they know how to explain things). A plus if you are both!

THE CHILDREN'S MAGAZINE WORLD

So what is the best way to break into the children's magazine field?

First, familiarize yourself with what is out there. Go to your local bookstore—one with a sizable magazine selection—and look for the kids' titles. You will see some old favorites that you remember from childhood, as well as new ones that are unfamiliar. If you work in a public library and have not browsed the current magazines in the children's area for a while, take a look.

You will see that there is an article for every child: humorous stories, articles for kids who like to make things, high-quality literary fiction, stories about kids who are making a difference in the world, celebrity profiles, mystery stories, puzzles of all types, science fiction stories, and much more.

THE CHILDREN'S MAGAZINE MARKET

Think about what you like to write or feel that you have a talent for, and prepare to go into more depth in your search for the right market for your work.

One common mistake of beginning writers is that they do not spend enough time in market research. The time you spend locating the magazines that are right for your story or article is well worth it; sending your work out to just any publication is a scattershot approach that more likely than not will end in rejection.

MARKET SOURCES

How can you find the best places to submit your work? Study the following sources. These books are available at bookstores or should be at most public libraries in the reference area:

Children's Writer's and Illustrator's Market. Cincinnati, OH: Writer's Digest Books, annual. Look in "The Markets" section for "Magazines." Here you will find a list of children's magazines and the preliminary information you need to submit your articles: addresses, phone numbers, and websites; editors' names; what types of material are needed; and how to contact. This is the information that editors want you to have so that they receive stories and articles that they can accept. Of course, there is much more to this reference tool, including book markets, lists of organizations, and helpful articles by published authors who were once just starting out, too.

Writer's Market. Cincinnati, OH: Writer's Digest Books, annual. This is the market source for writers of all types, and while the listing of children's magazines under "Juvenile" is

small, it is worth examining. Also check out the "Journalism and Writing" magazine section for titles of magazines to buy or subscribe to that will help you in your writing. As with the preceding title, this guide also features articles with great information for beginning and established writers.

WRITER'S GUIDELINES

The short entries for each magazine in the market books provide the basics for submitting. Most magazines publish more extensive writer's guidelines, which are invaluable for writers who want to submit articles successfully. In most cases, you can send for these guidelines with a letter and SASE (self-addressed stamped envelope). Many publications also include their writer's guidelines on their website.

PUBLICATIONS

Educate yourself about writing and publishing by reading periodicals for writers. Especially helpful are *Children's Writer,* a monthly newsletter, and the monthly magazines *The Writer* and *Writer's Digest,* which are for all writers, with occasional articles about children's writing. All three of these sources also include listings of markets.

You may wish to join the Society of Children's Book Writers and Illustrators (SCBWI). Membership includes the *Bulletin,* a bimonthly publication, and access to other society publications and regional newsletters.

TIPS FOR THE MAGAZINE WRITER

Send holiday or seasonal material well in advance of that time, usually six to nine months ahead. Some magazines publish theme issues. Editors will want either every article, or the majority in that issue, to reflect this theme. Editorial calendars for these publications are available with the writer's guidelines. Query first, unless the writer's guidelines specifically state to submit the entire article. A query letter is a one-page explanation of your article idea and your qualifications for writing it. Be sure to enclose a SASE with your manuscript or query letter. Follow guidelines to the letter. If the word count on stories is stated as no more than 500 words, do not send a 550-word story, no matter how good you think it is. When you are looking through sample copies of magazines, pay close attention to the style of writing, types of articles, and any special features like sidebars, and then make sure your submissions to the magazine follow suit. And look through more than just one issue; four to six is a good sample. Zero publishing credits? Try local publications, such as newspapers or city or regional magazines to build up your published articles file.

If you have a good idea and can express it with a fresh approach, you have a good chance of breaking into magazine writing. Editors are always on the lookout for good new writers who they can work with. Eventually, editors may contact you with writing assignments. So do your market research, send in your best work, and you may have a long-term relationship with that publication. And remember, your writing will inspire, inform, entertain, and influence children. What could be better?

WRITING BIOGRAPHICAL SKETCHES FOR PROFESSIONAL DEVELOPMENT

JANET BUTLER MUNCH

College librarians routinely handle requests for biographical information on the famous and obscure. Databases like Master Genealogical and Biographical Index, Marquis Who's Who on the Web, and Biography Reference Bank are mainstays in this research but are just a starting point.

Many specialized reference titles include biographical entries, such as *Encyclopedia of the Documentary Film, Encyclopedia of Science, Technology and Ethics, Historical Dictionary of the 1940s, The Crusades: An Encyclopedia,* and *Latinas in the United States: A Historical Encyclopedia.*

Librarians know these works from reviews in *Choice, Library Journal,* and *Booklist;* from browsing "Best Reference" sources; and from perusing catalogs. Other titles come to their attention through mailings, faculty recommendations, wide reading of library and specialized publications, examining reference holdings at other libraries, subscribing to selected electronic discussion lists and blogs, and visiting publisher exhibits at conferences.

Although librarians shape reference collections to meet users' needs, they may not even consider writing entries for works similar to those they recommend daily. Publishers, however, welcome contributions of biographical articles, which generally average 500 to 1500 words.

OPPORTUNITIES FOR PUBLICATION

Publication editors notify specialized journals and academic websites of planned reference works and the need for contributors on a prepared list of topics. Entries on notable individuals are generally included in such lists. Reliable websites that regularly feature calls for contributors are the following:

- *A Library Writer's Blog,* http://library writing.blogspot.com
- H-Net: Humanities and Social Sciences Online, www.h-net.org

Other leads present themselves through

- Referral by colleagues
- Searching for "call for contributors" in search engines
- Networking through professional organizations

WRITING THE BIOGRAPHICAL SKETCH

After seeing a contributor announcement for biographical entries, the college librarian generally submits an e-mail query to the editor. The editor usually responds with a list of topics (with word counts) that the planned publication will cover. The prospective contributor requests specific assignments and the editor generally asks for a statement of interest, curriculum vitae, and possibly a writing sample.

When the editor and contributor agree on the entries to be written, a contract is sent explaining the writing particulars (word count, deadline, compensation—if any—and rights). Some editors forgo contracts and just e-mail confirmation of assignments. Publishers can usually provide aspiring contributors with sample written entries for their planned reference work. Authors model their entries on the samples, focusing on writing style, formatting, length, references (not footnotes), and cross-references that are a staple in such publications. Examining imprints produced by the publisher or editor can also be instructive. The contributing author's submissions should be properly credited with his or her name and affiliation in the final publication. Avoid editors who cannot make this commitment.

Once the writing assignment is accepted, the contributor finds relevant source materials, reads them, and synthesizes them. These are the first steps in understanding the individual one is researching. Writing biographical sketches requires interest in the person assigned; ability to write clear, jargon-free, concise prose for informed laypeople; and a commitment to meet agreed-on terms. Writers must provide basic facts about the biographical subject, their main contributions, what propelled them to do what they did, how their work affected society or a particular field, and why their memory endures. Biographical research can be a window to other times, bringing individuals to life through a careful statement of facts, anecdotes, analysis of supporting materials, and interpretation of the person's contributions.

WHY WRITE BIOGRAPHICAL SKETCHES?

Oftentimes, college librarians have academic or faculty status and rank. Like their teaching faculty colleagues, they are expected to contribute to scholarship and publish. The academic model of librarianship differs from that of librarians working in school, special, or public libraries. Publish or perish, is a reality for library faculty who must survive annual reappointment reviews and ultimately tenure. This is where writing biographical sketches can help.

By writing biographical entries, college librarians have an opportunity to quickly break into print and begin creating a publication record. It is a mistake to think that only scholars or subject experts write biographical articles in reference works. Reading contributor profiles in specialized encyclopedias and dictionaries, found in typical college reference collections, tells a different story. It reveals that writers are drawn from specialists and nonspecialists, including freelance writers, advanced graduate students, and librarians. Writing short biographical sketches is not easy, but there is a good chance that well-researched and well-written entries will result in publication. This is because the editor or publisher has specifically requested coverage on this person and has a tight publication deadline.

WHAT CAN COLLEGE LIBRARIANS BRING TO BIOGRAPHICAL WRITING?

College librarians are the generalists in the academic environment. In addition to their MLS, they may have special subject interests or other graduate degrees. As the professionals dealing with information in the widest range of areas, good college librarians know the needs of their campuses. They see connections across disciplines and bring insights to research topics that may elude specialists.

Librarians may not think of themselves as scholars or writers. Yet they are highly skilled at finding information, accessing source materials, and determining their research value. Reference librarians are trained to search catalogs, complex databases, and search engines for information on specific topics. Subject experts marvel at the librarian's speed and efficiency in tackling intricate research assignments and gathering an impressive range of resources.

While the usual maxim to writers is "write what you know," librarians can draw on broad general knowledge and research ability to "write to learn." Writing biographical sketches is a way of sharing what is found while also making an important contribution to scholarship. The discipline of writing biography can also develop the budding author's confidence, paving the way for the demands of more in-depth studies published in peer-reviewed publications.

Examining the life of a person can lead to a richer understanding of society, events, and the cultural milieu of the time. Librarians use whatever primary or secondary sources are available to explain and interpret the contributions of their assigned subject. These sources can include diaries, correspondence, archival materials, wills, deeds, newspapers, books, journal articles, or obituaries. Contacting authorities or institutions with specific questions may also be needed. In using a variety of materials for research, the college librarian has a chance to know sources and repositories in a unique way. This all feeds back into the daily practice of librarianship.

HOW CAN WRITING BIOGRAPHICAL ENTRIES PROMOTE PROFESSIONAL DEVELOPMENT?

The nature of academic librarianship requires continual growth and development. By undertaking research, librarians test their limits and embrace lifelong learning. These efforts enliven professional practice and keep the workplace vital. Through their research and writing, college librarians can

- better understand the publication process
- contribute to scholarship and advance knowledge
- develop a track record of publications
- gain recognition for themselves and their college
- network with those engaging in similar research
- dare to learn and relearn databases and search engines
- discover new resources and repositories
- make more informed collection development decisions
- enhance their reference skills for daily work
- share insights in information-literacy instruction
- satisfy personal curiosity and stimulate new research interests

DO YOU WANT TO BE AN ANTHOLOGIST?

CAROLYN DAVIS

The term *librarian-anthologist* is a snazzy one that, like other composites such as *scholar-diplomat,* is more effective if bestowed on a person by others. I had been a writer, mostly of research topics and op-ed articles, for many years before I answered a call for submissions by e-mail from Carol Smallwood for an anthology that she and Cynthia Brackett-Vincent were developing on innovative experiences in women's lives.

I had had plenty of those, and I am part of the cadre of colleagues who frequently are asked how and if we can be librarians when our work very often is conducted out of the sphere of traditional libraries. I answered the call. The anthology, titled *Thinking outside the Book: Essays for Innovative Librarians,* was published by McFarland Publishers in North Carolina in 2008. It helped that a few months before I had begun a collection of expository vignettes of different stages of my life and had just written some about my research and facilitation experiences as a librarian. Although the editors deemed one of my stories to be outside the realm of traditional librari-

anship, they accepted two others to the developing anthology. Not ones to rest on their achievements, the team planned another anthology shortly thereafter. Its working title is *Contemporary American Women: Our Defining Passages.* My first submission was passed on, but another vignette that I more than doubled in length in three hours was accepted right on deadline, giving a taste of *The Front Page* kind of tension to my autobiographical short story.

Because I had such good luck in the genre, and had many more stories in the electronic chute of a vignette folder on my computer, it was gratifying that there was a demand for them. Carol pointed me to many other anthologies; as a sideline, among those that I investigated was one that I submitted a true story to for the *Chicken Soup for the Soul* folks for a pending anthology of cat stories (www.chickensoup.com/form.asp?cid=submit_story). Many websites host calls for submissions, for example, Growing Great Writers from the Ground Up (http://marthaengber.blogspot.com/2008/02/ie-10-seeking-essays.html). The American Library Association disseminates information about submissions and publications, and enables opportunities for networking with other authors and editors. One web page that has been helpful to me is www.ala.org/ala/aboutala/offices/publishing/products_and_publications.cfm. This page lists major ALA publications. Another useful site is ALA's Read Write Connect wiki (http://wikis.ala.org/readwriteconnect/), which links to many networking resources.

ARTICLE AND VIGNETTE WRITING: HOW TO BEGIN

Library schools offer excellent opportunities for students to begin to have their articles published, as faculty members are often involved in the editing and publishing of professional journals and newsletters for librarians and information specialists.

Sheila Intner, a professor at Simmons College, was the editor of *Technicalities: Information Forum for the Library Practitioner,* a newsletter for librarians and technology specialists. Sheila commissioned my first article about international library science when I went to Wales to attend the International Graduate Summer School, which was cosponsored by the Simmons GSLIS and the University of Wales at Aberystwyth. My article was well received and, pending my eventual move to Cardiff, a further commission followed from Sheila to write a series of articles for *Technicalities* titled "Tales from Wales." At that time, I was contributing to a Welsh journal also and my career as a writer of international librarianship was under way.

IS CONTRIBUTING TO ANTHOLOGIES WORTH IT?

There are a variety of topics that librarians speak and write about that are suited to anthologies. The reasons for librarians to invest resources in library science–based anthologies are many. A few of the important reasons are the following:

1. As a forum to address an issue or tell a story that is or has been significant to your professional experiences in the company of others' library sci-

ence experiences. Journals enable this, too, but an anthology allows for situations to be related in relaxed, biographical short-story formats. This format is easy to write as well as to read.

2. As a forum to network with colleagues. The development of an anthology is a somewhat more personal experience than that of contributing to a journal. Writing articles for professional journals is important, educational and, particularly to those in academia, generally necessary. Writing for peer-reviewed journals enhances one's professional standing and attractiveness to publishers. However, I have been able to participate in more of the marketing process of anthologies on behalf of the editors than I have submitting articles to journals. I have found that that work and the process of writing and submitting chapters for anthologies are rewarding, to a great degree because much of it was fun!

3. Building up publication credit and becoming better known in the field. I have received e-mail offering publication and employment options because one of the anthology editors pointed opportunities my way. The Internet is truly mightier than the mouth, and publication opportunities breed other opportunities. The diversity of the market is encouraging, as there are demands to hear from people who have had a multitude of experiences as librarians. The encouragement of librarians to conduct their own research is reflected in the number of publications accepting research articles on many different topics. If you as a librarian or your library as an organization is developing plans for different goods and services to offer, or if there have been situations that you've encountered on nearly any issue, an Internet search through the ALA, another professional web page, or some networking with colleagues will reveal a format through which to let the rest of the field know. Like the true literary treasure hunt that it can be, revealing multiple ways and means for publication, your searching and networking will reveal an increasing number of opportunities to enable us all to participate in the education of all of us.

THE LIBRARIAN-RESEARCHER WHO IS DISABLED

CAROLYN DAVIS

My role as a researcher and author of various aspects of disability can be said to have begun in childhood, because I was born physically disabled.

The treatments and understanding of the human body in the 1960s were fairly primitive by twenty-first-century standards, to a considerable degree because technology had not advanced enough to enable people to observe as much of the function of living bodies as they do today. However, attitudes regarding the practice of rehabilitative treatments were changing. Particularly notable to me in the early seventies was the vast improvement in 1970s New York from 1960s Rhode Island. That was a prerequisite for the tidal wave of information, new treatments, patient participation, and the multitude of possibilities that were to manifest during the following thirty years and beyond. People wanted to read firsthand, realistic accounts about living and working with disabilities. A market that had been small and sanitized, with "super humans" accomplishing much by endless work and fortitude, was simultaneously opening up and growing up. The laws and policies that had begun to develop at the demand of the World War II veterans obliged the public to hear truth and facts regarding the significant integration of people with disabilities into education, housing, and employment. People who were and are disabled have been telling their stories in writing. Librarians who are disabled and want to inform colleagues and others of situations that we have experienced, observed, and researched have niche markets for which to write. The Internet is a valuable tool to use to gain access to these markets. For example, www.ala.org, www.lisjobs.org, and a number of publishers of library science topics such as McFarland Publishers, which is based in North Carolina and located on the Web at www.mcfarland pub.com, as well as Greenwood Publishing Group at www.greenwood.com, and professional journals and newsletters, are all current or potential forums.

My publications that have my disability as one of their subjects include the following. Four of these publications tell of my work abroad.

"Combining Careers in Research," *Info Career Trends* 2, no. 3 (May 2001). http://lisjobs.com/career_trends/?p=99.

Davis, Carolyn, and Rebecca Barton, *Access Guide.* http://accessguidecardiff-online.blog .com. (As the facilitator of this project, I co-researched and coauthored this physical access guide to Cardiff, Wales.)

"The International Graduate Summer School in England and Wales," *Technicalities* 16, no. 2 (February 1996): 4.

"The Mobile Librarian," *Thinking outside the Book: Essays for Innovative Librarians,* ed. Carol Smallwood, 235–237. Jefferson, NC: McFarland Publishers, 2008.

"Some Experiences of an Internet Researcher," *Audio Visual Librarian* 22, no. 2 (May 1996).

MY ROLE IN JAMAICA

I conducted research on agencies that provided services to people with disabilities while a Peace Corps volunteer in Jamaica in 1997 to 1999. The national newspaper the *Jamaica Gleaner* published an article about the Jamaica Council for Persons with Disabilities, where I worked, and the research results to that time. The article, titled "For Love of the Disabled," appeared in March 1998 and led to a meeting between Dr. Marigold Thorburn and myself. Dr. Thorburn was a powerhouse who had developed national programs and agencies from scratch. We felt that the development of a national coalition would answer the needs of the then competing agencies. We began to develop forums to discuss this possibility with agency directors across the country.

In its newsletter *Hearing Hands,* published by the Jamaica Association for the Deaf (JAD; www.jamdeaf.org.jm/hearing-hands/), Iris Soutar, who is the director of the association, cited the importance of the coalition. The Jamaica Coalition is considered one of the most effective of its kind, thanks to the work of the agency directors and personnel who have shaped and currently maintain it.

MY ROLE IN WALES

After my term of service in Jamaica ended, I moved to Wales to conduct research in medieval Welsh history. Rebecca Barton and I also began to look at physical and psychological access to public places in Cardiff for people with disabilities. I published our results on a blog at http://accessguidecardiff-online.blog.com (no longer available).

HOW TO GET PUBLISHED

As stated earlier, there are niche markets both for research in the field of disabilities and for the life experiences of people with disabilities. Because librarians have basic training in research and reference methods, we have access to professions or subspecialties in research in a variety of fields, particularly librarians who have qualifications and experience in additional fields. I have found that the best way to begin to have my work published in library science, whether or not my disability was to be part of the story, was both to approach and to be approached by editors of journals and anthologies. Among the people with and for whom I have worked are: Professor Anthony Hugh Thompson of Aberystwyth, Wales, who was the editor in chief of *The Audio-Visual Librarian;* Sheila Intner and her successor Peggy Johnson for *Technicalities;* the multiconnected Rachel Singer Gordon at www.lisjobs.com; and Carol Smallwood and Cynthia Brackett-Vincent, the latter at Encirclepub.com, for their growing list of anthologies.

Our voices need to be heard and our chapters and books published. These projects not only educate and enlighten our colleagues but also can have an impact on others' quality of life. I strongly encourage anyone who is a librarian with a physical challenge to share her or his experiences with the rest of our profession.

WRITING REGIONALLY

STACY RUSSO

Several years ago I embarked on a writing project to combine two things I love: libraries and California. This project materialized in a book titled *The Library as Place in California* (2008). I structured my book around thirty-two chapters. Each chapter focused on a library I visited during research trips around the state. Most chapters also included discussions of the areas where the libraries were located.

During and after the writing of the book, I received questions from librarians about the nature of the project. Many expressed how fun the project sounded and said they thought they would enjoy similar writing. Others sought advice on writing and publishing. I always responded affirmatively that the project was definitely fun and provided any advice I could. What I discovered from my project, which I will share here, is that there are many publishing opportunities for regional writing tied to libraries. In addition, there are numerous professional benefits, which makes this type of writing unique.

REGIONAL WRITING

Most of us are familiar with the concept of regional writing, but it is important to review some of the more essential elements. Regional writing concerns the customs, history, and people of a specific area. The landscape may also be discussed, such as the urban environment, rivers, beaches, deserts, or forests. The focus may be quite narrow, such as a small town or city. It may also extend to an entire state or section of a country, such as the West or the South of the United States. Because most libraries provide services for their communities and preserve the culture of the surrounding area, part of the mission of libraries is inherently regional. This regional nature gives each library a distinctive story to tell.

GETTING STARTED

If you have an interest in regional writing, there are many avenues you may take. One way to begin is by focusing on a particular library or libraries. Here are a few broad ideas and questions to provide inspiration:

The region. How would you define the community the library serves? How does this library fit in with the demographics of the community? Does this library represent something special about the region? What role does the library play in its community? Does the library provide specific services and/or programs that reflect its community? Is the community diverse? If so, is the collection diverse? Do displays reflect the community? Have the demographics of the region changed over time?

Building and surroundings. If someone is visiting the region, why should this library be on the visitor's list of places to stop? What else is on the same block as the library? What is the neighborhood like? What will a visitor experience when driving or walking up to the library building? What makes this building and the surrounding area interesting?

History. What is the history of the library? What is the history of the region? What is the history of other libraries in the region? How do these histories combine? Have there been successes and failures in the library's history? Has the library been housed at different locations?

GETTING PUBLISHED

Library magazines. Writings with a regional focus are often sought after in library-related publications. If you peruse a few issues of *American Libraries,* for example, you will notice how there are often regional articles. If you happen to live in a state where a library conference is scheduled, this is another opportunity to publish. Attendees will be interested in visiting libraries in the area near the conference. Your article can be their tour guide! For this type of article, send a query many months in advance to the publication(s) that attendees likely read. For major library conferences, *American Libraries* and *Library Journal* are two possibilities.

Other publishing opportunities in the field include state and county library association newsletters.

General magazines. Opportunities for regional writing on libraries, however, extend far beyond library-related publications to include the following general categories:

- travel magazines
- regional magazines
- local newspapers

If you browse periodicals from these categories at a large newsstand, you will note the various titles for travel and regional magazines. Some, but not all, allow unsolicited submissions. Guidelines for writers may be found within the pages or on the magazines' websites. You are likely already familiar with local newspapers in your surrounding communities, but, if not, some light detective work will uncover these opportunities.

Books. If you feel ambitious and would like to write a book, the key will be locating a publisher that is open to material with a regional focus. Similar to magazines, you may target library-specific publishers or general publishers that include library or regional titles within their catalogs. It may also be wise to investigate smaller independent and local publishers. University presses are another option, because they are often interested in regional titles.

PROFESSIONAL BENEFITS

Early on I mentioned that there are potential benefits that come with regional writing on libraries. If this chapter has not enticed you enough, before ending, I will share these benefits:

Area expertise. As you become familiar with a region and the collections held at area libraries, your expertise can only help if you are serving on a reference desk.

Voice for your community and state. If you publish regularly about libraries in your area, you have the potential to be viewed as a spokesperson and promoter for libraries.

Regional networking. The only way to write well about libraries is to visit them. This allows you the opportunity to network with others in the field and build professional relationships.

Ideas for your library. Visiting libraries, where you will discover services, programs, displays, and unique uses of space, can only provide you with ideas to consider for your library.

With the numerous publishing opportunities, creative avenues, and professional benefits, regional writing projects have the potential to offer back as much as you put into them.

REFERENCE

Russo, Stacy. 2008. *The Library as Place in California.* Jefferson, NC: McFarland.

THE POET-LIBRARIAN

Writing and Submitting Work

COLLEEN S. HARRIS

Where does the poet-librarian find time for creative writing and submitting work? How do you begin to build a body of poetry you can be proud of but that also makes it into respectable journals, anthologies, or even your own chapbooks or full-length collection?

WRITING POETRY

Schedule time. The biggest challenge for your writing will likely be finding time. Because very few librarians work a strict forty-hour week, you may have to block time out of your schedule, perhaps get up earlier or postpone bedtime, and simply think of it as another time commitment. You'll be surprised, however, at how quickly including writing in your schedule becomes a natural addition to your daily routine, and how writing will become a habit.

Leave your office. Get out, take a walk, see people for lunch, or just enjoy the scenery. As a librarian, you likely come into contact with all sorts of people from all walks of life. Remember that even if you're a poet who writes about nature, your daily interactions with people and objects are fair game for your writing and may provide a good way to loosen up those creative mental muscles.

Join or build a writing community. Many cities maintain one or more writing groups that welcome new members—see which writing groups exist in your state or region. If you already know fellow writers, you should make a point to start a regular correspondence or meeting with them. In her book *How to Read a Poem . . . and Start a Poetry Circle,* Molly Peacock recommends scheduling an annual retreat with fellow writers, if possible, and using that time to share work (both your own and that written by others you admire), recharge your creative batteries, and solicit constructive criticism.

Revise. Few poets other than William Stafford can get away with having their first draft of a piece be their last. Developing a revision process will help refine your work. This process can include soliciting criticism from other writers, as well as reading your work aloud. You may discover things you want to change about the sound or tone of the piece that you didn't notice when reading it silently, or you may find that the poem isn't quite as clear as you thought it was. Don't be afraid to completely rewrite a piece—just remember to save your former drafts in case you need to go back to them.

SUBMITTING POETRY

Where to start. As a librarian, you are already at an advantage over other folks who may be interested in getting their poetry published. You have easy access to a number of tools for submission. In addition to *Writer's Market* or *Poet's Market,* your research skills and expertise are easily applied to researching your own personal interests. The Internet is a great place to do research on which markets prefer formal poetry, which prefer free verse, and which publish cutting-edge experimental and cross-genre work. *Writer's Market* now has an online equivalent available on a subscription basis at www.writersmarket .com and other free listings are available online with a little bit of research.

Do your research. If you write nature poetry, a literary magazine specializing in fantasy or horror is not where you want to send your work. Save your postage for markets suited to your talents. While most publishers recommend subscribing to get a feel for what work they enjoy, don't be afraid to take advantage of your library connections and check literary magazines out of the library or obtain them from interlibrary loan. You can also check the publisher's website for work samples and ask fellow writers who know your work what publications they recommend.

Submitting. Many writers find it most effective to set a block of time aside about every two months and batch mail submissions, crafting their cover letters, printing submissions, and stuffing envelopes. Be certain to check the publisher's website to see how they prefer to receive submissions. Also keep a record of what work you send where—if one publisher accepts a poem, you will have to remove it from other editors' consideration. You'll also want to be sure not to break the rule of no simultaneous submissions that some publishers enforce.

THINK ABOUT YOUR TOOLBOX

As a librarian, you are in a unique position to take advantage of the technology tools you are likely using in your everyday work. Think about it.

RSS feeds. You can subscribe to your favorite creative writing blogs and publisher sites, and get the latest announcements on calls for submissions or themed collections. You'll be in the know before everyone else!

Wikis. The various free wikis available make it very easy for you to start your own writing group with creative friends across the globe. You can share contest listings, writing prompts, and even create a long-distance workshop arena where folks can upload files and provide comments and criticism on one another's work.

Spreadsheets. Whether you're using Google Docs, Microsoft Excel, or some open-source software, it's a good idea to maintain a record of your submissions where you record the publication you're submitting to, the editor's name (if you have it), the title of your submission, and the date you mailed it.

As a poet-librarian, you are in a unique position to take advantage of the research and organization skills at your disposal, as well as new technologies. Developing good habits for your writing and submission processes will result in more polished pieces and better placement for your work.

DIVERSITY SHOUT-OUTS!
Writing Articles about Diversity

VANDELLA BROWN

A *shout-out* is a term today that means expressing and sharing good news and information about almost anything a person wants to write. Usually a shout-out involves a person telling others about the great job a person has done. Getting shout-outs into the library community is crucial, and there are many ways writers can go about doing it. I started with finding a subject about some specific aspect of culture, heritage, race relations, or activity and wrote about them. Many people look for popular and best-selling periodicals and serials to publish in, but I don't. I think the best place to start is with local publications. My first articles dealing with diversity and multicultural issues were with my local library's newsletter. I wrote articles about cultural programs that were happening in the libraries of Memphis, Tennessee. From there, I moved to

writing a regular column in an African American weekly newspaper about multicultural and bilingual literature for children, and when I began to write Afrocentric titles for a college bulletin, I got plenty of practice describing events, absorbing culture, and sharing awareness.

There are major tasks in writing about diversity and multiculturalism; they are finding the topics, creating a voice, timing, supporting a theme, and locating the market.

The ongoing task is presenting the information and keeping the faith in telling readers what they need to know about the diversity niche you've carved out in your writings.

The cultural news media loves to learn and share news about other cultures. I've always focused on writing about four minority groups that libraries serve: African Americans, Asians, Hispanics, and European immigrants. I look for printed magazines and newspapers that serve those reading audiences and that have news by and about them. I find the periodicals to submit to in grocery stores, at diversity conferences, on newsstands, and by word of mouth from other writers or readers. I let others know about my writing interests. And like they say, it's always better to write or collect information about something you have an interest in. For me, those cultures have been a part of my library's reading and diversity experience.

Creating a voice to report and write about your topics requires time and planning. I think about how long an article needs to be. I diagram the keywords, do any necessary research, and begin to make the news item different from anything that someone else has written before me. I like using popular phrases from African American culture, like Ebonics, or from other cultures, to set the tone. To me such language is catchy and colorful, and the meaning is usually fun to translate. When I wrote the article "African-American Fiction: A Slamming Genre" for *American Libraries* (November 1997), I knew the professional magazine would be interested if it contained elements about the African American reading culture, what kinds of people read African American fiction, what libraries are doing, and what makes that genre so different.

When the United States proclaimed its first national holiday in honor of an African American, I wrote the article "Martin Luther King Jr. Day: How Do We Celebrate It?" which was published in the *BSA Journal* (January 1987). This is a newspaper read by students, and I submitted the story to the college newspaper as an alumna. The article reflected what the day really means, which states would observe it, the surprise of which states would not, and why Americans should keep King's dream alive.

Finding the right time to share articles on diversity and multiculturalism is important to be able to publish in any specific area. Timing your articles could be important especially if you are looking for print in major publications. Knowing that October is Diversity Month or that June is Gay and Lesbian Pride Month could cinch your article for publication. The same is true for historical anniversaries and commemorations. Planning and timing a cultural or heritage article is a great way to provide shout-outs about diversity to the reading community.

Sometimes shout-outs are not news stories; they are empowerment in print. One such writing theme I enjoyed was to put together activities for Black History Month with the library community. In 2004, I chaired a committee of library staff and representatives of various agencies serving diverse cultural groups that met in Springfield, Illinois, to celebrate a Black History theme. Finding the words to entice audiences to the event on only a 14-by-17-foot poster involved being descriptive and thinking about timing and my market. The poster was a piece of marketing, but then the local paper picked up a similar format of the poster to publicize the month-long events. The poster was billed as "Black History Events you will not want to miss." The poster has become so popular that, in 2008, the committee and I were asked to produce something similar for the Commemoration of the Springfield Race Riot of 1908.

The Internet has made it much easier to find places for publishing articles about diversity. The Internet provides spaces for creating blogs and news articles. Sites like MySpace, Facebook, and YouTube are places to publicize diversity topics, or you could create your own web page and topics. Even though I use the Internet, I still prefer to locate possibilities with *Writer's Digest*. I still visit the local library and university periodical shelves to look through periodicals in which I would like to publish or contribute a shout-out, in the interest of showing the periodical editor what more diversity has to offer to the audience. I also e-mail or talk with magazine editors about my topics on diversity. I usually e-mail or send a query letter to a periodical editor before submitting a completed article.

Writing short shout-outs can provide the "skinny" on what's great to read. My article "Multicultural Children's Books for Reading," for *B. Visible Magazine*, focused on learning about many cultures through children's folktales available on audio. The article focused on bilingual books written in Spanish, Vietnamese, Chinese, and West African languages.

Writing articles about diversity in libraries is a way to reflect, support, inform, and build confidence in the writing market and readers. There is so much to share about culture and heritage—shout it out!

PART IV
FINDING YOUR NICHE ONLINE

BLOGGING TIPS FOR LIBRARIANS

MICHAEL LORENZEN

One of the newer methods of communicating within the library profession is blogs. Although not as prestigious as traditional writing, personal blogs can allow an author to reach out and spread ideas. For example, Jessamyn West has used her blog (www.librarian.net) to become well known in the profession. Thousands of people read her daily. While these new methods may or may not be as respected as the traditional journal literature, people do access and read them. They can bring a librarian a larger audience than any manuscript published in a traditional source. The Open Directory Project (www.dmoz.org/Reference/Libraries/Library_and_Information_Science/Weblogs/) lists 299 reviewed library and information science blogs as of July 1, 2008. It is clear that the colleagues of bloggers in the library profession are reading their blogs.

Starting a blog is easy. Keeping one going long term is much harder. It takes dedication to write on a regular basis. Further, writing for a blog is a visible activity that employers, potential future employers, and coworkers can visit and see. Many writers find this nerve racking, which may hinder the potential of the blog. Also, understanding the different technological options can be a challenge.

WRITE WITH A PURPOSE

When starting a blog, make a decision about the topics you will write about. Although you may allow yourself to write on anything occasionally, your blog should have a consistent theme that is attractive to readers. You should endeavor to keep most of your posts at your blog on this topic. If your posts are on wildly diverse topics, it will be hard for you to keep a regular readership.

Make sure you post to your blog at least several times a week. It's easy to start a blog, and many new bloggers post a lot at first. However, over time, the blog posts become less and less frequent. Set a schedule for writing and keep to it. If your blog has stale content, you cannot expect readers to visit often. However, do not just post anything either. Poor-quality posts can alienate readers and harm your reputation. Have a plan for your blog and stick with it. This will allow for regular, quality posting that will build up readership.

One technique for frequent (and rather easy) blog writing is to share sites and news articles with your readership. Are there articles from news sources that relate to the theme of the blog? If so, link to these articles, quote from them, and add your own commentary. This way of writing keeps people up to date and allows the author to express his or her views. It is also easier than writing a post from scratch.

Whatever you do, avoid writing about the library where you work. Do not share gossip. Do not criticize coworkers, supervisors, subordinates, or patrons. Be careful about mentioning your library at all. Surfers searching for information on your place of employment may find your blog from a search engine. Even if you think your post is positive, will library administrators agree that your post is what they want potential patrons to be reading about the library? Also be careful about expressing your views on controversial topics. It may feel good to share your political views online, but do you want it to derail a chance at a future job? Many potential employers search the Web for a candidate's name, and they may decide not to interview someone with viewpoints that differ sharply from their own. If you want to be controversial, that is OK. However, be aware of the possible consequences.

TECHNOLOGY ISSUES

The look of your site is important. Visitors will notice the overall look before they even begin reading your posts. As such, be careful when you choose your layout. Most blogging platforms offer multiple free templates to choose from. Pick one that is easy on the eyes with a simple layout and only one or two primary colors. Feel free to make changes to the template to make it unique to you. If you choose to run advertisements on your blog (such as Google AdSense), do so tastefully and with minimal visual disruption for readers.

Also make sure to register a domain name. Most blogging platforms offer a default "free" web address. However, mygreatblog.net is much more professional than say mygreatblog.blogger.com or mygreatblog .wordpress.com. Owning your own domain name will allow you to set up e-mail with your domain name as well. Domain names can be purchased for less than ten dollars a year. Registering for multiple years is a good idea. Whatever you do, do not forget to keep your registration current or someone may steal your domain name from you! If you have a domain name, you will need to get a hosting service for your blog, which also may cost a few dollars a month. Blogger (one of the most popular blogging platforms) offers free hosting for domains and is a favorite choice of many blog authors for that reason.

Finally, be sure to allow comments at your blog. Many readers will be excited by your posts and will want to contribute their thoughts. Allowing them to comment lets your blog grow into a community. However, be sure to moderate your comments. This extra step will require you to approve all comments before they are published. This slows down your readers a bit, but if you are diligent, it will not slow the process down much. Moderating comments allows you to delete the frequent comment spam attacks that all successful bloggers receive. Many webmasters, in an attempt to get links from your blog, will spam your comments. They may even disguise the submissions to look like they relate to your posts. However, the intent is to trick Google and other search engines into thinking that you gave their site a link from your blog.

CONCLUSION

Writing a personal blog allows you to share your ideas with the library profession at large. Be sure to carefully consider your writing options and the technological options you choose for your blog. These simple actions will help make your blog successful.

BLOGGING
Writing Op-Eds

MICHAEL DUDLEY

As many librarians are aware, blogs are an exciting venue for reporting on, exploring, and discussing current issues in librarianship. While many bloggers adopt a diarylike format or a more matter-of-fact newsy approach, there is another somewhat more complex form of blogging to consider, and that is the online editorial.

Blogs are a particularly effective way to address controversies in libraries, or hot-button issues that are making news in the mass media. For example, the impact of the PATRIOT Act on libraries has been the subject of many librarians' blog postings.

In the case of such important issues, timeliness can be essential, particularly when political time lines (such as votes in Congress or city hall or during election seasons) are at stake. The lengthy publication cycles for professional and academic journals can therefore work against your ability to make meaningful and timely contributions to a given debate. A blog, by contrast, offers a venue for immediate and public commentary.

The immediacy of blogging also, of course, has its disadvantages: an article rapidly composed in response to a media report or event and posted right away will reflect the conditions only as you saw them at the time; as the days pass and more time is available for reflection, the issue or how it is perceived may have changed substantially, as with your own ideas. In such cases, haste can be a liability.

The good news, though, is that with reflection can come revision and the possibility of expanding on your blogging in other venues.

Such blogging, if it is timely and informed and offers useful insights, becomes in essence editorial writing. Because one's opinion pieces, once posted on a blog, can have an impressive reach, getting publicized on services such as LISNews (http://lisnews.org) and then being cited by other peoples' blogs, they can end up contributing significantly to contemporary discourse about the profession and library issues. From there, it is a short distance to more traditional publishing: other websites or publications can pick up one's posts in their entirety and reprint them as op-ed pieces.

In the case of the response on the blogosphere on the USA PATRIOT Act and its impact on libraries, general and widespread opposition on the part of civil liberties groups and members of the public was fueled significantly by the sharing of information by librarian bloggers. What framers of the act had surely considered a minor provision—the ability of the FBI to obtain library patrons' records—has become perhaps one of the best-known, offensive, and (for the U.S. federal government) embarrassing aspects of the homeland security project.

As this example demonstrates, advocating for library issues through op-ed pieces can also be a way to disseminate information and ideas to the general public that might otherwise not be able to read them if they were confined to specialist publications. In this instance, however, because librarians were so vocal and public about their concerns related to patron privacy and the role of libraries in a democracy, mainstream media picked up the story and made it widely known.

As essential as libraries are to democracies, not all library issues are of such national importance or so controversial in nature. Being community-oriented institutions, public libraries are most important to those who live near them, which is to say their patrons. Therefore, the local media can be a prime venue for your work.

Most city newspaper editors welcome unsolicited opinion pieces from informed community members, and articles about public library issues are always of interest to members of the public. Obtaining a space on the editorial page might be as easy as sending the editor an e-mail to get his or her attention. You might make a follow-up phone call to state in brief what your article will be about, and of course, to direct him or her to your blog for a preview—although be sure to stress that you are open to revising and editing your work to meet the newspaper's needs.

This is a key issue for the blogger seeking other publishing venues: given the variety of potential publishing outlets (both online and in print), it's important to consider your potential audience. You may have to address several audiences, and all on the same topic! You might need to temper and qualify assumptions underlying op-eds directed at your colleagues—particularly ideological ones—for a local newspaper. As well, topics or approaches you might take on your own library issues blog may not be fully appreciated (or understood) by the readers of a more general interest or political website. And of course, where you might have oriented blog postings to specialist colleagues, you may need to recraft those postings to explain or remove library jargon and acronyms.

Speaking to a general audience also means addressing those who are not at all sympathetic to your ideas. As passionate as you may be about intellectual freedom and the freedom to read, there will be many readers of a city's newspaper who will be just as passionate about keeping certain kinds of library materials away from young people. Such passion can be mitigated to an extent by calm rhetoric and appeals to reasonableness: don't exacerbate a politically tense situation for your library by using inflammatory language or painting ideological opponents as extremists.

Much of this need to match your work with the right audiences also depends on the nature of the topics you choose to write about. The local newspaper may be more than happy to run an op-ed about local library funding or the latest controversial library materials, but it may not be all that interested in your thoughts on library technologies or the changing roles of librarians.

Before you make a decision to republish your opinion pieces, consider your own purposes and how republishing will meet your own objectives. Do you want to attract new readers to your own blog or find a new audience entirely? Are you promoting yourself as a commentator or your blog? The reason for this distinction is that running your blog entries as op-eds in external publications and on other websites may get you a wide audience, but this may not translate into traffic for your blog. After all, having read your article (even if your blog is credited as the source), readers may not click through to your blog.

My own experience with this is worth noting: a piece I wrote for my blog *CityStates: Commentary on an Urban World* (Dudley 2008a) on the political implications of the Batman film *The Dark Knight* was picked up (and retitled) by the alternative press site AlterNet (Dudley 2008b); from there it was widely cited by other commentators, including in the *London Times* (Goodwin 2008). However, the results in terms of hits to my own blog were minimal.

Adapting blog posts to an op-ed format also requires considering the different mediums. Hypertext linking offers the blogger conceptual shortcuts, so that necessary context and background need only be referred to in a complete sentence through which a link may be embedded for further reading. In an op-ed, where such linking is not possible, this context may need to be included, albeit economically.

This leads to the most fundamental of considerations when writing blogs with op-ed potential: stylistic conventions. Blog entries can be as simple as a personal anecdote or a signpost to items of interest on the Web. An editorial, however, should adhere to standard conventions of good journalism: it should have a hook to catch the reader's attention followed by concise statements as to the topic and purpose of the article. The reader should not have to struggle to figure these things out and should have no doubt where you stand on the issue. Finally, the piece should have a proper conclusion that reiterates points made previously.

Blog postings constructed this way make compelling reading and are attractive to editors of newspapers, magazines and other websites. If you are seeking out nonspecialist venues for your work, however, you will need to persuade both editors and readers that you are sufficiently informed on contexts outside your professional domain.

Adapting professionally or institutionally oriented writing for nonspecialist audiences does pose some challenges in terms of crossing disciplines. Where library jargon must be explained, so, too, should librarian-authors familiarize themselves with the professional or theoretical contexts relevant to the topic at hand. For example, an op-ed considering the location of a new library branch or the redevelopment of a downtown library should be informed by current thinking in urban planning and design rather than simply reflecting the concerns of the library board. This can mean not just extensive advance reading but also interviewing informed stakeholders.

Specialist librarians working in discipline-specific settings may find themselves writing for colleagues in several different fields. Blog postings or op-eds prepared for one set of colleagues can then sometimes be repurposed for another.

I have extensive experience in this regard. With a professional background in both librarianship and city planning, I have blogged on library, urban, and cultural issues for institutional blogs, and I appear as a regular blogger for the Planetizen urban planning website (www.planetizen.com/blog/29/). I have reformatted and submitted several of the postings I have prepared for these blogs to local and international newspapers, or they have run on external websites, notably AlterNet.

One of the primary lessons that I have learned from online publishing is that opining online is not a monologue but a conversation. One shouldn't be apprehensive about receiving online comments on your postings as they oftentimes will stimulate your own thinking on the topic. And of course, the more contentious the topic, the more likely the posting is to draw commentators and even unsolicited e-mail. In the latter case, if the letters are thoughtful and respond to the issue in a constructive fashion, I sometimes respond to the correspondents and ask if I can reprint their e-mail as blog entries.

Another thing to be prepared for is to be drawn in as a political actor on behalf of the issues about which you write. Local citizens concerned about their libraries may telephone and ask you to participate in citizens' groups or to speak to such. You may be called on by local media to speak on the issue for radio, television, or in the newspaper.

The act of writing blog postings of commentary and opinion or more commonly editorials is at its heart about being a shaper of opinions. You are attempting to persuade readers to consider perspectives that may be new to them, to communicate to policy makers that the course of action they are on is a mistake, to inform the public about conditions they may not have heard anything about. It is a serious responsibility and, depending on how successful you are with your rhetoric, can have positive or negative ramifications for your library, your community, and your own career as a librarian or a writer.

The key rhetorical position to bear in mind when considering this sort of publishing is reflexivity, that is, how you reflect on your role as a librarian in society and the role of the library as an institution embedded in society. Rather than sitting apart from social, political, economic, and cultural processes, the librarian-author is as much a part of those processes as the issues you write about. Therefore, the stance you take cannot be wholly objective but is rather that of a participant.

REFERENCES

Dudley, Michael. 2008a. "Batman and the 'End of 9/11': Overcoming America's Dark Night in Gotham City." *CityStates,* July 21. http://citystates.typepad.com/ius/2008/07/batman-and-amer.html.

———. 2008b. "Batman's Take on 9/11 Era Politics? Drop the Fearmongering." Alternet.org, July 25. www.alternet.org/movies/92385/batman%27s_take_on_9_11_era_politics_drop_the_fearmongering/?page=entire.

Goodwin, Christopher. 2008. "How Batman Became Cinema's Top Trump." *London Times,* August 17. http://entertainment.timesonline.co.uk/tol/arts_and_entertainment/film/article4524352.ece.

LIBRARIANS AS PERSONAL BLOGGERS

NICOLE C. ENGARD

When I changed my undergraduate path from creative writing to computer programming, little did I know that I would be a published librarian one day. Having never gotten the hang of creating realistic fictional characters, I turned instead to writing computer code and left the imaginary worlds behind. It wasn't until 2005, when I started my first blog, that I became a writer again.

BECOMING A LIBRARIAN BLOGGER

These days it takes only a love for sharing information and a little bit of time to become a member of what has been dubbed the "biblioblogosphere." The biblioblogosphere is made up of librarians, library lovers, and book fanatics who all write about their passion for the benefit of themselves and others like them.

To join the club, you just need a title for your blog and the desire to share information with your fellow bibliophiles.

In my case, I decided to stop sending e-mail to everyone I knew every time I found a new tool online and instead write regularly at *What I Learned Today* . . . (http://web2learning.net). My blog became a way for me to share my passion with others like me and to connect with other librarians across the world.

In three steps, you can be ready to share your passions with a worldwide audience as well.

1. Pick the title. The first thing you need to do is pick a name for your blog. This name can be as simple as using your name, like *David Lee King* (www.davidleeking.com), or something anonymous and catchy like *The Annoyed Librarian* (http://annoyedlibrarian.blogspot.com), or even something that explains what you will write about, like *What I Learned Today* . . . (http://web2learning.net). There are no set rules; you get to make your own!

2. Pick the platform. Before you can start writing, you have to pick the platform you want to run your blog on. With so many choices available for free or nominal costs, picking the right tool can be overwhelming. I'm a strong believer in kicking the tires

before making a commitment. Try some of the free and hosted options and decide which features you like and which you do not like. Once you have come up with a list of criteria, it will be easier to make your final decision. Some popular choices include

- Wordpress: http://wordpress.com or http://wordpress.org
- Blogger: http://blogger.com
- Typepad: http://typepad.com
- Moveable Type: http://moveabletype.org

3. Commit to the content. Just like any publishing endeavor, you must commit to write for your blog. There is no rule about how often you should write, but your readers will look for regular content on your site. It is best to set aside time at least once a week to write something for your blog. For some people, a set schedule helps them stay on track with their writing; others just write when they find something interesting to share. Whatever your style, it is important to keep the content coming so that visitors to your site always have something new to read.

WHAT SHOULD I WRITE ABOUT?

When coming up with inspiration for what to write on your blog, the possibilities are endless. I have seen librarians blog about libraries, gaming, technology, family travels, and what they ate today. Just like your readers expect consistency in your posting schedule, they will expect some sort of consistency in the topics you write about.

You will find that blogging as a publishing platform lends itself more to shorter articles with links to additional resources. Most people do not like to read full-length articles on a computer screen and may not read your blog regularly if your posts are consistently long. This is not to say that you should keep all of your posts short and sweet, just that you should find a good balance in post length.

Writing about your profession is usually the easiest for most of us because there is always something new that we are learning or experiencing on the job. If you are not interested in blogging solely for professional reasons, you will find that the library world is very open to colleagues who share stories of a personal nature. Writing online brings you in touch with people from all over the world who have had similar life experiences and can help you through tough times better than you might expect.

WHY BLOGGING?

Even today there are some who will say that blogging does not count as "real" publishing, but at a time when print journals are going online and digital publications are becoming the standard, blogs are a great way to get your colleagues to read your content. Blogs are also a more immediate way to get your research published. This is very important when you work in a field that is changing by the minute.

Keeping a blog with regularly updated content is also a great way to show your writing ability to potential publishers or employers. Putting your content in the public eye and maintaining a consistent audience will show that you can be responsible for writing on a large scale and keeping up with deadlines. Most important, it will also show your writing style and range.

CONCLUSION

For me, blogging has become both a great way to force myself to keep up with the profession and an amazing outlet for sharing my experiences. While my content is mostly about technology in libraries, I have occasionally thrown in a personal post or two and have gotten great feedback from the worldwide librarian community.

The most important thing to remember when starting your own blog is that it is supposed to be something fun for you. If you find yourself stressing about writing on your blog, maybe it is not the best publishing medium for you.

If you decide that you like writing for a diverse audience on a regular basis, just remember that you get to make the rules. You set your own writing schedule and content guidelines. Write for yourself and you will find that others want to hear what you have to say.

TEN REASONS TO PUBLISH AN ONLINE COLUMN

RUTH PENNINGTON PAGET

When I worked for accounting and consulting firms in Chicago and Paris, I learned how those firms used writing articles and books to establish their professional expertise in the business world. Businesses would come to these firms seeking proposals for audits and consulting in part because of the professional stature of the firms that staff publications created. Librarians can use this same technique of using the written word to create expertise as a means of currying public support for our organizations through online columns.

The following reasons for writing online columns figure among those that I have gleaned from my experience in writing the "Global Librarian" column during two years for the *Bayline* newsletter of the San Francisco Bay Area chapter of the Special Libraries Association.

1. LANDING AN ONLINE COLUMN IS EASIER THAN LANDING A PRINT ONE

If you have expertise in an area but have not published before, an online outlet may be ideal for you. It helps to query and then give editors two or three columns so that they can immediately place them on a publishing schedule. Standards are not lower on the Web, but cost and space limitations are much lower than in print, which makes it easier to add columnists. The secret is to remember to write for the reader's benefit and not your self-glorification.

One trend that I have noticed recently in my local paper is that it runs online columns as what appears to be a trial to gauge readership. The newspaper can see how the public responds to online columnists before giving them a column in the print newspaper this way. The online column promotes interaction with the paper as well when readers comment on the articles online.

2. CREATING A BUSINESS CARD WITH BRIO

An online column establishes expertise and provides a ready source of downloadable public relations material. For example, if you do presentations at your local chamber of commerce, you could staple your business card to printouts of your column and distribute them. Not only would attendees have your information, but also it would be easier for them to make personal recommendations to others about your library's services if they have something to share with their colleagues.

3. STAYING ABREAST OF NEW TRENDS

Writing a column will prompt you to stay current in your field of expertise. Your search for column ideas will cause this, and sometimes your readers or your editor will present you with ideas to write about.

4. KEEPING YOUR MESSAGE IN THE PUBLIC EYE LONGER

Print newspaper articles appear online in full text for about one to two weeks. After that, they show up in search engines in a newspaper's archives with only one or two sentences describing the content; for full text, you generally have to pay for the article.

Online newsletter columns generally appear in search engines as full-text versions. Having expertise-laden articles available to the public free of charge could make the difference in obtaining an article in the newspaper or a television spot when the media is researching a topic, getting the public to vote on a library bond, or encouraging donors to fund programs at your library.

5. USING ONLINE COLUMNS AS A NETWORKING TOOL

As a column writer, you have a perfect forum for interviewing movers and shakers in and out of the library world. If you cannot physically go to a different part of the country, try a telephone interview or even an e-mail interview.

6. WRITING OUTSIDE THE LIBRARY FIELD

Other librarians know how our field works and how vital it is. To expand that knowledge to other audiences, librarians must be present in other venues. The sampling of areas here shows how librarians can create a presence in fields outside of library science:

- helping a small business with marketing research in a chamber of commerce newsletter
- providing health and wellness information resources in a gym's newsletter
- contributing to student success in a school online newsletter
- discussing sources for funding for a nonprofit's newsletter
- describing how to do genealogical research at the library in a genealogy newsletter
- providing reading readiness tips to a day-care association's newsletter
- sharing literacy skills information with an adult school newsletter

7. HONING YOUR WRITING SKILLS

Practice and a skillful editor's techniques will make the blank page or blank screen hold no qualms for you. If you need a creative budge, Twyla Tharp's *The Creative Habit* may be what you need.

8. PROMOTING YOUR LIBRARY'S BENEFITS TO THE PUBLIC

Collect your online columns, print them out, and put them in a binder for the public and visitors to peruse at your library. This collection informs the public and would, in the ideal case, encourage them to make personal recommendations about how your library benefits the public to other patrons, the media, politicians, and foundations.

9. PROMOTING EMPLOYEE KNOWLEDGE

Not only do online columnists learn from their writing, but the entire staff can benefit from reading these columns as well. Placing hyperlinks with article annotations on library intranets provides staff with access to the latest trends and norms in the profession.

10. SETTING THE AGENDA

The best benefit of writing an online column is that you can create topics of discussion among audiences that may have never been aware that a library does more than lend books. Instead of waiting for others to recognize and write about the contributions of libraries to the economy, education, and community, librarians can spread that message themselves with online columns in the right venues.

WRITING FOR LIBRARY WEBSITES

BETH M. SHEPPARD

EASE ON DOWN THE ROAD

A great web page, like an effective highway billboard, conveys information quickly and precisely. Billboard content is driven by practicality. A traveler speeding down an interstate cannot read a full paragraph of small print. By the same token, an ad that is too simple is obscure. One races by and wonders, "What was that sign about?" Web pages, the billboards of the information superhighway, must also be comprehensible and concise.

WHAT ABOUT TEXT?

Content that includes written text is essential to most library websites. Creating prose for the screen, however, is not as easy as it seems. Andrew Dillon (1994, 3) once remarked, "It is clear that simply transferring paper formats to the electronic medium is insufficient and often detrimental to use."

Luckily, in the fourteen years since Dillon penned these words, several basic precepts have emerged for the effective presentation of text on the Web. They involve the triad of format, organization, and substance.

EASY ON THE EYES: FORMAT BASICS

The Web allows myriad choices for presenting text. Still, not every selection is wise. Some decisions may actually slow down the reader. A few rules, though, will help you keep on course.

Contrast. Make certain that your text stands out from the background. A dark backdrop requires a very light text shade of text or one of a complementary but distinct color. Also, avoid red and green combinations, which are associated with colorblindness. Indeed, an estimated 8 percent of the male population has this vision deficiency (Muter 1996), so sensitivity to color is vital.

Fonts. The selected font must be easy to read. Think about it. How many sites have you seen with script or loopy typefaces? Crisp typefaces like Calibri, Arial, or Verdana make it easy to scan text. Frank Thissen (2004) also recommends Coinn, Georgia, Myriad, and Minion for their clear shapes. That is not to say that elaborate fonts should never be used. Certainly a designer may wish to match a specialty font with specific content. But design effects must be balanced with readability.

Justification. Paragraphs in which only the lines on the left side are aligned are the easiest to read. Centered text and right-justified text should be used sparingly, if at all. Text that is fully justified (both sides aligned) is the most difficult to read, because spaces in the middle of the line are awkwardly stretched and compressed.

Line length. Shorter lines are better. The average line should contain eight to ten words (Grabinger and Osman-Jouchoux, 1996).

ROAD SIGNS POINT THE WAY: ORGANIZATIONAL ELEMENTS

Some studies show that reading from the big bulky cathode-ray tube monitors that still linger in many libraries is 28 percent slower than reading from paper (Muter 1996). This means that web authors must help readers. A variety of markers facilitate comprehension of text.

Paragraphs. Paragraphs should be shorter than they would be on paper. In addition, more space between paragraphs makes blocks of text appear as distinct units.

Bolded keywords. To aid with scanning, a few essential words might be rendered in bold, though avoid the colors used for hyperlinks!

Bullets, lists, numbering, headings. Short headings, bullets, and numbering make content easier to absorb at a glance. These devices are particularly useful for lengthy texts.

HAVE SOMETHING TO SAY: SUBSTANCE MATTERS

On the Web, many sites compete for a reader's attention. Despite this there are ways to make the most of the medium and create appealing text.

Simplify. Word choice and sentence structure should be trouble free. Complex sentences, ponderous vocabulary, and parenthetical remarks should be eliminated wherever possible.

Shorten. Steve Krug (2006) puts it best. Most words on websites just take up space. Krug advises eliminating superfluous instructions and greetings. He even recommends ruthlessly cutting out half the words on a given web page.

Avoid scrolling. Humans like to take life easy. They don't want to chase down information. The wise web author thus puts the most important ideas at the top of the page. That way they might be read before the reader wanders away. Along these same lines, long text blocks that extend beneath the visible screen area and require scrolling should be avoided. Don't rely on the reader to do the work!

Don't forget the obvious. Sometimes those who write web text are too familiar with the library they are promoting and neglect vital pieces of information. The name of a library, for instance, doesn't necessarily convey what type of library it is or what sort of services it offers. Phone numbers are essential, yet sadly often forgotten. Julie M. Still provides additional guidelines for content in her book *The Accidental Webmaster* (2003), as do Susanna Davidsen and Everyl Yankee in their text *Web Site Design with the Patron in Mind* (2004).

Change often. Regularly adding fresh content encourages repeat visitors. Don't let announcements about book sales, holiday hours, and the summer reading program linger for more than one business day after the event has taken place.

Keep it legal. Library websites should model the ethical use of information. Follow copyright guidelines and add appropriate attributions, if any.

READY TO ROLL

With the text written, take it for a test drive. Feedback from actual users will let you know if you are on track. If a few patrons who represent your target readers have no difficulty with the text, then you are ready to roll!

REFERENCES

Davidsen, Susanna, and Everyl Yankee. 2004. *Web Site Design with the Patron in Mind: A Step-by-Step Guide for Libraries.* Chicago: American Library Association.

Dillon, Andrew. 1994. *Designing Usable Electronic Text: Ergonomic Aspects of Human Information Usage.* London: Taylor and Francis.

Grabinger, R. Scott, and Rionda Osman-Jouchoux. 1996. "Designing Screens for Learning." In *Cognitive Aspects of Electronic Text Processing,* ed. Herre van Oostendorp and Sjaak de Mul, 181–212. Norwood, NJ: Ablex.

Krug, Steve. 2006. *Don't Make Me Think! A Common Sense Approach to Web Usability,* 2nd ed. Berkeley, CA: New Riders.

Muter, Paul. 1996. "Interface Design and Optimization of Reading of Continuous Text." In *Cognitive Aspects of Electronic Text Processing,* ed. Herre van Oostendorp and Sjaak de Mul, 161–180. Norwood, NJ: Ablex.

Still, Julie M. 2003. *The Accidental Webmaster.* Medford, NJ: Information Today.

Thissen, Frank. 2004. *Screen Design Manual: Communicating Effectively through Multimedia.* New York: Springer.

CONFESSIONS OF AN AMAZON.COM REVIEWER

CORINNE H. SMITH

My name is Corinne, and I'm a reviewaholic. I can't stop writing about books.

I can trace my addiction to the early 1990s, when I was the reference coordinator for a university media department. I answered the call to write reviews for a new publication, *The Video Rating Guide for Libraries.* The process was exhilarating. Free videos showed up, and all I had to do was watch them and write about them. I summarized, analyzed, and described the most appropriate audience for each piece. A few months later when the next issue arrived in the office, I could see my remarks and my byline in print. What fun!

When I subsequently relocated and found work in a high school library, I also sought an outlet for more review writing. I signed up with *The Book Report,* a magazine designed for school librarians. Several times a year, a box of books appeared on my doorstep. My assignment was to outline the essence of each one in fewer than 350 words. No problem. I knew the routine. And in the end, I could donate the best of those review copies to our own library.

Then one day during a districtwide meeting, a fellow librarian raved about a wonderful new online book jobber she had discovered: Amazon.com. We oohed and aahed as she chatted about ordering books, paying for them with a credit card, and getting the books within days. Our minds reeled with the possibilities. The World Wide Web was just coming into its own, and no other company was offering such a service at the time. "People can post book reviews on the website, too," she said.

My ears perked up. *The Video Rating Guide* had folded after five years of operation, and I was experiencing reviewer withdrawal. Perhaps my next opportunity lay on the Internet. I looked at the site and was disappointed. Very few visitors had donated reviews. I posted a handful for the best books I had recently read, just to say I had taken a stab at it. After all, I was still getting regular deliveries from *The Book Report.*

Something changed around the turn of the century. Amazon seemed to be always in the news and at the forefront of web activity, led by quirky but business-savvy Jeff Bezos. We librarians began searching for titles on Amazon instead of in *Books in Print,* which was too expensive for many of us to buy. We bookmarked Amazon on our circulation and reference desk computers. It was gradually becoming an invaluable resource.

When Larry McMurtry of *Lonesome Dove* fame released a thin nonfiction volume called *Roads: Driving America's Great Highways,* I thought it might be a good book to review online. I myself was a lover of long-distance travel. I got a copy, read it, and quickly crafted and posted one paragraph of commentary. I clicked the Submit button and didn't give the description another thought.

But the next time I landed on my Amazon profile, I saw that my ranking had improved significantly. What was going on? You see, Amazon.com ended (and still ends) each posting with the question: "Was this review helpful to you?" Anyone can click and vote Yes or No, except for the reviewer him- or herself. Evidently dozens of visitors found my *Roads* rumination good enough to hit the Yes button. My magic number improved as a result. We had no name for this phenomenon back then, but we can recognize it now as an early version of Web 2.0. Anyone could post, and anyone could provide feedback. This was an illustration of the power of the Internet.

I watched my position rise with each Yes vote my words received—climbing from the No. 30,000 range to around No. 12,000—and something stirred in me. I was an only child who craved external validation. Now I could get it merely by writing a few sentences and sharing them with the world. I was hooked. Amazon.com was my enabler.

I scoured my bookshelves at home. One at a time, I checked each title for an Amazon review. Those that had none were fair game for me. I bought star stickers to mark the spines of every book I wrote about, so that I could check the status of my personal collection with a quick glance. My preoccupation with Henry David Thoreau exploded into a full-blown obsession. I felt the need to analyze every book about Thoreau that I could get my hands on. I soon learned that while adding descriptions of older books improved their online appearance, that approach was not the best way to acquire new votes. A few transcendentalist fans appreciated my work, but the general public didn't see those critiques that I had labored so long over.

The trick, then, was to evaluate potential best sellers. Surely those listings would attract the most hits. That's when being a librarian came in quite handy. By then I was working in a public library, where we were in the business of providing the newest and the best for our patrons. I sliced open Baker and Taylor boxes with glee, rejoicing in the fragrance of printer's ink on tidy wood-pulp sheets, even while I examined the contents for potential review material. Sue Grafton mysteries and John Grisham nonlegals were my favorites. I read them overnight before we put them out on the new release shelves. My goal was to beat to the punch the No. 1 Amazon.com reviewer, the speed reader and former librarian Harriet Klausner. Sometimes I succeeded; often, I did not. But posting the first review did not guarantee getting the most votes, either.

My online opinions followed the format I was required to produce for the print journals. From the start, I wanted my postings to be more than trite ether fluff. Ideally, the review would begin with a summary of the book (without giving away the plot if it was fiction) and end with a note about the target audience. Several paragraphs would suffice. I grew to love this self-inflicted composition challenge. After all, I was voluntarily providing readers' advisory on a global scale. But I sometimes questioned my motives. Was I doing it for the readers or to see my own name and words on the screen? I wasn't sure. Were my online reviews any less professional than my printed ones? The jury was out on that one. Could I admit in public that I wrote reviews for Amazon.com? Or was that confession tantamount to boasting that one's avatar was well known on Ever-Quest?

Nevertheless, in January 2007, I reached Top 1000 Reviewer status on Amazon.com. A special moniker appeared beneath my byline. That's when the tables turned. I became a marketing commodity. Now publishers, publicists, and authors contacted me, flooding my in-box with solicitations. "We've noticed that you've read X," the messages began. "Perhaps you would like to read Y as well. We'd love to send you a review copy." It was flattering to receive such transmissions, for they often praised my previous work. How nice! To some of them I gave the nod; to most, I said no. I barely had enough time to devour books of my own choosing.

I managed to post an average of one review per week, and I edged a bit higher in the Amazon ranks. I received e-mail from fellow readers who agreed or disagreed with my assessments. I received e-mail from authors who thanked me for my kind words, if I offered them. At book signings, I began to quietly explain to authors that I had reviewed their titles on Amazon. Some acknowledged me politely. One novelist replied, "Oh, I don't read reviews." But when I introduced myself to John Matteson, who was then promoting *Eden's Outcasts: The Story of Louisa May Alcott and Her Father,* he stood up and hugged me. He had read my review and had welcomed it, as he hadn't gotten much positive press to that date. We chatted at length and exchanged e-mail addresses. Later, we conversed online only once or twice. I expected no more from an author-critic relationship.

Soon enough, I found myself overwhelmed by reviewing assignments, which included ten music CDs for Rambles.net and a stack of reference books from *Library Media Connection,* the successor to *Book Report.* I was forced to take stock of my writing life. I met all of my deadlines, but I knew I had to make a choice. I resigned from all print periodical obligations. The Internet owned me and my keyboard.

On April 12, 2008, from out of the blue, I got a message from John Matteson. "Dear Corinne: You have probably heard by now that *Eden's Outcasts* was honored this week with the Pulitzer Prize for Biography. The award has made me all the more appreciative of people who saw merit in the book before these late events. I just wanted to write and thank you for your marvelous encouragement at a time when it was most needed." I was stunned. I felt myself shaking, and I felt tears coming. Of course John and his book deserved the Pulitzer. But he need not thank me. I was only a rah-rah girl on the publishing sidelines. Validation? I now had more than I could have ever wished for. I was both proud and humbled. Surely I would never come closer to that international honor myself. Suddenly this act of writing and posting reviews was no longer a game, no longer a meaningless, annoying personal habit. The world could and did read my paragraphs. Had a Pulitzer judge seen my words? I shuddered.

Late in 2008, the Amazon.com execs changed their metric of ranking reviewers. Quality was now rewarded over quantity. The new algorithm included the percentage of Yes votes over No votes. Because I had an approval rating of 91 percent, my rank flew from No. 796 up to No. 266. At the same time, No. 1 Harriet plummeted to No. 445. I had finally beaten her; but it had taken a rule change to do so. It was enough. I was satisfied.

Even though I'm now writing a book of my own, I still try to submit a review each week to Amazon.com. After all, I have an online reputation and that Top 500 Reviewer status to maintain!

PROMOTING BUT PROTECTING YOURSELF ONLINE

CORINNE H. SMITH

It's a fine line to tread: you want to publicize your work without risking your personal safety at the same time. Here are some tips for keeping your online approach sensible, professional, and secure.

1. At least once every three months, examine each instance of your Internet presence. Look at your own website; your listing on the site of an employer, publisher, and/or publicist; and any background bios you have posted on blogs or social networking pages. Is the information accurate and consistent each time? Does it promote you and your work in the best possible light? Will a visitor recognize you as the same individual in each place?

2. Remember that your original writings are considered published once they are posted online. Give each piece its own web page. Release your inner cataloger! Add metadata tags that reinforce your authorship and guarantee that searchers will land on your work. For each page, you or your webmaster should embed a blue-bar browser title containing the composition title and your full name, a variety of keywords drawn from your subject matter, and a 150-character description summarizing your writing. The latter will show up beneath your link on any search engine results list.

3. Protect your e-mail address from most spammers by not hot-linking it. Consider embedding the information into a graphic or spelling out each element on the screen (e.g., "name at domain dot com"). If you prefer, ask visitors to complete an online form to contact you.

4. Protect your exact location by refraining from posting your street address online. Saying that you live in southern California or along the coast of Maine may be enough. If you need to offer a surface mail contact, consider using a post office box or the address of an employer, publisher, or publicist (if appropriate).

5. Protect yourself from possible identity theft by not mentioning your mother's maiden name in any biographical sketch. If you have school-age children, you might consider keeping them anonymous as well.

On the brighter side: relish the networking framework that the Internet offers. You will gain more leads and contacts than you may have thought possible.

TURNING *SEQUELS* INTO A DATABASE

JANET HUSBAND

HARDCOVER SUCCESS

Sequels: An Annotated Guide to Novels in Series was a surprising success. It was among the top sellers of the American Library Association's 1982–83 list. A second edition was published in 1990 with the help of my newly recruited coauthor, a skilled reference librarian and a relentless worker who just happens to be my husband, Jonathan. Together we learned how to use our new Apple II computer to compose and store text. The third edition in 1997 was much easier to update.

But by 2002, it was clear that the Internet had taken over the world and I began to worry about the future of *Sequels.* Surely print reference tools would soon be archaic. And though our now fairly sophisticated computer skills made updating and revising the work easier, it had grown to a rather intimidating size over the years. What had started as 362 one-column pages had become 598 two-column pages plus an extensive subject index.

WEB MASTERY

A quick look at the *Boston Yellow Pages* assured me that there was no lack of website developers in my neck of the woods. I narrowed down the field by checking websites and requesting brochures, and finally I talked to a few sales representatives from companies that I thought might be interested in my small project.

After visiting and interviewing several companies and getting estimates, we settled on a small company west of Boston. Their nineteen-page proposal was very detailed, listing the industry standards they would meet, such as

- Markup specifications based on the latest HTML and CSS2 guides

- Compatibility with the latest Netscape and Internet Explorer browsers

- Load time of less than twelve seconds on a 56K modem

- Screen resolution of 800 by 600 pixels

The proposal also specified the programs they would use: Dreamweaver, MS-SQL, and Adobe Photoshop, among others. I showed these technical pages to everyone I knew who had a smattering of website knowledge and I was reassured by their positive responses.

Judging the functionality of the proposed program was trickier. Home page, order page, log-in page—these seemed fairly straightforward. We asked to have a scope page and a sample page added. During our interview with the sales and programming team, we had described in detail the search capabilities we wanted. I was impressed that the proposal reflected our needs with reasonable accuracy: they had actually understood what we were talking about. Yes, we would be able to search by author, title, character, subject, or keyword.

After meeting once again with our team of programmers to modify and clarify, we signed a contract for $11,500. In six weeks, we would have our software.

PROGRESS

Well, of course, it was not quite that easy, and it took a lot longer than six weeks. But the process was new and exciting and fun. Naming our product was no problem this time; *eSequels* seemed the obvious choice. I searched the Web; no one else was using it.

My guidelines for writing the brief text for each web page were avoid jargon, be succinct, and make the reader want to subscribe. The real work of writing, editing, and entering the authors, titles, and annotations into the database would be done after the design stage. We knew that would be a long and laborious process.

I hated the first graphic proposed by the designers—a very uninspired photo of a girl reading. I wanted something distinctive, and I found the perfect work in Winslow Homer's 1877 watercolor *The New Novel,* which shows a young woman engrossed in reading. I thought it would give the website a classic look. I wrote to the owner of the work, the Springfield Art Museum, and the museum very kindly gave me permission to reproduce the painting as long as I gave them proper credit. They sent me a jpeg image that I forwarded to the designer.

Having this key feature simplified the rest of the design work. Background color, font types, and button style were chosen to coordinate with Winslow Homer's artwork. Each web page took shape on a test site that I could watch being created. The programmers and I decided on each element together.

PROBLEMS

Naturally, along the way misunderstandings developed. For instance, the programmers initially allowed us twenty titles per author and were amazed when we told them that some of our series would run to forty titles or more—series by John Creasey, Erle Stanley Gardner, and Ed McBain, to name just a few. They were equally surprised to learn that Agatha Christie created five detectives—Poirot, Miss Marple, Ariadne Oliver, Tommy and Tuppence, and Superintendent Battle. But they cheerfully devised ways to handle very lengthy series and five different series under one author, although Roman numerals caused them considerable trouble.

The one thing that stumped them was the librarian's practice of ignoring the initial article of a book title: *A, An,* or *The.* Type "Big Sky" into any auto-mated library network, and the search results will display as *The Big Sky.* What seemed obvious and simple to us was baffling to them. Eventually, we settled on placing the article after a comma at the end of a title.

When we were satisfied with the design and functionality of our site—in just more than four months—the developer recommended a web hosting company that could register our domain name, put us online, and keep us reliably online for about $600 per year. We took the developer's advice, signed up, and watched our site go live.

PHASE 2

The next phase would be to fill up the database with the information from the print edition; revising and updating entries; and researching, writing, and entering data for all the new series created since the last edition of *Sequels.* This has become our avocation in retirement.

In April 2008, we began marketing www.eSe quels.com with a direct mailing to six thousand public libraries and advertising in *Library Journal.* Our subscriber list is growing every day. And every day we add new authors and titles to keep *eSequels* up to date.

PART V
MAXIMIZING OPPORTUNITIES

WRITING FOR PUBLICATION AS A STATE OF MIND

DIANE STINE

Two years after receiving my MLS, I interviewed at an academic library for a position as a serials cataloger. At that institution, librarians enjoyed faculty status. For retention and tenure, it was necessary to be involved in professional activities and to have some publications.

One of the people I met on my interview was an assistant university librarian. She explained to me that a librarian's rank was not tied to her position. She was a full professor, not because she had such a high-level job in the organization but because "she had a list of publications as long as her arm." This image was etched into my mind's eye and when I was hired there, it was my goal to emulate her.

I immediately began to think about publishing and soon realized that the first important step in writing for publication is to have a topic you really care about. Also, if you can talk about a subject, you can write about it. Fortunately for me, AACR2 came out just about this time. The cataloging world was buzzing with rumors about what changes these new rules would bring about.

Well, the rules finally reached our hands. As I perused the rules for serials in microform, something I had two years of experience cataloging, I saw that the rule for description of the publication area stated that the information to be provided would be for the place of publication, publisher, and publishing dates of the microform, not the original serial.

I was outraged. How could a journal or newspaper with a nonunique title (which describes most of them) be identified if the publisher statement said: Ann Arbor, Michigan: University Microfilms. I harnessed this energy and began to write my first article, "The Cataloging of Serials in Microform under AACR2 Rules," which was published in *Serials Librarian.*

This is when I realized another important point in setting your mind to writing for publication. Every time I had to document procedures for staff working with me or write a report, I thought about what I could add or change to make my written document a publishable text.

In 1991, I was working as a cataloger at another academic institution when OCLC issued new procedures for cataloging using its utility. The documentation was quite cumbersome. To learn the new procedures myself, and make them understandable to clerical staff, my supervisor and I began to rewrite the documentation in more simplified language. We ended up with two volumes that were published by the Illinois State Library and used in their workshops to train libraries using this new system (*Searching PRISM* and *Editing on PRISM,* with Georgine Brabec).

Once you are tuned into writing for publication, you notice opportunities everywhere. At the academic library where I was the selector for materials for the Russian department, the professors asked me to purchase *The Modern Encyclopedia of East Slavic, Baltic and Eurasian Literatures* for our library. When I was ordering it, I learned that the publishers were looking for people to write articles for upcoming volumes. I immediately volunteered and was assigned to write entries on two Russian art magazines.

Soon after this, I saw a notice of a Slavic institute at the University of Illinois at Urbana-Champaign where scholars could come and use their library, which was one of the few that held issues of these journals. In addition, the library had many resources for background information for my research. I applied to attend the institute and was accepted. At the time I was living in New Mexico.

Fortunately for me, my university had a committee that granted funds to defray travel costs for scholarly pursuits, so I applied for a grant. Wow, three items for my tenure portfolio: acceptance into the institute, receipt of a travel grant, and two published encyclopedia entries.

There's no doubt that once you are in the writing-for-publication frame of mind, each activity leads to another connection, which can lead to another publication. When I was cataloging textbooks, I was annoyed at the plethora of duplicate records in OCLC. Because textbooks come with many accompanying materials, libraries tended to catalog whichever pieces they owned. If a library owned the teacher's edition and a workbook, that is what was in the cataloging record. If a library had a student edition with some maps, it cataloged those pieces.

At this time, I was cataloging a lot of filmstrip sets. The rules for these ancient relics stated that the film reels were the main item and the cassettes, booklets, study guides, and so on, were all listed in accompanying material and a contents note.

I thought, why not catalog textbooks the same way. Following my rule that if I cared about a subject I would write about it, I wrote another article, "Suggested Standards for Cataloging Textbooks" published in *Cataloging and Classification Quarterly*.

Some members of the American Library Association, Association for Library Collections and Technical Services, Cataloging of Children's Material Committee saw my article and asked me to serve on the committee, which I did from 1993 to 1998, as chair from 1995 to 1998. This committee has published several editions of a book titled *Cataloging Correctly for Kids*. While serving on the committee, we were working on the third edition and I wrote one of the chapters, "Automating the Children's Catalog," once again reinforcing my point that writing for publication and professional activities lead to more of the same.

Another time I was on an Illinois Library Association committee, which had the task of editing the June 1985 issue of *Illinois Libraries*. Again, my committee assignment led to publication. I contributed to the issue with an article on the adequacy of library education for serials librarianship.

Working with others on an article or book is yet another way of getting into the writing-for-publication frame of mind. Besides committee members, coworkers make great coauthors because they are often interested in the same subject.

In my first faculty status position, I teamed up with two other librarians, Connie Thorson and Russ Davidson, from our library to see how other academic libraries handled faculty status. We devised a survey and published: "Faculty Status for Librarians: Querying the Troops," in *College and Research Libraries*. At the same institution, we were deciding whether to retain the position of personnel librarian when ours left and the director appointed me and Janet Fredericks and Judith Bernstein to a committee; we wrote "The Personnel Officer in the Medium Sized Academic Library" for *Journal of Library Administration*.

So—get an idea, get mad, grab a partner, join a committee. If you don't know how else to begin, do a survey and start writing for publication.

THE ACADEMIC LIBRARIAN AS WRITER

JANET BUTLER MUNCH

Academic librarians with faculty status must accept performance criteria that focus on excellence in librarianship, service, and scholarship. Yearly reappointments and finally tenure provide strong motivation for librarians to write and publish. The "publish or perish" mantra is reinforced in the professional literature. What receives less emphasis, however, is the intrinsic value of active engagement in research and writing for the librarian. These activities not only refine and deepen knowledge of a topic but also sharpen thinking and analytical skills.

The academic environment can be a virtual idea incubator that

- brings together scholars and researchers from a range of areas

- supports collaborative efforts

- presents ongoing lectures and seminars across disciplines

- provides the employee fringe benefit of free classes

- maintains library resources that can be a springboard for research

- has technical expertise to support research and writing

GETTING STARTED

Once the new academic librarian internalizes the library faculty model, the next step is picturing oneself as a writer capable of producing a publication. The impact of seeing one's name on a first published work can dispel the question "Can something I write be published?" To achieve some sense of oneself as a writer, the following exercise can prove helpful.

Use yourself as the author and write a complete bibliographic citation for an article that you would like to write. Word process the citation, boldface and enlarge it, and put it on your desk. Look at it. Think about it.

You can revise the citation or even change the topic.

Brainstorm and write down, in short phrases, what you know about the topic.

Examine what you wrote and look for connections or patterns.

For a week or two, spend fifteen minutes daily logging what you have done to explore the topic. Did you search for books, skim tables of contents, search databases, or read articles?

Review your log and zero in on what needs to be done.

Write a 100- to 150-word abstract on the article you would write. Ask yourself why this topic is significant and what audience should read it.

Begin a focused literature review. Think about how your proposed publication will expand what is known and contribute to the literature?

WRITING AND THE WORKPLACE

Viewing the workplace as a laboratory for research projects can be played out for any issue affecting the library. In-house research might focus on user satisfaction with a website, evaluating a book jobber, or information literacy assessment. Examining the local situation and reading the professional literature put the study in a larger context. The benefits of research accrue to the library and can make an important contribution to the field.

Many colleges offer professional development funding to faculty that can be used to underwrite travel, manuscript preparation, image digitization, or equipment. Leave time may also be available for faculty working on research and publication. Money and time can be the two biggest impediments to professional development, and it is important that library faculty use whatever offerings are available. Unless specifically barred, library faculty should claim opportunities to apply for internal grants and leaves.

Librarians should not underestimate their tremendous networking capabilities. They meet campus teaching faculty through committee meetings, departmental liaison work, providing reference services, teaching to course assignments, and assisting in grant literature reviews. Some of these collaborations result in research discussions, joint publications, assistance with research methodology, or even offers to review manuscript drafts. External collegial connections through electronic discussion lists and association work can also pave the way to writing opportunities. Professional conference presentations benefit from audience feedback and can eventually result in manuscript publication.

WHAT COMMITTED WRITERS KNOW

Writing is a creative process and cannot be forced. When not writing, one should be thinking and reading broadly. Good writing is a reflection of concise thinking and analysis.

Carrying a pad and pen allows the writer to think on paper while waiting in lines or for appointments. Memory fades just like the name scrawled on wet beach sand will gradually disappear as waves roll in. Jotting down thoughts reminds the writer to verify a fact, check a citation, read another article, or change a phrase in a manuscript.

Keeping a daily log of activities is a self-monitoring technique that leads to progress in completing a manuscript within deadline.

Committing to write a certain number of words daily or for a certain amount of time makes sense once the writer is well grounded in the subject.

A writing block might mean that the writer has not sufficiently mastered the topic. The subconscious stews on problems when we do the ordinary things like sleeping. Today's writing snag may flow more easily tomorrow simply by waiting to proceed.

Writers set boundaries. They let the answering machine take the call. They read their e-mail at set times. They close their doors to think, write, edit, and rewrite.

SURVEYS AS A WRITING PROMPT TO GET STARTED IN PUBLISHING

DIANE STINE

As you get involved with professional organizations and begin to write for publication, people sometimes ask you to write an article or a chapter for a book or to work with them on a publication. In this instance, it is harder to get started because you haven't picked the topic yourself, so you haven't been thinking about or talking about the subject.

Devising a survey to gather data on your topic is an excellent way to begin if the topic is amenable. Surveys also give you access to a topic you might not know anything about and information that is not available elsewhere.

Once I was a member of a committee that was editing an issue of a library periodical. The committee members were all working in or had experience working in the field of technical services librarianship because the issue was devoted to education for technical services. Although I had two cataloging classes in library school, I only had one course on serials librarianship, which was taught during a four-week January intersession and covered all aspects of serials. I did not feel that this prepared me for working with serials and wondered how many library schools were teaching courses devoted to serials and/or containing a module on this topic.

When preparing your survey, it is important to first determine your purpose: the outcomes you expect. Then, as with any other article for publication, you need to find out what other research has been done on the topic. In my research, I found evidence of two earlier surveys that had indicated that training for serials librarianship was not sufficiently covered in library schools, and I wanted to see what strides had been made.

I devised a survey and mailed it to all of the library schools accredited by the American Library Association. In this case, it was very easy to determine the participants for my survey because there are a finite number of library schools.

What I wanted to find out was, first, did the library school teach a serials course? If so, how often, was it required, and what percentage of the students took the course? Then I listed serials-related topics and asked which ones the course covered. I found out that while library schools were making a genuine effort to add serials-related subject matter to their curricula, few students took the course.

Another time I was asked to write a chapter for the book, *Young Adults and Public Libraries,* edited by Mary Anne and C. Allen Nichols. The topic was partnerships in the public library. I didn't know a lot about the topic, so as part of my background research, I sent a survey to local libraries asking them about the types of partnerships they had formed.

Surveys are also a good way to find out how other libraries are doing something that your library is interested in pursuing. They are also a good way to show your library administration support for a particular point of view.

When I became the serials cataloging team leader at an academic library, I was surprised that all of the other serials catalogers were paraprofessionals and that the position did not require previous cataloging experience. I personally had five years of paraprofessional copy cataloging experience with books before I ever touched a serial, and I found it difficult to teach staff all of the intricacies involved in cataloging along with the eccentricities of serials. Also, this was

almost thirty years ago, and the OCLC database was not as comprehensive, especially for serials, and the records were not as reliable as they are today. This led to my surveying other medium-sized research librarians about their staffing patterns and led to the article "Serials Department Staffing Patterns in Medium-Sized Research Libraries" for *Serials Review.*

In conducting this survey, I wished to determine how many of the libraries had a centralized serials department; of those that had one, what tasks they handled; and what level of personnel were assigned to the tasks. Because our library had a centralized serials department, I could then compare us to the respondents that also had this type of organization. Then I asked about the tasks handled because our department consisted of three sections: ordering, cataloging and processing, and serials check-in. I was mainly interested in the tasks performed by the cataloging personnel and whether they were professionals, paraprofessionals, or clerical. I assigned these terms on the basis of an article I had read while doing research for my survey.

For the survey, first I asked if the library had a separate serials department. If the answer was no, I wrote "no need to continue, but please return the questionnaire." Of course, I mailed self-addressed stamped envelopes with the surveys. I listed all of the tasks performed by our serials department and had column headings asking for the number of clerical staff involved, the number of paraprofessional staff involved, the number of professional staff involved, and whether the process was manual or automated. This way, the respondents had to fill in only a limited amount of information. The rest of the survey involved circling the types of materials ordered and then the types of materials cataloged by their serials departments.

Pick your topic, do your background research, choose your participants, and design your survey. It is vital to make the survey easy for the person answering it to ensure the highest number of surveys returned. Use multiple choice, fill in the blank, circle the answers that apply, and so on, whenever possible and always include a self-addressed stamped return envelope. Write up the results of your research and survey and you will have a written document ready for publication.

EDITING BOOKS

WAYNE JONES

So, let's say the assignment you have from the publisher is to edit a book on a broad library and information sciences topic, a book that you don't write yourself but for which you solicit authors for the various chapters. Where do you start? What are the parts of the assignment that you have to do, and what do you leave to the chapter authors? Is there anything for you to do at all except wait for the authors to do the work for you, fix a couple of commas here and there, and then send the whole thing off to the publisher?

One of the most important tasks of the editor is to take that broad topic, research what has been previously published on or around it, and then decide what take or slice or flavor of the topic this book will have. It is hard to overestimate how essential and vital this part of the editing process is, because if it is not done well (or at all), the result will be a book that has already been written or, perhaps even worse, a book on a promising topic but with large, obvious gaps for which you should have solicited chapter authors to write. So, choose an approach to your topic that has not been done before and get a comprehensive suite of well-informed authors to cover it well.

Solicit each potential author by an individual e-mail, explaining clearly and succinctly what the book project is; the exact subject matter you want him or her to cover; and the most important details about length, deadline, style, and so on. Don't overwhelm during this first contact, but make sure that the authors know what they would be committing themselves to. For the potential authors that decline for any reason, thank them for taking the time to consider your project, and then find someone else to write that chapter. For those who say yes, thank them even more and have full guidelines ready: how long the chapter should be, in what physical or electronic format it should be submitted to you, the style for footnotes or endnotes, the deadline, and so on. Even though the publisher may ultimately want you to submit the completed book on paper (even multiple paper copies), don't burden your authors with this requirement, which generally slows down turnaround time: if possible, just ask them to send the chapter as a Word or rich-text document attached to an e-mail.

A word about another essential part of the editing and publishing process, and one that will affect you several times: deadlines. Your book is likely one of many on which the publisher has many editors, both internal and external, working, and so in short: respect the deadline that the publisher has given you and plan your work with your contributing authors accordingly. Don't ask the publisher for another week, or a few days, or even a single extra day just because something unexpected has happened at work, or you got sick unexpectedly, or your computer crashed, or any other perfectly understandable reasons that make sense for you but may cause serious scheduling problems for the publisher. Always provide wiggle room for yourself and for your authors: plan for the fact that a few unplanned things will happen, and provide them time to be over.

Be clear with the chapter authors about what exactly your editing policy is. An editor should never make assumptions or guess at anything, but one viable policy is to correct obvious errors silently on behalf of the authors, but to query those same authors when anything substantive is wrong or if there is a passage or sentence or word that you just can't figure out. This really is a service that you are providing to the authors, saving them before their words end up in print, because it's likely that if their editor can't understand the writing, then readers won't either. Always be available to the writers and give them time on the phone, by e-mail, or in any other reasonable way they might want to communicate with you. Answer their questions clearly and promptly: don't let an e-mail sit in your in-box for days while the author languishes, waiting.

My own experience has been that contributed chapters fall into three basic categories. A few are a breeze to edit, the majority are middling, and another terrible few will be (ahem) challenges for one reason or another. The 90-10 rule probably applies: you will spend 90 percent of your editing time on 10 percent of the contributions. Don't begrudge that of the authors or think that it is anything strange; simply accept it as a statistical fact of the process.

When you are actually reading and editing the chapters, it is important to be attentive to the macro and the micro. As you read each chapter, ask yourself whether the structure and the arrangement make sense to you. No, you won't be an expert on all the details of the subject matter, but of course you will know enough to expect each chapter to be logical and comprehensible. Query the author if anything doesn't make sense to you. As for the micro, these are the typical things that most people probably think editors are solely concerned about: spelling, usage, punctuation, the minutiae of note style, and so on. The authors may not (and should not) be cavalier about such details, but generally speaking, they will be more concerned with the content of the chapters than with anything else; do them a favor as a good editor and make sure the details are right. A note on notes: my experience has been that most writers, quite understandably perhaps, don't have

the time or inclination to pore over the *Chicago Manual of Style* or even a shorter guide trying to track down the intricacies of citation, so make sure the guidelines you provide to the authors include examples of the most common bibliographic entities they will likely cite (e.g., book, chapter in book, website, article in journal).

Once you've submitted the edited chapters (on deadline!) to the publisher, the main remaining step for you to be involved in as editor is proofreading. Be aware that, during the proofreading stage, it is generally not possible to make major changes to the text, only relatively minor corrections. Spend most of your time on the chapters before you submit them to the publisher—read and reread them—to make proofreading fairly trouble free. Some publishers will also allow you to compile the index to your own book (also done at the proofreading stage), and if you know how to do this, you should. However, don't underestimate how difficult it is to compile an index or how long it takes.

Finally, be patient with any delays in publishing and always keep your contributors informed of progress.

NURTURING A BOOK CONCEPT TO PUBLISHING SUCCESS

Lessons Learned from a First-Time Book Editor

DEBORAH H. CHARBONNEAU

Developing a book concept into a publishing success involves discipline, management, and creativity. Furthermore, understanding the scope of work involved in the book publishing process can be one challenge facing library practitioners who are contemplating taking on such a project. Therefore, the aim of this chapter is to demystify the process of publishing a book by offering practical advice from a first-time guest book editor who has collaborated with international contributors. In particular, lessons learned about identifying a potential topic for a book, writing a book proposal for the publisher, and negotiating the book contract are highlighted. In addition, important skills needed for publishing success are described.

IDENTIFYING A BOOK CONCEPT

The book-publishing journey is a time-consuming, yet rewarding, process. When formulating an idea for a book, it is important to consider some of the reasons for wanting to write a book. According to Goetting, Miguez, Curry, and Richard (2007, 3), there are "many reasons why a librarian might want to publish." For instance, potential authors may wish to share their knowledge, experience, or expertise with their peers, and writing a book offers a way to reach a wide audience. In addition, publishing can generate interest on a focused issue. From personal experience, publishing a book became an exciting opportunity to work with several contributors to help shed light on important issues and to explore particular topics in-depth. Some authors may also envision that their books could be used as textbooks to help inform students. Furthermore, writing offers the advantages of name recognition, resume enhancement, professional networking, and career development (Gordon 2004).

Understanding the reasons for wanting to write and who the potential readers are will help conceptualize and refine the book idea. Conducting a review of the literature to determine what has already been published about the topic is also a crucial step in this process. Overall, selecting a topic that one is passionate about, assessing whether there is a need for the book, and identifying potential readers are important considerations when formulating an idea for a book.

LOCATING A PUBLISHER

After identifying a possible idea for a book, the next step is to perform some background research to find a suitable publisher. One useful approach is to locate publishers with books on similar topics by searching online via WorldCat, exploring publisher websites, visiting publisher booths at conferences, and browsing catalogs from publishers. Another recommendation is to assess the quality of books from potential publishers by reading book reviews of their publications and obtaining copies of their books from interlibrary loan for inspection. If feasible, consider contacting the authors of books from a prospective publisher to inquire about their experience with the publisher.

Furthermore, contacting a publisher to inquire whether there is interest in a particular topic is highly recommended. This will let the author know whether the idea is worth pursuing early in the process. In addition, the publisher may provide helpful suggestions and guidance for refining the idea. If there is interest from the publisher, the next step is to prepare a compelling book proposal to convince the publisher that the idea is worth the investment.

PREPARING A BOOK PROPOSAL

The main purpose of a book proposal is to elicit interest from the publisher. Guidelines for preparing book proposals are generally available on the publisher's website or sent directly to authors who are invited to submit a book proposal. However, most book proposals share several common elements. A book proposal typically includes an annotated table of contents describing the chapters and content of the planned work, a description of the intended readership market, and information about the proposed author for the book. It is also essential to research the competition to effectively demonstrate how the proposed book is unique and how it contributes to the profession. In addition, publishers often ask for a sample chapter or a writing sample as part of the book proposal package.

NEGOTIATING A BOOK CONTRACT

If the book proposal is accepted, the publisher will prepare a contract to be signed by both the author and publisher. Several items are often specified in the book contract. These include the length of manuscript, delivery date of the book manuscript, and royalties paid to the author. Some clauses in the contract are standard. However, authors may want to investigate provisions allowing the author to retain the rights to a future electronic version of the book and the ability to post the work, or a portion of it, in an institutional repository. The contract also states whether an index is needed, which typically falls under the responsibility of the author. If there are plans for several authors to contribute to the book, then each contributor will need to sign a contract. Therefore, negotiating a book contract requires a careful review of the language in the contract, understanding the terms of the contract, and negotiating with the publisher for any desired amendments.

CONCLUSION

Book publication "represents a substantial investment of time, effort, and money by both [the] publisher and author" (Schuman and Harmon 1997, 20). For authors contemplating writing a book, cultivating a book from an initial concept to printing entails a series of stages. These stages range from identifying a possible book topic, locating a suitable publisher, sending an inquiry to a publisher to determine whether there is interest, and preparing a compelling book proposal. Whenever a book proposal is accepted, then the task of the book author evolves. As such, the author next focuses on writing the book manuscript, coordinating any contributions to the book by additional authors, and delivering the manuscript to the publisher for review and feedback. Therefore, for book publishing success, a variety of skills are needed including being an effective writer, negotiator, coordinator, marketer, and problem solver. In summary, publishing is a great challenge, and understanding the overall process of publishing a book increases the likelihood of moving from book concept to publishing success.

REFERENCES

Goetting, Denise, Betsy B. Miguez, Sheryl M. Curry, and Susan M. Richard. 2007. "First-Time Book Publishing: Negotiating the Perils and Pitfalls." *Technical Services Quarterly* 25 (2): 1–18.

Gordon, Rachel S. 2004. *The Librarian's Guide to Writing for Publication.* Lanham, MD: Scarecrow Press.

Schuman, Patricia G., and Charles Harmon. 1997. "From Book Idea to Contract." *Library Administration and Management* 11 (1): 19–25.

EDITING A LIBRARY ASSOCIATION MAGAZINE

WAYNE JONES

Most library associations produce some kind of magazine for their members. In fact, the receipt of a regular magazine (often they're quarterly or monthly) is often a much-cherished benefit by the members of a wide range of associations, whether national, state or provincial, or even more local. The editorial teams that work to edit and publish them vary in size and operating procedure, depending, of course, on the size of the magazine's readership or print run, the frequency, the complexity of the publishing process, and a hundred other things that may or may not apply to one or other magazine. Many associations also have no printed magazine at all, simply an online magazine or presence that may be updated continually or regularly. The following paragraphs present the main components of the editorial team for a typical library association magazine.

The regular columnists. Regular columnists are the members of the team who take responsibility for the editing of a column that appears in every issue. Editing in this sense may mean either actually writing the column or soliciting someone else to do the writing: in the latter case, the columnist would then play the role of what most people think of when they think of editors, that is, working with the writer on revisions, putting the column in the magazine's style, copyediting, and so on. The topics that each columnist writes about or solicits are the ones that are at the core of what the members of the particular association are interested in and that they would consider necessary for the magazine to cover.

The feature writers. Feature writers are generally not members of the editorial team per se but have been solicited by any member of the team to write about an issue of topical or timely interest to the readership. Often these features are completely unsolicited: a reader who knows about the magazine or is a member of the association simply submits an article to a member of the team, asking whether the magazine would be interested in publishing it.

The association executive. Many associations set up their magazines so that members of the executive staff of the association (e.g., the executive director, one or more or all board members) are also part of the editorial team. The idea is to provide very broad oversight for the general direction of the magazine, and in some cases, the executive may choose to be involved in the regular process of editing as well.

The editorial board. The editorial board members are advisors to the magazine, often recruited because they are already very involved in the profession and can identify others to write for the magazine. Editorial board members may even solicit directly themselves. An active and engaged editorial board can be essential to ensure that the magazine remains relevant to the readership.

The managing editor. The managing editor oversees the logistics of putting each issue together:

setting deadlines, liaising with the publisher or printer, cajoling writers to get their copy in on time, coordinating proofs, and so on.

The editor in chief. The editor in chief coordinates all of the foregoing activities.

Depending on the frequency of the magazine, the editorial team is always either finishing off one issue or starting the next. Often the deadline for the final go-ahead to the printer is met for the current issue and then it's immediately time to start thinking about putting together the lineup for the next one. A lot of the work of editing an association magazine, as for any magazine, involves deadlines: a deadline for getting copy from the writers, a deadline for column editors to have to submit edited copy to the managing editor, a deadline for submission to the printer, a deadline for first proofs, a deadline for second proofs, and on and on.

It's extremely important for the editor to be well organized, to stay on top of what aspects of the work are done and remain to be done—otherwise the timely production of the issues can be seriously compromised. The editor has to keep control of the broad goals of the magazine and the big tasks associated with regular production, but he or she also has to be mindful of details that demand attention at nearly all stages of editing. An important tool in this latter regard is the style sheet or style guide, which records many of the decisions and policies that the magazine has decided to follow: dictionary, stylebook, style of citations, house style for numbers and dates, certain spellings and treatment of specific words, and so on. A well-developed style sheet can save the editors and columnists the time of having to revisit various options (*website* or *Web site*? serial comma or not?) and can provide valuable guidance to the writers. Make it available right on the association's website.

As for those macro issues, the main one on the production side is to always be planning a few issues ahead. What topics or events are coming up that the magazine needs to cover? It is also essential that the editor always have articles that can be used in the current issue if necessary: a thin magazine, one without copy, is no magazine at all. Finally, the editor should keep in mind who the readers are and, as simple as it sounds, always supply them with the kinds of things that they want to read.

EDITING CONFERENCE PROCEEDINGS

STEPHANIE MATHSON

Are you well organized? Do you meet deadlines on projects easily? Are you a tactful communicator? Do you typically work well with other people—including coauthors or coeditors? If you can respond yes to these questions, then you should consider volunteering as a conference proceedings editor.

For academic librarians appointed as tenure-track faculty members or quasi faculty members working in a continuing appointment system, publishing is of grave importance. Editing conference proceedings provides us with interesting publishing opportunities that may be outside of (but perhaps related to) our own scholarly research and writing areas. Compiling and editing conference proceedings are large projects that reappointment and tenure committees look on favorably; however, do not let the amount of work scare you away. By planning your editing project and holding your contributors—and yourself—to firm deadlines, the task is manageable.

Earlier this year, I served as coeditor of *The Thirteenth Off-Campus Library Services Conference Proceedings,* the proceedings for a biennial national conference that my institution sponsors and publishes. (The papers in the proceedings will also be published in 2009 in the *Journal of Library Administration.*) Only by happenstance was I asked to coedit the proceedings. My only previous experience was coediting my state library association's newsletter for two years. The editor of the last proceedings was the head of the department that organizes the conference; when she took a new job last year, she asked me to serve with her as coeditor of this year's proceedings to preserve continuity in retaining a member of my institution's staff as an editor.

With these things in mind, I encourage you to volunteer to edit newsletters of the professional organizations to which you belong. That will give you great experience in corresponding with contributors, editing articles, and meeting myriad deadlines. From there, look for opportunities to edit more and different kinds of publications such as conference proceedings.

When you agree to edit (or coedit) proceedings, you may also automatically become a member of the conference advisory or programming board. If that is indeed the situation in which you find yourself, you will have responsibilities beyond those of an editor. You may be asked to review paper and poster session proposals. (This will be helpful in that you will know what the papers are about when you receive the drafts.) Your contributions—as an editor and/or board member—will be acknowledged at the conference. You may also have the opportunity to introduce speakers or facilitate workshops during the conference. All of these activities are great additions to your vita.

Once you find yourself serving as an editor or coeditor of conference proceedings, familiarize yourself with the publication standards that contributors must follow. Are they to draft papers following the guidelines of the American Psychological Association? Are they to use some other format? If you have the opportunity to do so, talk to the conference manager about reviewing the requirements for the call for papers before they are publicized. This not only will give you the opportunity to revise the guidelines as you see fit (especially if you are an experienced editor) but also will allow you to start planning your editing schedule. Here are questions to consider:

- What is the deadline for proposals?
- When will contributors be sent their letters of acceptance?
- When will the completed papers be due?
- When is the conference?
- Will the proceedings be published before or after the conference?

Caveat: If copies of the proceedings will be distributed at the conference, your turnaround time to edit and compile the manuscript will probably be quite short. Do not let that prospect frighten you, but it is an important question to ask of the conference manager before you agree to serve as editor.

When I agreed to serve as coeditor, I was able to review the paper guidelines and make changes in format requirements and rewrite some of the text regarding the graphics included in the contributed papers. These revisions made the directions clearer to authors and undoubtedly saved my coeditor and me some headaches once we began receiving drafts.

We had a fairly short turnaround time in editing drafts, communicating with writers regarding suggestions and corrections, and compiling everything necessary for the manuscript of the entire proceedings. I spent several hours each weekend for three consecutive weeks reading and editing papers.

Fortunately, I was able to spend some time working on this project during the week, too. In total, I spent approximately 120 hours editing (nineteen of thirty-two papers), corresponding with authors, and compiling all of the materials (papers, poster session abstracts, and introductory sections) over two months.

My coeditor and I had only one face-to-face meeting during which we began compiling all of the papers into one document. All other communications we had with each other were via e-mail or phone, and that worked well for us. No doubt, though, it was advantageous that my coeditor had compiled the previous conference proceedings by herself.

The effort I put into this editing project was well worth it. The proceedings were well received by the Off-Campus Libraries Services Department and the conference attendees. Not just a niche publication, proceedings have an audience beyond just the contributors and conference-goers. Subjects covered included library instruction via course management software, database tutorial creation, and conducting focus groups of distance education students.

In the end, editing conference proceedings—though time consuming—was easier than I had anticipated. My compensation for my work as editor, advisory board member, and moderator of three presentations was a waiver of the conference registration fee and reimbursement for my airline ticket and hotel expenses during the conference.

Here is a quick list of tips to keep in mind if you are thinking about editing conference proceedings:

- Work with a coeditor if you are inexperienced.
- Be knowledgeable about the publication format authors must follow. (Remember that as the editor, you may have leeway in deciding which standard is used.)

- Be firm with deadlines but flexible if contributors have work or personal emergencies and you have some time during which to wait for their final papers.

- Revise individual papers carefully. Do not rewrite papers, but clearly communicate needed changes and, if necessary,

your rationale for the changes with the authors.

- Proofread the completed proceedings manuscript carefully for everything from page numbering to odd-looking margins and fonts.

- Enjoy the conference!

STRATEGIC PUBLICATION

ROBERT S. NELSON

Mapping one's yearly publication strategy is important for a long career as a writer. It requires writers to examine aspects of their writing style, their upcoming projects, and their nonwriting commitments. Deliberately aligning these elements will foster better writing habits, increase productivity, and help stave off burnout.

TO THINE OWN SELF . . .

The greatest factor when starting to create a yearly publishing plan is honesty. Our egos want us to believe that we will be able to have that two-hundred-page manuscript done in a month. In reality, that manuscript may take a year or more to complete. To delineate what to publish when, you must first examine what you write and how you write.

If your focus is writing research papers, you must attempt to discern the amount of time needed to collect and analyze responses, as well as to manage unintended outcomes. Allot time to deal with recommendations from peer reviewers. Other factors can cause your time line to shift. Carefully considering the many influences on the writing of research paper is necessary to judge correctly the amount of time needed to complete a project.

Creative writing represents a different challenge. Allowing time for creative works to ferment is important to quality writing. It is also an important consideration when attempting to discern your yearly publication trajectory. How long does it take a poem to feel complete? For some poets, the answer is never, but in most cases, there is a definitive point at which a poem has reached its final form. As you work, you need to track this process. This will allow

for a reasonable approximation when calculating the time needed to complete a project. For fiction, there is a substantial period of development and evaluation throughout the course of the work. Character sketching, plot line summaries, and other tools require time to prepare. These things should be accounted for when honestly assessing the amount of time needed to complete a work of fiction.

THE MOST WONDERFUL TIME?

Now that you have determined the time needed to complete a project it is important to consider when you should begin. For writers, a calendar is the next best writing aid next to the thesaurus. The notion of all writers being free spirits answering only to the dictates of the Muses is romantic but a bit unrealistic. A writer's life is just that, a life. Doctor's appointments, work requirements, weddings, and other issues all compete for the same time as your writing. A quick consultation with a well-maintained calendar would mitigate some of the intrusions a life can have on a writer's efforts.

If you require three months to complete a research article, a quick review of your calendar will provide you with a good approximation as to when you should begin. Writing and publishing for research require long stretches of deep concentration. You would be ill advised to start a research project during the winter holiday season. Distractions abound at this time of year whereas the postholiday season (February to April) is less likely to contain disruptive events. If your writing relies on referenced research, you should also consider library availability when planning start dates.

Poets and novelists may not need to consider distractions like holidays, but other events can be factors in completing projects on time. Travel plans may be both a positive and a negative influence on creative writing. If a series of poems concentrates on a particular place and your travel plans require you to be away from that place for a period, it will affect your ability to work. On the positive side, the distance may foster a different perspective on the subject. For novelists, interruptions and distractions may be beneficial. Planning to complete a certain number of chapters before an event such as a wedding or a houseguest's arrival will allow you to take a short hiatus from writing without feeling the guilt that is sometimes associated with such breaks. The change in pace may also assist in figuring out a plot line.

MULTITASKING

Once the calendar has been set and the work is under way, you can consider what to do in the lulls. As various forms of writing require different attentions and work ethics, it may be best for you to space out your projects with a decided rhythm. This will help stave off boredom and burnout. It can also help to avoid market saturation in any one area.

If you send out a set of poems for consideration, why not attempt to write an essay or even a short research paper while waiting for letters from the publisher? Developing a poem, essay, or article rhythm allows you manipulate your working habits and the calendar to your advantage. For the novelist, in the pauses between chapters or larger book sections, consider conducting and even publishing research on issues, places, or events your characters must contend with. This is an excellent way to multitask as a writer.

EASIER SAID

Writing is so subjective that it is difficult to prescribe an effective plan of any kind. What is not difficult is knowing and understanding that publishing quality writing takes time and that you must assess how much time you need, how best to manage that time, and what to do with the spaces in between. This will extend your writing career and make you a much happier writer in the end.

LIBRARIANS AS FIRST-TIME BOOK EDITORS

NICOLE C. ENGARD

When I was in middle school, I wrote my first book. Unfortunately, it was the kind of book only a mother could love. So, when I was approached by a library publisher to write a book for librarians to love, of course I jumped at the opportunity. There was one catch of course: this book was to be written by more than twenty authors and I was going to have to edit everyone's work.

GETTING STARTED

The first step was to come up with a formal proposal including a book summary, target audience, and sample table of contents. This process may be different depending on the publisher you are working with. While the first two items on my guidelines were relatively simple, it was the sample table of contents that required several hours of thinking.

I decided to find chapter authors through word of mouth instead of submitting a call for proposals. A call for proposals is sent out to mailing lists, outlining the book and what would be expected of authors. Then authors would submit their chapter ideas to the editor for review. Both options are valid ways to find contributors for your book, but using word of mouth allowed me a bit more control over the influx of ideas and questions.

COMPILING CONTENT

I started with some suggested contacts I received from the publisher. When I contacted potential authors, I simply asked whether they had any recommendations for other authors. Using this method I was able to find twenty-seven authors around the world to contribute to the book (a number that changed throughout the process).

When compiling your content, you want to make sure that you avoid having too much overlap in your chapters. I chose to have several introductory chapters on my topic, but made sure that all three were authors who brought a different point of view. I also tried to find projects that used many different techniques so that, in the end, the book would be a well-rounded guide for librarians of varying experience levels.

GUIDELINES

Make sure that you have an outline of chapter-writing guidelines for your authors. The more information you provide, the less likely it is that you will have to do major rewriting. I chose to use online tools provided by Google that would allow me to store my guidelines online. I wrote up several documents using Google Docs (http://docs.google.com) and was able to share them with my authors. This way I knew that everyone had the same information.

I also requested that my authors write their chapters using the same tool so that they could share their work with me and I could offer suggestions along the way. This also guaranteed that I would have all chapters submitted in the same format, making it just a little bit easier for me to make everything uniform in the end.

DEADLINES

While you will have a deadline from the publisher for the final draft of the book, as an editor you have to decide how much time you will need to edit the work of others and give your contributors a deadline that you can work with. Always keep in mind that there will be requests for extensions and/or authors pulling out of their commitment, and you'll need to accommodate accordingly.

One option is to stagger deadlines so that each bunch of chapters comes in at a different time. This will allow you to edit the work over a longer time period. I chose to have all of the chapters submitted at the same time giving me five months to go through the works submitted and edit them for publication.

EDITING

Once you have the chapters in hand the hard part begins. As an editor, you have to step back from your own personal style and look at the chapter submitted to you objectively. When working on a guide for librarians, you do not necessarily need the entire book to have the same tone, you just want your chapters to be well written and useful to the reader. This was the hardest part for me, to not push my personal writing style on my authors' chapters.

It is important to spread out your editing time so that you can keep a clear eye on what you are reading. Start by skimming through the chapters to get a feel for the content that your book will include. Then spend some time on each chapter individually. Once you have gone through the entire book once, go through it again. Even though your title is editor, the community will expect you to be the expert on the topic of your book.

CONCLUSION

The process of editing a book is going to be different for each person and publisher. Once you have the guidelines from your publisher, sit down and think carefully about how you want to approach your new project. Do you want to put out a call for proposals? Do you want to find authors on your own? How much time will you need to edit the chapters submitted to you?

The most important tip I can provide is that you have to be flexible. Be prepared to have authors who do not meet your deadline, expect authors to send you works that are not up to your standards, and be prepared to work harder than you ever imagined. I went into this project thinking it would be easier than writing an entire book on my own, but it was just as hard, if not harder, to be the editor of a book.

PUBLISHING BY LEVERAGING NEW TECHNOLOGIES

ALINE SOULES

The traditional method of publication has been to write an article, submit it, and wait for acceptance or rejection. While this method is still valid, there are many more opportunities to publish today, making it much more exciting.

E-mail, electronic discussion lists, blogs, wikis, websites, and social networking are all venues for your creativity. I belong to many electronic discussion lists and contribute occasionally after proofing what I write.

With blogs, you don't control all the content, if others comment, but with wikis, you can restrict contributions to yourself or give rights to only those you choose, although the end result may not clarify who wrote what. A major challenge with these forms of publication is to get people to visit them, but they are searchable on the Web for those who are interested in the topics.

Websites are more work than blogs and wikis and are often the face of your organization. They convey information, promote your organization, and facilitate online interaction with users. Organizations are also jumping into Facebook, MySpace, and Second Life. For example, the California Academic and Research Libraries group has had a website for a long time, but in its latest PDF newsletter, it announced a presence on Flickr and Facebook.

So how do you make this work for you? The Librarian in Black, a longtime blogger, has created a franchise out of good topics, good writing, hard work, and publicity through her blog, Flickr, and her website. On Google, I also found a blog about her website.

I've found it useful to combine these tools for a niche set of audiences. For example, I teach a two-credit information literacy course, first face-to-face, now hybrid, and soon online. I store material and grades on Blackboard, our campus learning management system, but I use external wikis and blogs because they are the real information world in which students will work. I ask each student to create a blog on Blogger.com for their assignments. They may keep their blogs private, but most students don't bother.

In summer 2008, our library redesigned its website, requiring librarians to change their subject pages. I chose to create a basic website from the library template, but I primarily use it as a jumping-off point to other sources, including my supplementary wiki pages and a couple of my modules. I have the flexibility to change the wiki, yet if our website is revamped again in future, I won't have to redo the whole fabric of information I'm building. (See http://library.csueastbay.edu/guides/english/.) I am also collaborating with Sarah Nielsen, the coordinator of our MA in teaching of English to speakers of other languages program, to embed information literacy in a redesigned curriculum (see http://tesol csueb.wetpaint.com).

Modules are the latest publication endeavor in our library, involving PowerPoint presentations with voice-over or other combinations of text and media. We are now creating an interactive map and exploring film for a library welcome. These creations require knowledge of some software (e.g., Camtasia, Captivate, VoiceThread, Premiere) and added assistive technology capabilities. You can output to the Web, MP3, and iPods. It's time consuming but fun, and it provides a new form of publication. For a great example, see the Weigle Information Commons Music Video created by University of Pennsylvania students at http://wic.library.upenn.edu/about/musicvideo.html.

LEVERAGING TODAY'S OPPORTUNITIES FOR MORE TRADITIONAL PUBLICATIONS

All of the foregoing can lead to presentations, articles, and further writing opportunities. Possibilities are often announced on electronic discussion lists. Submit a proposal if you have something to offer. If you don't feel confident enough to propose on your own, find a partner. Don't worry about rejection; everyone's rejected sooner or later. Ask for feedback if your piece is rejected. Sometimes that's more valuable than the experience of proposing. Sooner or later, you will be offered an opportunity.

While seeking shorter-term opportunities, you can pursue a research project for a more traditional research paper you submit for peer review. As the process takes many months, it's good to keep other projects going.

An opportunity to present can also lead to publication. The last time I presented, at the American Library Association's Summer Conference in 2008, an editor from *New Library World* came up to me afterward and asked me to write an article for the online peer-reviewed journal. I submitted a couple of months later and my article will appear in 2009.

At some point, you may decide to tackle the challenge of a book chapter or a book. You need a concept that's uncommon enough to attract an editor, because of either the content or the angle you intend to take on the subject. You also need to plan your time. You can handle smaller pieces along with your full-time job, but a book is different. I responded to a call for chapters, submitted a proposal, asked someone I barely knew to be my partner, enjoyed writing, and made a great new friend. You'll find the chapter and my partner listed on my resume page at http://libraryresume.wetpaint.com.

WHAT DO YOU WANT?

Once you start, you'll find out whether writing is for you. You'll note that I say "writing," not "publishing." Some people pursue publication for tenure and promotion, not because they like writing. With the increasing variety of opportunities, however, you have more chances to find what suits you best. Try things. I've written in all the forms I have described here, modules being my latest adventure. Writing is my passion and I hope that it will be yours, too. Publication is simply the icing on the cake.

MY VERY OWN ISBN NUMBER
A Librarian's Path to Publication

JAN SIEBOLD

It is my belief that for people to accomplish their goals, they must affirm and visualize them on a regular basis. During those days when I was trying to get published, one of my frequent visualizations involved going to the fiction shelf in my library and seeing a book written by Jan Siebold nestled between ones by Anna Sewell and Shel Silverstein, picturing my book titles on numerous award lists.

I imagined a student painstakingly laboring over a cereal-box book report based on one of my books. I rehearsed what I would say to students (and knew what I would wear!) when I would be invited to do author visits at schools. And I knew that when the ISBN agency assigned my first book its ten-digit ISBN number it would outrank my Social Security number in importance to my life. (I wondered if an ISBN tattoo would be considered over the top for an elementary school librarian.)

This may be a good time to mention visualizations to avoid. Among them are imagining piles of your book for sale in an aisle of the local dollar store, finding your book in a box of discards awaiting a trip to the garbage, and seeing one of your books placed under the leg of a computer projector to raise the image's screen height.

The positive visualizations provided the necessary fuel for me to keep sending my writing to publishers. Fortunately, as a working library media specialist, I had a rewarding job that also provided me with income as one manuscript after another was rejected.

In high school and in college, my formal writing training had been limited. I often tell students that my best training as a writer comes from being a lifelong reader. However, at the time, I felt the need for some type of writing class.

I attended the summer workshop Teaching Writing Using Museums and Local Resources at the Smithsonian Institution. During the two-week seminar, I participated in activities and writing assignments in each of the Smithsonian museums, including the National Zoo.

Our class met back at Smithsonian headquarters at the end of each day to compare notes and to read what we had written. For the first time, I experienced the support and feedback that a writing group can provide.

On arriving home from the Smithsonian workshop, I signed up for a community education writing workshop, and again was fortunate to find a group of helpful and supportive fellow writers. After the class ended, a small group of us continued to meet as a writers group.

At both writing workshops, and from everything I had read or heard about writing, it seemed that one of the tried-and-true rules of authorship is that a writer must write every day. I resisted this idea at first, finding that I was able to summon the words whenever I was inspired to write. However, during what I have since named the "Age of Rejection," that inspiration was more and more difficult to find.

At that same time, my niece had begun writing for her college newspaper. She was given daily writing assignments with very short deadlines. Her writing quickly became much stronger and prolific. Her editing skills improved greatly. She blossomed into a writer of amazing depth and insight. I was duly impressed and gave the rule about writing every day new consideration.

I began looking for alternative ways to practice my writing skills and to broaden the avenues of opportunity for publication. I found that editors of newspapers, newsletters, and professional journals are always on the lookout for pieces. After all, most of them have daily, weekly, or monthly publication schedules and require an ongoing supply of well-written articles.

I received my first monetary compensation for an article that I wrote for the *Buffalo News.* I had written about the neighborhood observations that I made while walking two miles to work every day. I received a first-place award in a New York State United Teachers journalism competition for a feature article that I wrote about starting over in a new school after my library position was cut. The *Artifacts* newspaper featured my piece about watching the sun rise from Cadillac Mountain in Maine.

The checks and awards were welcomed, but much more important were the boosts in confidence that I received from seeing my words in print. They helped to negate the frustration and sense of hopelessness that I was feeling about my children's book manuscripts.

By writing every day, I also began to notice that ideas started to flow more freely. Many of those ideas came to me while I was out walking, and it became difficult to remember all of them. I started to carry a small notebook and pencil wherever I went, lest I forget a gem of a writing topic. From a mail-order catalog, I ordered small notebooks and pencils that are worn like a necklace.

I started keeping paper and pencil on my bedside table for those middle-of-the-night inspirations. In fact, it was one of those nighttime ideas that led to the idea of structuring my book *Rope Burn* (Albert Whitman, 1998) around well-known proverbs. If I hadn't reached over in the dark and scrawled the word *proverbs* on a piece of paper, I'm not sure that book would have come together as it did.

After several years of receiving big, bad brown envelopes containing manuscript rejections, I came home from school one day (Monday, February 3, 1997, at 4:10 p.m., thank you!) to find instead a white business envelope with a publisher's return address. Folded neatly and exquisitely in that envelope was a publisher's letter of acceptance. I will never forget how I felt after reading it.

Since that day, every one of my previously mentioned positive visualizations (except the tattoo) has come true. As librarians we are in the unique position of being surrounded by examples of literary inspiration. We have the inside scoop on publishers and trends. We have opportunities to attend author and illustrator presentations. Newspaper and professional journal editors are constantly appealing for articles.

The writing itself must come from within, but we are fortunate to be surrounded by resources that can help us along the path to publication.

MAXIMIZE YOUR OPPORTUNITIES TO GET PUBLISHED

GABRIEL MORLEY

Breaking into publishing is not as hard as it might seem, especially if you know a few tricks of the trade and are willing to do some writing pro bono to establish your reputation and quality of work.

Editors are busy people. They are always on the lookout for good writers who are easy to work with and dependable. Establishing yourself as a professional will give your writing career some longevity. Getting started is often the most difficult part of the process. Don't try to write a full-length three-thousand-word feature article if you've never done it before. Work up to that level by building your portfolio of published clips with smaller, shorter pieces.

One of the easiest ways to obtain a publishing credit is by doing book reviews. Book reviews are typically short and based on the publication's specific guidelines. Dozens of journals and magazines publish reviews of new books. Librarians are perfectly suited to write reviews, and just because you're a librarian, doesn't mean you have to limit yourself to library-related publications. (The same goes for professional articles.) Expanding your publishing horizons can take several paths. Here are a few:

Consider a range of publishing sources such as journals in management, math, education, and the sciences.

Obviously, some of the material in other professional journals will be too esoteric unless you have prior knowledge of the subject specialty. So exploit your undergraduate degree. For example, if you have a BS in engineering, consider reviewing engineering books for journals in that field. Editors will be impressed with your technical knowledge.

Take stock of yourself. Think about things you do and how you might be able to turn your own experiences into a review or article. For example, if your hobby is training dogs, keep your eyes open for dog-training books to review.

Once you've picked up a few bylines, you may want to attempt a feature article. The first thing to do is research your topic to find out whether anyone has written similar articles. Try EBSCO and Google. Doing preliminary research on your topic prevents you from looking like an amateur when you contact an editor proposing an article on something the magazine just covered. If an editor has published something similar to your idea, simply adjust your topic to give it a fresh angle.

If no one has written about your subject recently, the next step, if you are a beginner, is to write the article. Yes, write the article before you contact editors. Write the whole article. I know many writers will stomp their feet and say I'm wrong; but, when you query an editor with an idea, the first thing the editor will do is decide whether your proposal is a good fit for the publication. If it is, then the editor will check your background and previous publishing experience.

If you have little or no experience, the chance of an editor accepting your proposal is slim because plenty of people have great ideas, but you have to be able to actually write the article. Just because you can sum up the article in three to five sentences and write a nifty cover letter doesn't mean you can put together a cohesive article following all the elements of style under strict deadline. Why should an editor take a chance on you? You need to prove yourself.

If you have already written the article and enclosed it with your query letter, the editor can make a decision immediately. You have eliminated the risk the editor must take by giving you an assignment.

Many individuals disagree with me on this point. As an editor, if I don't know you, I would rather see a completed article to prove you can do what you say you can. As a writer, writing the whole article first is somewhat of a gamble because you might not find a home for it. As a beginning writer you are better off writing the entire article and trying to get an editor to work with you on the basis of your submission.

If you are an experienced writer with previous publications (clips), it is in your best interest to query editors rather than write spec articles (i.e., articles that you write without a commitment from an editor).

Before you submit anything, you should pay special attention to your manuscript and query letter. Your first impression will go a long way toward earning an assignment. If your work is sloppy or wrong for the publication, you will be dismissed immediately.

Proofread. Have someone else look at your article and query letter. It must be error free.

Follow submission requirements. Find out how the publication wants articles to be submitted. Most magazines accept electronic submissions. Ask for a copy of the publication's guidelines and follow them exactly.

Be succinct. Your query letter should be short and to the point and should contain your personal and professional qualifications. Summarize your article.

Include something about why people will want to read your article. Is it timely? Is it a new trend? Is it a new look at an old problem?

Cater to your audience. If you're writing for a math journal, keep that in mind as you're writing. Make sure your style fits the magazine.

Be on time. Production schedules are usually four to six months in advance and can be more. Do not miss your deadline. Your editor will put you on "The List."

Getting published is often about finding the right magazine or editor. Don't give up if you're turned down the first few times. Keep after it. An academic librarian friend of mine recently sent out a story thirteen times before it was accepted and published. Think of topics that will attract attention or create buzz. This is what editors are looking for as well. Seek out topics that are of interest to you. If you can find a topic that fits your interest, it will make the article better and your publishing experience more enjoyable.

INTERVIEWING FOR PUBLICATION

PATRICK RAGAINS

Today's readers crave authenticity. With the exception of an autobiographical narrative, nothing achieves this quite like an interview. Interviews in magazines such as *Library Journal* and *American Libraries* cover a range from noteworthy directors and leaders in the publishing industry to authors, educators, and innovative frontline librarians. These magazines normally publish interviews only when conducted by staff writers and editors. Your publication outlets for interviews include state, regional, and specialized library publications (such as ACRL section newsletters). You may also conduct interviews for historical purposes, which I cover at the end of this chapter.

WHY INTERVIEW?

Personal narratives are compelling. Librarians read interviews to discover the keys to professional success: how to lead or reach an elusive target audience for library services.

BACKGROUND RESEARCH ON YOUR SUBJECT

Avoid asking your interview subject anything you can find in background research. If you are interviewing a public library director, come to the interview with knowledge of the community, current developments (such as new services or facilities), and the library's challenges. If you're interviewing an author, read his or her latest work and criticism, and be able to discuss the work's setting, similar works, and authors.

ARRANGING THE INTERVIEW

If you plan to interview an author, artist, educator, librarian, or mid-level administrator, you can usually contact your subject directly. Top-level administrators, including agency heads, normally have staff screen their calls and e-mail. In either case, a phone call or e-mail is an acceptable way to establish contact. You should introduce yourself and give your affiliation. Explain why you're requesting an interview (e.g., to coincide with a library opening or, for an author, to publicize an upcoming talk or book signing) and tell where and when the interview will be published. Ask for an appointment of a specified length (usually no more than forty-five minutes to an hour, although you can still conduct a good interview in less time). Indicate your availability and set up a meeting time and place. If you will conduct the interview over the phone, verify the number that you will call to reach your subject. Tell him or her whether you plan to record the interview, because some people are uncomfortable having their voices recorded.

AUDIO RECORDING

You should record your interview with a reliable, portable audio recorder especially if you intend to publish it in question-and-answer format. Good battery-operated digital recorders currently start at about $200. These devices record in common file formats, such as WAV, and can convert to MP3 for easy storage and e-mailing. Keep fresh batteries and a DC adaptor handy.

CONDUCTING THE INTERVIEW

When you arrive for the interview, start with a question that will encourage your interviewee to relax and talk at some length about his or her recent work. Listen and be prepared to ask follow-up questions, such as, "You said you envision the new library as a focal point for the community. How will that happen?" This is only an example, but the point is to ask questions that elicit expansive and authentic responses. A bit more about authenticity here: your interviewee will likely have an agenda to promote. For instance, I've interviewed performers who see their audiences somewhat differently than I do. Explore your subject's perspective, but probe enough to keep the interview broadly informative and more than simply free advertising. Remember that it's your job alone to achieve balance and inform your readers.

PREPARING THE INTERVIEW FOR PUBLICATION

Transcribe the recording as soon as possible after you've completed the interview. Edit the interview for publication by excising fillers (e.g., uh, um), revising disfluencies into standard sentences (e.g., "The building is beautiful and people . . . you see people here at all hours" becomes "The building is beautiful and you see people here at all hours"), and rearranging text into a narrative that flows logically for the reader. Write an introduction providing background about the person and the reason for the interview. When the interview is published, notify the interviewee and send a copy to him or her, along with your thanks. If your editor plans to post the audio file to websites, you should obtain prior permission from your subject.

ORAL HISTORY INTERVIEWING

By the 1920s and early 1930s, ethnologists, historians, and musicologists were using audio recording as a documentary tool. American historians launched large-scale interviewing projects shortly after World War II; today, most sizable manuscript repositories in the United States house oral interviews. The current StoryCorps project allows family members and friends to interview one another and archive their recordings at the Library of Congress (www.storycorps.net).

While collecting oral testimony is a respected research activity, oral histories are not always widely published. Librarians interested in collecting oral history should become familiar with the Oral History Association's "Evaluation Guidelines." This pamphlet address matters such as ethical and legal guidelines, equipment use, and responsibilities to interviewees, the public, archival institutions, and the historical profession.

Librarians have created several oral history projects of their own. The Medical Library Association has a model program designed to promote the history of the association and health sciences librarianship. Two smaller collections are Careers in Librarianship, housed at Indiana University's Center for the Study of History and Memory, and Boston Public Library's New England Round Table of Children's Librarians. These collections and others in all subjects are a nationwide treasure trove for authors seeking primary sources for historical research.

LIBRARIANS AND THE LOCAL LITERARY COMMUNITY

Making Space on the Same Shelf

LISA A. FORREST

If you're like most writers, you probably have boxes of unpublished work—much of which has never made it past the rejection-note phase of the publishing process (if you've actually gotten as far as submitting). Many poets I know usually start out by eagerly sending a few poems to some big-shot magazines (raise your hand if you've ever sent a poem to the *New Yorker, Poetry,* or the *Atlantic*), just hoping that maybe their poem will be "the one." Let's be honest—the chance of getting a poem published in a national magazine is pretty slim. As director of the Rooftop Poetry Club reading series at Buffalo State College, I often counsel less experienced writers on how to promote their work. While it's great to have high aspirations (I would never discourage anyone from trying!), I always remind fellow poets not to overlook local networking and publishing prospects. But where does one begin? Here are a few pointers to keep in mind when attempting to break into the local scene.

ALL POETRY IS LOCAL

Bob Dylan didn't start out his musical career touring Europe—he began playing in a coffeehouse in Dinkytown (an actual neighborhood in Minneapolis) and later made important connections in Greenwich Village. The point is, all artists start somewhere—and it's usually in their own communities. It can be easy for writers to be reclusive and simply ignore the community aspect of the craft—but in doing so, they also shut out possibilities for networking and creative collaborations. Imagine Kerouac without Ginsberg and Burroughs. Consider the importance of the Black Arts Repertory Theatre within the black arts movement. Community really does matter.

IT'S YOUR TOWN, TOO

The local writing scene can seem a bit cliquey when you're the new kid on the block. But remem-

ber, there's a first time for everyone. Grab a friend and check out the local literary happenings in your town. Most community newspapers have weekly listings of readings, workshops, and writing groups. As they feature readings from local authors, independent bookstores are often great places to break into the literary scene. Our local used-book store has a community room that can be rented out for readings and events.

DON'T JUST LOOK, TOUCH

Many bookstores carry small press and little magazine publications, including handmade poetry chapbooks and zines. These can be a great source of inspiration for your own work and help you to make connections in the community. If you read something that you enjoy, why not contact the writer and tell him or her so? You might just make a new connection in the process.

MAKE A CHAPBOOK, SHARE A CHAPBOOK

Today's desktop publishing tools allow one to easily self-publish. Promote your work by creating your own chapbook to give to fellow writers—or circulate the work of others by establishing your own zine. How-to books and art stores (check out the beautiful papers) are excellent sources for bookmaking inspiration. Think of your own chapbook as material for trade, and take these with you when you attend (and give!) readings.

TAKE OUT AN AD

Is your town short on literary happenings? Why not start your own open mic or reading series? Coffee shops, tearooms, libraries, bookstores, bars, park spaces—all can be really interesting places to host readings. The Rooftop Poetry Club uses the rooftop garden of the E. H. Butler Library (Buffalo State

College) for its meeting space. Informal workshops and formal classes can also be great places to make connections with fellow writers. In the spirit of Gertrude Stein, consider organizing a literary salon for your writerly acquaintances.

HEAR ME OUT

Don't forget audio venues to showcase your writing—such as radio and Internet podcasts. Our local NPR station hosts listener commentaries and has sponsored a poetry show. There are a number of poets in Buffalo who have their own blog-talk radio programs that feature interviews and readings by local writers. Ask around. You'll be surprised what you hear.

FACEBOOK ME

Don't ignore the importance of social networking sites, such as Meetup.com and Facebook. Social networking sites are a convenient way to connect with other writers, share your work, find out about local happenings, discover calls for work, and advertise your own literary events. I've been introduced to many fellow writers through the world of Facebook. When we do finally meet in person, there is already a feeling of camaraderie. When you're new to the scene, it's easy to feel like an outsider—but social networking tools can help you meet established writers, publicize your work, and achieve social recognition in and outside of your own community.

THINK OUTSIDE THE BOOK

Community poetry projects offer unique publishing opportunities. I've participated in or organized community poetry projects using vintage postcards, library catalog cards, discarded 35 mm slides, and topographical maps. Look past your own publishing endeavors to have success with your own writing career. As librarians, you are already in a natural place of leadership—so why not use your position within the literary community?

POLITICS AND POETRY

If all of this sounds too political for you—try thinking of being political as being participatory. Just as one participates by submitting a poem to a magazine, writers participate by becoming involved in the literary community. If good things happen (for example, you get published) because of the connections you make, this is simply a side effect of your involvement in the community. Now get out there and participate!

THE LITERARY WORLD NEEDS LIBRARIANS

Writers love librarians. When attending literary events, don't be afraid to introduce yourself. You'll soon discover that these strangers aren't as intimidating as they first appeared—and as fellow writers, you obviously have something in common. Librarians—already in a natural position of literary leadership—are perfectly suited to take on such roles as reading series organizer, zine publisher, or literary salon host. With a little effort, unique networking and publishing opportunities are yours for the making.

hope that you made it to these last few pages in the book only after you've read all of the preceding chapters, because taken together they form a comprehensive corpus of advice, guidance, and encouragement that should set you well on your way to starting—and finishing—one of a whole range of possible writing projects.

Of course, there's always a good reason not to be writing. You have work to be done during the week and perhaps into the weekend. There are family and friends, obligations, events, chores and errands and responsibilities. Somewhere in the midst of a hectic twenty-first-century life you may be able to carve out some so-called free time, but perhaps the last thing anyone wants to do then is to be thinking about work again. And not only thinking about it but also analyzing your thoughts and fashioning them into clear, concise, comprehensible words.

However, if there's a single theme that I could contrive to cover the nearly one hundred pieces in this book, it's that this achievement is demonstrably possible. Yes, you have to start somewhere: pick your topic, do your research, and write your first sentence. And then you have to power through the temptation, the raging urge, to leave the thing unfinished, to do something else productive instead or just to relax a little. Persevere. Write a first draft, read it over, have an informed colleague read it over again for you. Stand back, give the process a little time, and then have at it again, writing, rewriting, editing, making your work the best it can be. Oh, and the end result: final draft submitted, the decision of the editor, and finally your hard-fought and well-wrought prose published. Or you could keep it simple and direct: start a blog and have your first posting on the Web before you go to bed tonight.

Before any of that, though, you need to do a little background reading to become more informed. If you haven't read the chapters yet, go back and have a look at them all. I particularly recommend the one on page . . .

—**Wayne Jones**, head of Central Technical Services, Queen's University, Kingston, Ontario, and editor of *Access* and *E-Journals Access and Management*

PAUL BLOBAUM is an associate professor at Governors State University Library, University Park, Illinois, and a subject librarian for the College of Health and Human Services. His website credits include *Health Science Librarians of Illinois Newsletter* and the Association of College and University Policy Administrators. His work has appeared in *John Steinbeck Encyclopedia* (Greenwood Press, 2006), *Journal of the Medical Library Association, Introduction to Reference Services in Academic Libraries* (Haworth, 2006), *Serials Librarian,* and *Journal of Hospital Librarianship.*

VANDELLA BROWN, a diversity librarian at the Illinois State Library, obtained her MLIS from the University of Iowa. Her work has appeared in *American Libraries* and *ILA Reporter.* Her recent book is *What Is a Zawadi to We? A Poetic Story of Kwanzaa and Gift Giving* (Lumen-Us Publications, 2007). She appears in *Who's Who of American Women.* A miniature book collector, Brown presents workshops about family reunions and celebrating Kwanzaa.

DR. JOHN R. BURCH JR. is the director of library services at Campbellsville University. He reviews books for *American Reference Books Annual, Choice: Current Reviews for Academic Libraries,* and *Library Journal.* He is the author of *Owsley County, Kentucky, and the Perpetuation of Poverty* (McFarland, 2007) and the compiler of *The Bibliography of Appalachia* (McFarland, 2009). He coauthored, with Tim Hooper, *Campbellsville University* (Arcadia, 2008).

DEBORAH H. CHARBONNEAU, a librarian at the Vera P. Shiffman Medical Library at Wayne State University in Detroit obtained her MLS from the University of Pittsburgh. Her publications have appeared in *Journal of the Medical Library Association, Journal of Consumer Health on the Internet,* and *Evidence Based Library and Information Practice.* She edited the book *Global Information Inequalities: Bridging the Information Gap* (Oxford: Chandos Publishing, 2008).

TOM COOPER, the director of Webster Groves Public Library in Webster Groves, Missouri, earned his MLS from the University of Missouri–Columbia. He has also worked as a library technician for St. Louis County Library, a collection development associate for St. Louis Public Library, and adult services librarian at Richmond Heights Memorial Library. Since 1996, he has reviewed books for the "Sunday Books" section of the *St. Louis Post-Dispatch.*

CAROLYN DAVIS is a librarian, researcher, and development specialist. A GSLIS graduate of Simmons College, her publications include articles in *Thinking outside the Book: Essays for Innovative Librarians* (McFarland, 2008), *Info Career Trends* (www.lisjobs.com), *The Audio-Visual Librarian* (Aberystwyth, Wales), and a series for *Technicalities: Information Forum for the Library Practitioner.* The author of twenty-eight publications and presentations, she is the author of, *How to Write Persuasively* for ABC-CLIO.

GEORGIE DONOVAN (MLS, University of Arizona; MFA, University of Texas at El Paso) is acquisitions librarian at Appalachian State University. She coedited *Staff Development Strategies That Work* (Neal-

Schuman, 2009) and has published articles in *Library Administration and Management, C&RL News,* and *Charleston Conference Proceedings;* encyclopedia articles in *The Eighties in America* (Salem, 2008) and *Great Events from History* (Salem, 2007); reviews in *Counterpoise;* and poetry in *Figdust* and *The Rio Grande Review.*

MICHAEL DUDLEY, a librarian and researcher at the Institute of Urban Studies at the University of Winnipeg, Canada, has published peer-reviewed articles in *Journal of Planning Education and Research* and the online journal *Theory and Event,* and he has contributed a chapter to *Multimedia and Planning,* forthcoming from SpringerLink. He is on the editorial board of *Progressive Planning* magazine, is a regular blogger for Planetizen.com and citystates.typepad.com, and contributes occasionally to Alter Net.com.

NICOLE C. ENGARD, MLIS, writes technical documents and tutorials for librarians at LibLime and teaches classes for librarians on technology topics. She has contributed articles to *Computers in Libraries, Online, Journal of Web Librarianship, Thinking outside the Book: Essays for Innovative Librarians* (McFarland, 2008), and *Library Mashups: Exploring New Ways to Deliver Library Data* (Information Today, 2009). She was named one of *Library Journal*'s Movers and Shakers in 2007.

ANIKA FAJARDO is a writer and librarian living in Minneapolis. She has a MLIS from San Jose State University, and her reviews of women's fiction regularly appear in *Library Journal.* Her writing has appeared in various publications, most recently in *apt: an online literary journal* and *Savvy Women's Magazine.* She is currently working on an anthology called *Let Them Eat Crêpes: Stories and Recipes Featuring the French Pancake* (http://eatingcrepes.com).

LISA A. FORREST is a senior assistant librarian for SUNY College at Buffalo and the founding member of the school's Rooftop Poetry Club. She is the recipient of the 2008 Excellence in Library Service Award from the Western New York Library Resources Council, and a 2007 and 2008 Pushcart Prize nominee. Her poetry has appeared in a variety of publications, and her first collection of poems, *To the Eaves* (2008), is available from BlazeVox Books.

JOHN GLOVER, the reference librarian for the humanities at Virginia Commonwealth University, obtained his MLIS from the University of Washington. He has been published in *Beneath the Surface: 13 Shocking Tales of Terror* (Shroud, 2008), *City Slab, Fantasy Magazine, Goblin Fruit, LIScareer,* and *Urban Library Journal.* Any time of day or night, he is liable to be scribbling furiously in a composition notebook, trying to bring order out of chaos.

COLLEEN S. HARRIS, associate head of access and delivery services at North Carolina State University, has been published in *InfoCareerTrends, Sow's Ear Poetry Review, Wisconsin Review, Main Street Rag, descant, Appalachian Heritage,* and *Library Journal.* Her full-length collection of poetry, *God in My Throat,* is from Bellowing Ark Press, 2009. An avid jigsaw puzzler and slave to her basset hound, she is completing her MFA in creative writing at Spalding University.

ROBERT P. HOLLEY, a professor of library and information science at Wayne State University, obtained his doctorate from Yale University and his MLIS from Columbia University. His most recent edited book is *Cataloger, Editor and Scholar: Essays in Honor of Ruth C. Carter* (Haworth, 2006). "Libraries as Repositories of Popular Culture: Is Popular Culture Still Forgotten?" in *Collection Building* (2007) was selected as one of the best three articles of the year in that magazine.

JANET HUSBAND, a Rutgers graduate, worked at the Free Library of Philadelphia, then moved to Massachusetts to become acquisitions librarian at Quincy Public Library, where she compiled the first edition of *Sequels.* Subsequently she was director of the Rockland and Cohasset Public Libraries. She is now involved with www.eSequels.com, her online version of *Sequels.* She also has edited newsletters for the Massachusetts Board of Library Commissioners and the Massachusetts Library Association.

WAYNE JONES, the head of Central Technical Services at Queen's University in Kingston, Ontario, Canada, was previously head of serials cataloging at the Massachusetts Institute of Technology and at the National Library of Canada. He has worked as a freelance editor, edited books about serials and e-resources (most recently *E-Journals Access and Management,* Routledge, 2008), published articles and reviews, and currently is editor in chief of the Ontario Library Association's official magazine, *Access.*

SIGRID KELSEY is full librarian, electronic reference resources and web development coordinator, with the Louisiana State University Libraries. Kelsey has coedited *Outreach Services in Academic and Special Libraries* (Haworth, 2004) and *Handbook of Research on Computer Mediated Communication* (IGI Global, 2008), served on editorial boards, edited a column for *Louisiana Libraries,* and appeared in *RUSQ, The Reference Librarian*, and *Information Technology and Libraries.* She's an active member of the Louisiana Library Association.

DOUGLAS KING, special materials cataloger at University of South Carolina, obtained his MLIS from the University of South Florida. He has published reviews in *Library Journal, portal: Libraries and the Academy, OLAC Newsletter,* and *Journal of Electronic Resources Librarianship.* He has also coauthored an article for *OCLC Systems and Services* and contributed to *A Day in the Life: Career Options in Library and Information Science* (Libraries Unlimited, 2007).

MICHAEL LORENZEN, head of reference services at Central Michigan University, received his MLS from Kent State University. He has published in *Research Strategies, Illinois Libraries, Journal of Library Administration, College and Undergraduate Libraries, MLA Forum,* and several books. He won the Michigan Library Association Information Literacy Award in 2008. He lives in Mount Pleasant, Michigan, with his wife, Julie, and his sons, Calvin and Caleb.

DAWN LOWE-WINCENTSEN, Portland operations librarian at the Oregon Institute of Technology, coauthored *A Leadership Primer for New Librarians* with Suzanne Byke (Chandos, 2009). Her leadership articles and book reviews appear in *Public Services Quarterly, Info Career Trends,* and *The Proceedings of the Australian Library and Information Association New Librarian Symposium* (2006). Her MLIS is from Louisiana State University, and her BA in creative writing from Linfield College.

DR. MARGARET READ MACDONALD, associated with the King County Library System near Seattle, is author of more than fifty books (including seventeen picture books), which draw on her library background and her folklore Ph.D. (Indiana University). Among her award winners are *The Great Smelly, Slobbery, Small-Tooth Dog* (August House, 2007), *Peace Tales: World Folktales to Talk About* (August House, 2005), and *Ten Traditional Tellers* (University of Illinois, 2006).

DR. MICHELYNN MCKNIGHT, assistant professor at Louisiana State University School of Library and Information Science, developed the course Publication for Librarians. Her work has appeared in such journals as *Journal of Academic Librarianship, Journal of Documentation,* and *Journal of Hospital Librarianship;* she cowrote *Mathematics Education Research: A Guide for the Research Mathematician* (McKnight, Magid, Murphy, and McKnight, 2000); and she has

edited newsletters, served on editorial boards, and contributed chapters to *Information and Emotion: The Emergent Affective Paradigm in Information Behavior Research and Theory* (edited by Diane Nahl and Dania Bilal, 2007) and *The Medical Library Association Guide to Managing Health Care Libraries* (edited by Ruth Holst, 2000). Her book *The Agile Librarian's Guide to Thriving in Any Organization* will be published in 2010.

DR. ANN MARLOW RIEDLING is an associate professor at University of South Florida. Her nine textbooks have been published by Linworth, Neal-Schuman, Libraries Unlimited, and others, and include *A Guide to Becoming Information Literate in the 21st Century* (two editions). A two-time Fulbright Scholar in *Contemporary Authors,* her forthcoming books include *Extreme Searching for Teens: Curricular Tools* and *Reference Skills for the School Library Media Specialist: Tools and Tips* (3rd ed.).

KAY MARNER is a paraprofessional library assistant in outreach services at Ames (Iowa) Public Library. She works on APL's Bookmobile and manages select youth collections. Marner is the author of *Dog Tales: The Adventures of Smyles,* published by Ames Public Library (2006) in conjunction with its early literacy outreach project, Project Smyles, which Marner pioneered. Marner freelances regularly for *Adoptive Families* and *ADDitude* magazines, and she blogs for ADDitudeMag.com.

STEPHANIE MATHSON, a reference and instruction library at Central Michigan University, earned her MLIS from Wayne State University. Her work has appeared in the *Journal of Access Services* and *College and Undergraduate Libraries,* and she coauthored a chapter in *Academic Library Outreach: Beyond the Campus Wall* (Greenwood, forthcoming). A member of Beta Phi Mu, she is currently working on an MA in English language and literature.

NANCY KALIKOW MAXWELL, library director at Miami Dade College North Campus, is a frequent contributor to *American Libraries* magazine. Her most recent book is *Sacred Stacks: The Higher Purpose of Libraries and Librarianship* (American Library Association, 2006). She received the National Albert Clark Prize in 1997 for religious essay writing. Her writing has appeared in the *National Catholic Reporter, Reform Judaism, Lilith,* and *Tikkun* magazines, among others.

GABRIEL MORLEY is director of the Pike-Amite-Walthall Library System in Mississippi. He has an MLIS from the University of Southern Mississippi and is copyeditor of *Mississippi Libraries.* Prior to becoming a librarian, he was a daily newspaper editor and reporter for seven years. His work has appeared in *Library Journal, Louisiana Libraries, Mississippi Libraries,* and *LIBRIS,* as well as *Thinking outside the Book: Essays for Innovative Librarians* (McFarland, 2008).

ELIZABETH MORELLI, collection development librarian for Richmond Public Library, Richmond, Virginia, received her MLS from the State University of New York at Geneseo. She has published book columns, essays, and editorials locally in *Style Weekly.* Since 2003, she has served on the Praeger Publishers' Library Advisory Board. In 2007, she was the first place recipient of the Margaret Kinnan Rawlings essay award in conjunction with Writing the Region Workshop.

DR. JANET BUTLER MUNCH, associate professor and special collections librarian, Lehman College, City University of New York, has contributed to *Historical Dictionary of the Gilded Age* (Sharpe, 2003) and *Colonialism: An International, Social, Cultural, and Political Encyclopedia* (ABC-CLIO, 2003) and has published articles in *College and Research Libraries* and *Urban Library Journal.* She has chaired the Professional Development Committee of the Library Association of the City University of New York.

ROBERT S. NELSON is the Library Instruction Coordinator for the College of Staten Island, CUNY. He began his library career as a school librarian in 1995. His published works include articles on instructional effectiveness and information-seeking behavior, a book chapter on keyword searching, and an ACRL-published CLIP Notes on plagiarism policies and academic libraries. His poetry has appeared in *Volition, Bathhouse, Fluent Ascensions,* and *Downtown Brooklyn.*

BETH NIEMAN, a librarian at Carlsbad Public Library in Carlsbad, New Mexico, is the author of a popular weekly book column, "Footnotes," for the *Carlsbad Current-Argus.* Her articles on child care have appeared in *Parent Life* and *Newsweek,* and she is a contributor to *Breakfast New Mexico Style* (Sunstone Press, 2009). Beth is a member of the Land of Enchantment Book Award Committee for the New Mexico Library Association.

MARY NORTHRUP, reference librarian at Metropolitan Community College–Maple Woods, Kansas City, Missouri, obtained her MLS from the University of Wisconsin-Milwaukee. Her publishing credits include articles in *Book Links, Children's Writer, LMC,* and numerous other periodicals, and two

books: *American Computer Pioneers* (Enslow, 1998) and *Short on Time, Long on Learning* (Linworth, 2000). She is a member of the board of directors of the Missouri Center for the Book.

VALERIE J. NYE is head of public services at Fogelson Library at the College of Santa Fe. She has cowritten two books, *Postmark Milledgeville: Flannery O'Connor's Correspondence in Archives and Library Collections* published in 2002 by Georgia College and State University and *Breakfast Santa Fe Style* published in 2006 by Sunstone Press. She is currently coauthoring and editing a third book that will highlight libraries in New Mexico.

RUTH PENNINGTON PAGET, supervising librarian for youth services, Monterey County Free Libraries System, California, has published more than ninety-five articles about multicultural work environments, reviews of ethnic restaurants, art criticism in the magazine *Art and Antiques,* and business articles in *Commerce in France.* Among her five books are *Eating Soup with Chopsticks: Sweet Sixteen in Japan* (AuthorHouse, 2003) and *China Hand: From the Great Wall to Olive Ball and Beyond* (iUniverse, 2005).

PATRICK RAGAINS is business and government information librarian at the University of Nevada, Reno. Patrick edited *Information Literacy Instruction That Works: A Guide to Teaching by Discipline and Student Population* (Neal-Schuman, 2006), which received the 2008 Ilene Rockman Publication Award from the Association of College and Research Libraries' Instruction Section. He has published articles in leading professional journals and is active in the ACRL Instruction Section.

FAYE C. ROBERTS wrote a weekly newspaper column while director of Columbia County Public Library in Lake City, Florida. Other published works include "Florida's Library Leadership Program" in *Interface,* the publication of the Association of Specialized and Cooperative Library Agencies (Fall, 2007) and "Hiring for Outreach" in *From Outreach to Equity* (American Library Association, 2005). Roberts currently serves as executive director of the Florida Library Association.

STACY RUSSO is instruction librarian and coordinator of reference and information services at Chapman University. She is the author of *The Library as Place in California* (McFarland, 2008). She is a regular book reviewer for *Library Journal* and has also reviewed for *Serials Review, Feminist Collections,* and *Feminist Teacher.* A book and animal lover, she lives in southern California with her husband and their three cats.

ELAINE SANCHEZ, head of cataloging and metadata services at Alkek Library, Texas State University–San Marcos, obtained her MLS from University of Texas at Austin. Books, chapters, and surveys include *Emerging Issues in Academic Library Cataloging and Technical Services* (Primary Research, 2007), *Introducing and Managing Academic Library Automation Projects* (Greenwood, 1996), and *Academic Library Cataloging Practices Benchmarks* (Primary Research, 2008). Her journal articles are found in *Technical Services Quarterly* and others.

BRUCE R. SCHUENEMAN is head of systems at Texas A&M University–Kingsville. His publications include *The French Violin School* (Lyre of Orpheus, 2002); a book chapter in *Giovanni Battista Viotti: A Composer between the Two Revolutions* (Ut Orpheus Edizioni, 2006); *Minor Ballet Composers* (Haworth, 1997); and articles in various journals, including *Fontes Artis Musicae, Music Reference Services Quarterly, Strings, Humanities Collections,* and *Notes: Quarterly Journal of the Music Library Association.*

BETH M. SHEPPARD, Ph.D., is director of the United Library at Garrett-Evangelical and Seabury-Western Theological Seminaries in Evanston, Illinois. She holds an MLS from Emporia State University and graduate degrees in religion from Princeton Theological Seminary and the University of Sheffield. She has published in *ATLA Proceedings,* authored numerous book reviews in the field of biblical studies, and serves as section editor of bibliographic essays for *Theological Librarianship.*

JAN SIEBOLD, a school library media specialist in East Aurora, New York, since 1977, received her MLS from the University of Buffalo. She has served as NYLA Secretary, and she received the NYLA/SLMS Cultural Media Award in 1992. She is the author of *Rope Burn* (Albert Whitman, 1998), *Doing Time Online* (Albert Whitman, 2002), and *My Nights at the Improv* (Albert Whitman, 2005), three middle-grade novels on numerous award lists.

CORINNE H. SMITH, a cataloging and reference librarian at Anna Maria College (Paxton, Massachusetts), has worked in a variety of library venues since 1979. Her book and media reviews have appeared in *The Book Report, Library Journal, Library Media Connection, The Video Rating Guide for Libraries,* and on Rambles.net and Amazon.com. She is writing a book-length manuscript about Henry David Thoreau's 1861 trip to Minnesota.

ALINE SOULES, a library faculty member at California State University, East Bay, has earned an MSLS, an MA, and an MFA. She has been published in journals, in books, and on the Web, both in the library and in the creative writing fields. Recent examples include publications in *Against the Grain, New Library World, Handbook of Research on Electronic Resource Management, Kenyon Review,* and *Houston Literary Review.*

ELIZABETH A. STEPHAN, business librarian at Western Washington University, received her MLS from the University of Wisconsin–Madison. She has been published in *Journal of Academic Librarianship, College and Undergraduate Libraries,* and *Academic BRASS.* She was assistant editor and editor of *Mississippi Libraries* for three years. Stephan edited ten books while at Krause publications, including *O'Brien's Collecting Toys, Toys and Prices,* and *Toy Shop's Action Figure Price Guide.*

DIANE STINE, librarian at Warren-Newport Public Library, has been published in many journals, including *Illinois Libraries, Serials Librarian, Serials Review, Cataloging and Classification Quarterly,* and her most recent publication appears in *Public Libraries* (January/February 2007). She has written chapters for books including *Cataloging Correctly for Kids* (American Library Association, 1998) and *Young Adults and Public Libraries* (Greenwood, 1998), entries for *The Modern Encyclopedia of East Slavic, Baltic and Eurasian Literatures* (Academic International, 2002).

KRIS SWANK, library director at Pima Community College, previously worked for the Thunderbird School of Global Management and an educational nonprofit in South Africa. She has contributed to *Library Journal, American Libraries, Educational Technology Research and Development, The International Directory of Business Biographies* (St. James, 2005), and *The Successful Academic Librarian* (Information Today, 2005). Her short story "Bitter Honey: A Minoan Mystery" was published in *Orchard Press Mysteries* (2008).

KATHRYN YELINEK, the coordinator of government documents at Bloomsburg University of Pennsylvania, earned her MLIS at the University of Pittsburgh. Her essays and short stories have appeared in *flashquake, Thereby Hangs a Tale, Literary Traveler, Mindflights,* and *Dragons, Knights, and Angels,* among others. Within library science, she has written for *College and Research Library News* and *PaLA Bulletin.* Her book, *The History of South Mountain Restoration Center,* was published in 2001.

You may also be interested in

Librarians as Community Partners: Including 66 focused snapshots of outreach in action, this resource showcases the creative solutions of librarians searching for new and innovative ways to build programs that meet customer needs while expanding the library's scope into the community.

Writing Reviews for Readers' Advisory: Whether the ultimate goal is writing reviews for a library website, book club, or monthly handout, or freelancing for a newspaper, magazine, or professional journal, you will find plenty of ideas and insight here.

Hiring, Training, and Supervising Library Shelvers: How do you find good library shelvers and keep them for more than a few months? Tunstall gives practical advice to help you do just that with a complete overview of how to hire, test, train, and retain shelvers.

Is Consulting for You? Ulla de Stricker shows how your skill-set can be applied to a range of consulting activities from highly specialized, focused activities to broad strategic efforts.

Order today at www.alastore.ala.org or 866-746-7252!